Interior Gardens
Designing and constructing green spaces in private and public buildings

Haike Falkenberg

Birkhäuser
Basel

1

7–140

TYPOLOGIES OF INTERIOR GARDENS

2

141–176

GENERAL BASIC PLANNING

Foreword

Many companies increasingly see interior planting as part of the design for a modern working environment. But permanent planted spaces are also being introduced in a variety of spaces and buildings types: private houses, medical facilities or public buildings.

A garden's different elements can be transferred to other garden types, independently of its context and typology. Given that, the collection of projects in the first chapter of this book should also be considered on two levels: as a cross section through the various indoor garden typologies, from the vertical garden to the atrium; and then as examples of the different conceptual approaches to the subject of planting in detail, from the abstract plant wall carpet to natural-looking garden design with the usual elements such as paths, water, walls, trees, bushes, ground cover etc.

The selected private indoor gardens that deviate formally from familiar traditional conservatory planting serve primarily to improve the atmosphere in the space, and the air quality. They create private, sheltered places to spend time in or retreat to, and the variety in their design takes account of occupants' individual needs.

Most of the planting examples are public projects that can act as buffer zones within the building's air conditioning system, and they often help to communicate company values. The individual elements in these large gardens can usually be reproduced on a smaller scale and in different contexts.

Three projects demonstrate the use of wall planting systems. This relatively recent form, the vertical garden, is particularly suitable for planting 'difficult' spaces and is closely linked with interior design. Products and applications for the various systems are rapidly being developed by specialist companies.

Plants have a large number of positive qualities, which these work in a variety of ways within any approach to planting. Physical and chemical effects, such as filtering pollutants out of the air, are particularly important for interiors, along with the symbolic impact created, for example by integrating nature into our mainly urban habitat. Living greenery enhances people's sense of well-being and their efficiency, and is also scientifically proven to help sick people to recover.

Ideally, indoor gardens should be designed in close co-operation between client, architect and green space planners, who will bring in other specialists such as lighting planners or planting experts. The principles involved in design planning, such as determining function, location and size, and the form and orientation of the planting, are presented in the second part of this book.

Indoor gardens are not restricted to particular climate zones, and the project selection in the first chapter is correspondingly broad in geographical terms. On the other hand, structural aspects such as thermal insulation, glazing, lighting and plant selection also need to be considered, according to use and climate zone; this is addressed in chapter 3. A list of plants in the appendix complements the information about materials and construction.

With the exception of the new design for the Devonian Gardens Indoor Park in Calgary, which is due to re-open in 2011, all the projects selected are completed gardens. Each location has its own individual parameters, and the examples that have been functioning well for years are an important source of valuable experience when planning new gardens.

This book is intended to present design possibilities for indoor gardens, pass on the fundamentals of construction, and provide stimulus for further research and personal interpretations of the indoor planting. Personally, I am looking forward with great excitement to innovative developments in indoor gardens.

HAIKE FALKENBERG

On Interior Landscaping

Effective interior landscape design, construction and management require a special appreciation of the way plants define a particular environment. Collaboration between the architect, the client and the landscape designer plays a key role in producing an environment that is aesthetic in its choice of materials, but achieves maximum functionality of the space. Maintaining a relationship between the building architect and the landscape designer is vital throughout all phases of the design and build process. Interior landscape design is a niche market, pairing specialists in landscape design with progressive architects and clients who understand the value of living plants.

Mature, flourishing living features are often unexpected elements within interior spaces. Much of the appeal comes from the juxtaposition of natural elements with man-made features. The CanWest project (now the Postmedia building) used a combination of hard and soft materials. The walkway opens up movement through the building, and the circular seating areas set along the path are tucked into the garden, allowing employees to sit and be immersed in a green space 12 months a year. Seating areas are deliberately geometric, to contrast with the natural planting arrangement. The plant material selected flourishes in dryer soil and air. The humidity level of the building needed to be maintained in order to avoid the build-up of condensation on windows. Plant materials that require wet soil will raise the humidity of the building and can lead to problems with the building envelope, the growth of mould and mildew, and insect infestations.

Our goal was to achieve a tropical effect without raising the humidity levels in the building drastically. Dry tropical plant selections tend to be slower growing, and so require fewer replacements for plants that outgrow the space. Some of the specimens at CanWest are over 20 years old. Once the design and construction plans are complete, extensive waterproofing is the primary phase in building an interior landscape. Damage due to leaking water can cause serious problems to a building's foundation and contribute to many of the issues that discourage more extensive application of interior landscaping.

Many of the challenges often encountered in the construction phase can be avoided by thorough planning during the design phase. Moving quantities of plant material, much of which can be very large, is a problem if access to the interior of the building is limited. Entrance points are rarely wide open, so consideration is required in the design phase to limit the size of the elements. The weight of materials must also be considered at the design stage, as stone and other hardscape elements must be moved by hand, since machine access is usually not permitted. Organization, detailed planning, and skilled workers are all vital to ensuring timely progress.

Indoor gardens provide immeasurable benefits to the staff who work within the building. Aside from the obvious improvement in air quality, the gardens can reduce noise, increase motivation in the workplace, and decrease absenteeism due to respiratory illnesses, while contributing to improved feelings of overall well-being. In particular, the interior landscape at CanWest creates a sense of community by providing a gathering place for the employees to enjoy.

PETER GUINANE
CEO ORIOLE LANDSCAPING, TORONTO, CANADA

Typologies of
interior gardens
1

With reference to international projects, the following chapter presents the different types of inner gardens:

— Vertical Gardens → **p. 12**
— Small indoor plantings and gardens in private homes → **p. 26**
— Open and enclosed inner courtyards and patios → **p. 48**
— Atria and large conservatories → **p. 78**

Types of planted gardens under glass that are not primarily intended as places for people to spend time in, such as botanical gardens or zoological parks, are not included here. Greenhouses of that type are usually intended primarily for the protection and controlled cultivation of plants, or for food production; their construction is simple and the light-permeable outer shell is traditionally single-glazed, although it may also include film or sheeting. The greenhouse effect plays a decisive role in heat gain in these structures, which are generally not otherwise heated. They are also often equipped with irrigation and shading systems. And even though they are not included here, much interesting information about gardens inside buildings can be garnered from plant cultivation and agricultural designs; for instance, materials generally used in tomato production were used for the atria of the Alterra building → **p. 120.**

The boundaries between the categories are fluid: there are overlaps in terms of architectonic design, with various possible interpretations. This typology should not be viewed too dogmatically – it is only a loose grouping based on the key features of each design. If the designs were classified differently (by function, for instance), they would be grouped differently.

The exceptional diversity of the projects presented here is intended to demonstrate the full spectrum of design possibilities for plants inside buildings. To varying degrees, the descriptions of the designs here concentrate on the aspects that are relevant to the planting and its functions. Many of the design ideas, design elements, and constructions included here could be applied to other projects on a different scale or with different functions.

The exceptional design, size, layout, and functions of the Sky Gardens at the Fusionopolis building in Singapore means that the project is in a class by itself. It could be seen as a vision of a future in which architecture and planting exist as an inseparable whole, with the use concept including ecological concerns, energy conservation, and people's general well-being.

VERTICAL GARDENS

These vertical gardens demonstrate the use of wall planting in enclosed inner spaces or in an open but secluded inner courtyard in a private home. What all these designs have in common is that they have no contact with the ground. The whole installation – base structure, substrate, plants, and supply of water and nutrients – is secured to a vertical supporting wall.

Despite each installation being unique, these designs are not experimental projects – they are tried and tested systems by specialist firms, each adapted to specific localized conditions. Wall gardens can fulfil the same range of requirements in different types of buildings as other indoor garden types, and have the advantage of saving space. The aesthetics, however, are as important as the function: wall planting adds interesting possibilities to the interior architecture design range that can be integrated into many design concepts.

— Planted wall in the inner courtyard of the Morris House, Richmond, Australia → p. 12
— Planted lift shaft and canteen in the Tryg insurance company headquarters in Copenhagen, Denmark → p. 16
— Vertical garden at the headoffice of the Mannheimer Swartling law firm in Stockholm, Sweden → p. 22

SMALL INDOOR PLANTINGS AND GARDENS IN PRIVATE HOMES

The size of a planting doesn't matter – a well-placed bed or plant container can change the whole look of a space and fulfil various functions. A small leaf volume can be enough to improve the quality of a small space, dampening noise or forming part of a route system. A small planting may be enough to create a visual connection between the indoor and the outdoor space – as demonstrated by the Seattle Public Library project → p. 38.

Our examples of unusual small-scale designs provide creative suggestions for integrating plants into any building type. We have intentionally excluded 'traditional' private glazed conservatories, because these extensions of the living space, often decorated with plants in tubs, have already been well documented (see bibliography) and because their design and construction principles are not significantly different from the guidelines and sample projects presented in this book.

— Roofed pation with garden terrace in the Foothills family home, Pokeno, New Zealand → p. 26
— Loft apartment with indoor garden in Düsseldorf, Germany → p. 30
— A tree in an Athens appartment, Greece → p. 34
— Planting concept for the Seattle Public Library, USA → p. 38
— Planting concept for the office space at the Combined Traders Company, Haarlem, the Netherlands → p. 42

OPEN AND ENCLOSED INNER COURTYARDS AND PATIOS

An 'inner courtyard' is a space surrounded by building structures on all sides, generally with a rectangular floor plan and open to the sky. An 'atrium' contributes to the lighting of a building's interior, and may be roofed over. 'Patio' originally meant a Spanish inner courtyard – a feature found in noblemen's palaces, but also in small houses, where it would provide an extra living and meeting place and help to cool the building. Open patios traditionally include large or small potted plants, which may be hung from the walls. Central elements include a fountain, or other water feature, and seating.

Some of the designs presented here are for airspaces several storeys high, which can be viewed from a variety of different heights, making the planting look different (as in the Chelsea Harbour Design Centre in London, the Can-West (Postmedia) building in Toronto, and the ESO hotel rotunda in Chile). There are two open courtyards presented here that have completely different functions: an enclosed, secluded area in a private home (see the roof apartment project with garden courtyard in London), and a quiet place in a school building (see the Giardino delle Ninfe project).

ATRIA AND LARGE CONSERVATORIES

An atrium was originally an inward-looking central space in a private house – a feature of Roman architecture. Over the past few decades, a new architectural model and new materials and techniques have led to the atrium being reinterpreted in a number of ways. What all these multi-storey glass-covered courtyards and halls, some of which are very large, have in common is that they are transparent and open to the sky. An atrium may be a climate-controlled space that can be used all year round (such as the Genzyme Center), or a glass structure that acts as a thermal buffer zone.

Glass structures serve to house plants and people, to protect them from the weather, and to moderate changes in external temperatures. They benefit from the greenhouse effect and are therefore not heated (or are heated only by the exhaust air from the adjacent rooms). These light-permeable constructions have to fulfil the static and construction requirements for occupied rooms (as in the Covent Garden and Alltours projects). Conservatories were originally built to house (and preserve) sensitive plants during the winter. Today, the word is usually understood to mean a transparent or semi-transparent structure or part of a building where people can spend time. The walls and the roof may be wholly or partially glazed. All the usual construction and building regulations for habitable buildings must be met. The greenhouse effect is useful in keeping the inner space warm and can help to optimize the energy budget in unheated constructions that are thermally separated from the main building. Specifically, such spaces can act as an air buffer by providing prewarmed air to be channelled into the heated parts of the building. For heated conservatories, heat protection glass must be used, and the roof and ceiling must also be insulated to prevent heat loss through thermal bridges.

A planted wall in the inner courtyard of the Morris House

VERTICAL GARDEN: Fytogreen Pty, Ltd.
ARCHITECT: Michael Morris of Morris Partnership Architecture and Planning Pty Ltd.
COMPLETION: 10/2009
LOCATION: Richmond, Melbourne, Australia

PLANNING ASSIGNMENT

Vertical planting of the freestanding boundary wall of a narrow two-storey courtyard with view protection.

CONTEXT

This little inner-city single-family home plot is hemmed in by tall buildings on two sides. Nevertheless, including a narrow courtyard in the plan and setting the two-storey house back from the street created plenty of interior space, with a range of views of the outdoors.

The central courtyard is surrounded by the building on three sides, with a free-standing metal wall on the remaining side. The courtyard can be entered and used, but its function is primarily visual. It can be seen from almost all rooms of the house through the large windows that look onto it. The courtyard expands the living space and provides the interior with daylight. At the same time, the freestanding metal wall protects the privacy of the inhabitants from the neighbouring apartment block.

CONCEPT

The narrow inner courtyard and its low surface area suggested the idea of planting the metal wall with two 8 m vertical gardens. They are a major decorative element for the house, and this garden cannot be seen into from outside. The wall faces west and is protected from the wind and partly by the house. The Australian grasses and ferns offer an interesting contrast against the hard, shimmering metal surface. The lush greenery and the combination of different leaf structures and textures looks lively and gentle – an effect enhanced by the fluid arrangement of the plants as laid out in the planting plan 5 → p. 15, which looks like an abstract painting.

The design, planning and construction of this wall were carried out by the architect in close collaboration with the Fytogreen planted walls company, in order to have the best possible construction. Several layers of perforated aluminium sheeting are secured on both sides to a steel substructure on three untreated steel supports. Alucobond Spectra Cupral is a material that changes colour depending on the light and on the angle it is seen from. The holes in the upper section are small so that it conceals more, while their diameter increases lower down, leaving the metal supports visible.

1   The two planted vertical garden beds are flush with the aluminium wall cladding in the narrow, two-storey inner courtyard of a private house.

The colour, transparency and texture of the wall are different at different times of the day. The spaces for the planned planting modules for the two Fytowalls were cut out of the aluminium, and containers made from plastic-coated, watertight plywood with an overall surface area of 10.5 m² were fitted into the gaps to house the wall planting systems and all installations. The outer edges of the planting modules are flush with the aluminium surface.

The modules have standard dimensions of 100 × 50 × 15 cm and consist of a special hydroculture substrate. This non-soil substrate can absorb large amounts of moisture and transport it upwards by a wicking effect. This means that the plants only have to be provided with water and nutrients via the drip tubes laid between all rows of modules for 5 to 10 minutes every day.

The standard parameters for the Fytowall – orientation, light, direct sunlight, air movement, shade, temperature and precipitation – were checked on site. The supporting wall that anchors the hooks for the plant modules can support 88 kg/m². After the supporting wall was completed and the necessary water and electricity supply had been fitted, the concealed irrigation system was added. In the event of municipal restrictions on water use during a drought, the planted wall will be supplied from rainwater tanks integrated into a natural stone wall along the access path.

The planted walls firm had started growing the plants in the modules 12 weeks before the Fytowall was installed, so that when they were installed in the wall, leaf cover was at about 80%. Moisture sensors and a control unit were provided to regulate the amount of water and nutrients required by the plants and the duration of the supply each day.

After completion and checking of all installations, the individual plant modules were hung on the stainless steel fastenings mounted on the wall. The actual planting was completed in a few hours.

Completion services included installing and checking the control apparatus and the drip pan, which catches any excess water at the planted wall's lower edge and channels it into the house's drainage system. The drip pan is 20 cm deep – 5 cm deeper than the planting modules – so that it can catch any water dripping from the leaves.

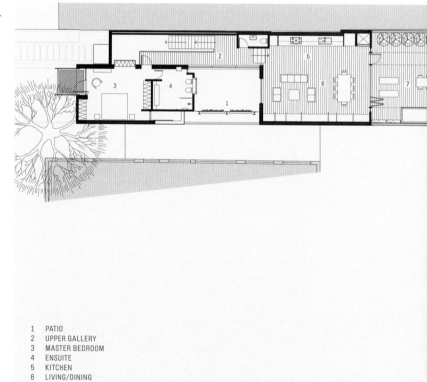

2 Layout of house with courtyard.
3/4 The vertical gardens are framed in perforated aluminum
    sheeting. The fine pattern of holes in the upper half provide privacy
    protection from the neighbouring apartment buildings, while
    the large holes lower down leave the untreated steel supports visible.
5 Fytowall planting plan.

1   PATIO
2   UPPER GALLERY
3   MASTER BEDROOM
4   ENSUITE
5   KITCHEN
6   LIVING/DINING
7   DECK

2

3

4

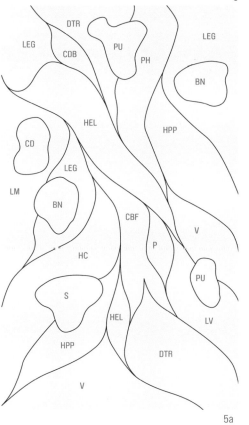

5a

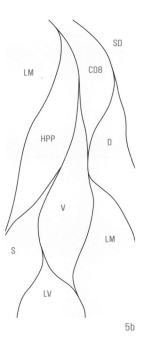

5b

LEG	Liriope 'Evergreen Giant'	*Liriope 'Evergreen Giant'*
HEL	hellebore	*Helleborus*
DTA	Dianella	*Dianella*
LV	Liriope variegata	*Liriope variegata*
BN	bird's-nest fern	*Asplenium australasicum*
S	elkhorn fern	*Platycerium bifurcatum*
HPP	alum root	*Heuchera purple plum*
CBF	Serbian bellflower	*Campanula poscharskyana*
PH	Pteris hendersoni	*Pteris hendersoni*
HC	mother spleenwort	*Asplenium bulbiferum*
LM	lilyturf	*Liriope muscari*
P	Pratia	*Pratia*
V	common violet	*Viola odorata*
SM	Ophiopogon japonicus 'Nana'	*Ophiopogon japonicus 'Nana'*
SD	Ophiopogon 'Snow Drops'	*Ophiopogon 'Snow Drops'*
D	hare's foot fern	*Davallia*
CDB	Dalmatian bellflower	*Campanula portenschlagiana*
CD	rainbow fern	*Calochlaenda dubia*
CDB	Campanula portenschlagiana	*Campanula portenschlagiana*
CD	Calochlaenda dubia	*Calochlaenda dubia*

5

Planted lift shaft and canteen for the headquarters of the Tryg insurance company

PLANTWALLS: Green Fortune
ARCHITECTURE, DESIGN: Built Identity, Copenhagen, Denmark
COMPLETION: 2007–2011
LOCATION: Ballerup, Copenhagen, Denmark

PLANNING ASSIGNMENT

Vertical planting in an office building: as a cladding for a lift shaft, as a sound-dampening feature, and the eye-catching 'café tree' meeting place.

CONTEXT

This new interior architecture and design concept visually represents and reinforces the merger of two large insurance companies – on the outside and on the inside. The Copenhagen company Built Identity created a renewal concept that went far beyond simply renovating the building.

After analysing the company's list of values, they created a new and vital corporate identity. The values of humanity, innovation and energy were incorporated into an organic, visionary and distinctive design.

The tree as a metaphor is an important element, recurring throughout the building. This is why several vertical wall plantings were part of the plan from the beginning: they represent the tree, and their natural liveliness contrasts with the pale-coloured, unadorned Scandinavian interior.

There are also 'tree' elements in the entrance area (roots), on the lift shaft (trunk), in the 'cafe tree' (crown), on the floor elements in the lift shaft (branches), and in the offices (fine twigs with leaves and flowers).   →

1   The café tree in the canteen is an eye-catching feature and a meeting place. At the same time, both the planting and the panels installed in its interior reduce noise.

CONCEPTS

Planting of the round lift shaft

The company's Copenhagen headquarters consists of eight buildings. In a multi-step process, these have been redesigned and partially enlarged. They are connected by an elongated, roofed access space known as 'The Street'. This 'Street' is a two-storey transit area that receives plenty of sunlight through a glass roof and glass facades on the gable sides. Apart from a strip of red floor tiles, white predominates – which makes the planting on the round lift shaft in the middle of the access space all the more striking. The varied green of the plants contrasts distinctly with the functional, clear inner space. The different shapes and volumes of the leaves and stems and the movement of the overhanging planting give the space depth, warmth and structure.

The Plantwall structure is an inorganic fabric in which plants can flourish. It is only 75 to 80 mm thick, and can bend to fit around rounded walls. The planting begins a few centimetres above the ground, and can be seen from several different heights. The selection of plants takes the conditions into account, featuring plants from warm climates that thrive at a lighting strength of 700 to 1000 lux. Spotlights mounted around the upper edge of the shaft **2** optimize the light provision (the daylight falling through the glazed roof is insufficient because the isolating glass blocks much of the red end of the spectrum). The automatic watering and nutrient supply building systems are housed in a small box. Maintenance is largely confined to checking regularly on the health of the plants and making sure that the supply system is functioning properly.

2

3

Planting in the canteen

Before the redesign, the large canteen was an uncomfortable, cold and noisy room used for taking quick meals. Since the redesign, the visitor enters a bright café through the new entrance area. It has a new eye-catching feature and meeting space: the 'café tree'.

The sides of the square 'café tree' structure are covered with the same Plantwall system as the lift shaft. Because the plant elements are only 75 to 80 mm thick, they do not impose any additional loads. There are noise-absorbing panels inside the café tree's steel structure that significantly improve the space's acoustic qualities. All the electricity and water conduits are integrated into the cladding so that they do not affect the simple design of the visible structure. The planting, with its large leaf volumes, actively contributes to the spatial climate by absorbing sound and increasing humidity in the air. The artificial lighting had to satisfy two requirements: adequately supplying all plants with light, while keeping the canteen free of glare.

The redesign shows that well-designed shared spaces can contribute to a strong corporate identity. Workers at the Copenhagen headquarters use the canteen and café throughout the day as a new multifunctional work space: for working on laptops, for discussions with colleagues or customers, and for breaks. The combination of artificial and natural elements creates a 'living house' where employees and customers can feel welcome, meet up, and work together. The design seamlessly combines practical use and communication – indoors and outdoors.

2 In this narrow space, the additional lighting needed for the plants creates a play of light and shadow that changes throughout the day.
3 From a distance, the round wall planting looks like a massive trunk. Closer to, one becomes aware of the texture, scent, moisture and movement of the plants.
4 Floor plan of traffic areas with lift shaft.

4

5

5   The café tree symbolizes development,
    harmony, balance and growth.
6   The compact wall planting system places
    no extra demands on the loadbearing
    structure, allowing the café tree to be a
    freestanding structure.
7   Floor plan of café tree.
8   Construction principles of café tree.
9   Cross section of café tree.
10 Detail of drip gutter.
11 Detail of corner.

6

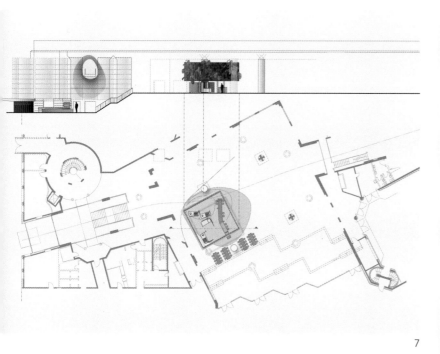

7

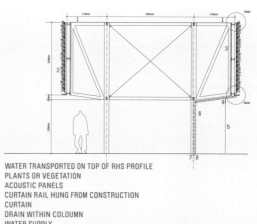

1   WATER TRANSPORTED ON TOP OF RHS PROFILE
2   PLANTS OR VEGETATION
3   ACOUSTIC PANELS
4   CURTAIN RAIL HUNG FROM CONSTRUCTION
5   CURTAIN
6   DRAIN WITHIN COLOUMN
7   WATER SUPPLY
8   DRAIN

9

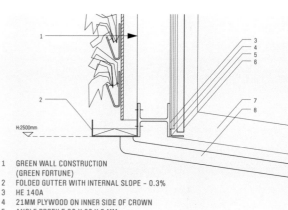

1   GREEN WALL CONSTRUCTION
      (GREEN FORTUNE)
2   FOLDED GUTTER WITH INTERNAL SLOPE - 0.3%
3   HE 140A
4   21MM PLYWOOD ON INNER SIDE OF CROWN
5   ANGLE PROFILE 60 X 30 X 5 MM
6   PERFORATED ACOUSTIC PANELS,
      METAL TYPE AS LUXLON, WALL CLADDING W-H1000
7   RHS 120 X 60 MM
8   DRAIN 56 MM

10

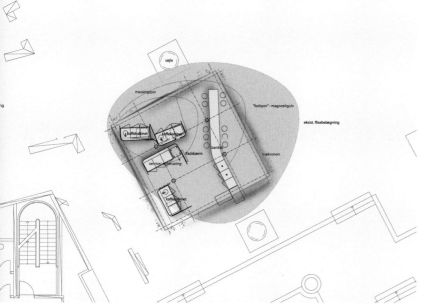

8

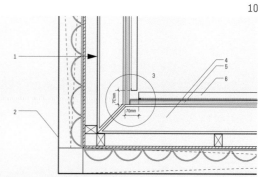

1   GREEN WALL CONSTRUCTION (GREEN FORTUNE)
2   FOLDED GUTTER WITH INTERNAL SLOPE - 0.3%
3   ACOUSTIC PANELS FIXED WITH EQUAL DISTANCE TO THE CORNER,
      INACCURACY IS REGULATED TOWARDS RHS-PROFILE
4   HE140A
5   PLYWOOD ON INNER SIDE OF CROWN - 21 MM
6   PERFORATED ACOUSTIC PANEL, METAL TYPE AS LUXLON,
      WALL CLADDING W-H1000

11

Vertical garden at the head office of Mannheimer Swartling law firm

PLANT WALL: Green Fortune
ARCHITECT: Strategisk Arkitektur
PROJECT DESIGN: Gretchen Milliken and Jonas Ericsson
COMPLETION: 2008
LOCATION: Stockholm, Sweden

PLANNING BRIEF

A wall of greenery integrated into the marble wall cladding to enhance the company's profile and to enliven the traditionally styled interior architecture.

CONTEXT

The Mannheimer Swartling legal practice is an international legal advice firm. The spectacular new office building, which has 14,000 m² of usable space, plays an important role in getting the firm's message across – as is expressed by the architectural language and generous volumes of this steel and glass building, in which the materials and colours of the interior – marble, wood, muted colour tones – are based on classical ideals.

CONCEPT

The client requested that a planted wall be included in the interior design. The vegetation seems to grow directly out of the marble facade cladding adjacent to the broad access steps in the atrium's foyer area. The greenery of this vertical garden does not make it look as if nature is breaking into the building – instead, it fits into the space's design as if it was an elegant wall covering.

This kind of 'plant wall' is usually installed in a climate-controlled, heated interior space where the temperature does not significantly deviate from 200 °C. The location factors – especially temperature, humidity and light – are analysed and used to determine what plants will be used.

In this interior space, there was insufficient daylight even for shade-loving plants, because the atrium's glazing almost completely blocks the light wavelengths used by plants. A way of providing light for the whole expanse of the wall had to be found. Ten metal halogen lamps on mountings projecting high above the steps are trained on the green space in such a way that the individual species each receive the amount of light they require. This lighting scheme also makes the wall stand out more and emphasizes the aesthetics of the planting. →

1   The 'plant wall' complements the broad access steps of the Mannheimer Swartling, a large law firm in Stockholm.
This 70 m² plant wall is one of the largest designs by Green Fortune, which specializes in wall plantings in interiors.

The wall planting has other uses besides its aesthetic and communicative functions: noise reduction and improvement of climate by binding dust, filtering out pollutants, and increasing humidity. However, the dryness of the air within the office (as with most office buildings, the air here can become very dry in winter) can also damage the plants, making it important to choose suitable species. The regular checks during maintenance are particularly directed towards preventing attacks by pests, such as spider mites, occasioned by dry air.

The planted wall is a closed system, with drip tubes supplying the plants with a water-nutrient solution. After the tubes and conduits for the automatic irrigation system and the subconstruction had been installed on the supporting wall, the textile modules for the plant roots were attached. All the connections and mountings are hidden in the wall niche. The control unit for the automatic irrigation system is easy to access, but is discreetly hidden in a wall cupboard. A gutter along the green wall's lower edge collects excess water and channels it into the building's drainage system. This gutter is integrated into the facade's marble cladding and is concealed from above by overhanging plants. After the law firm's supporting wall had been prepared, applying the modules and the planting only took two weeks.

A plant wall brings greenery into a building without reducing the usable space. The vegetation often imposes no more requirements on the planning, construction and budget than any other wall covering – natural stone, for example.

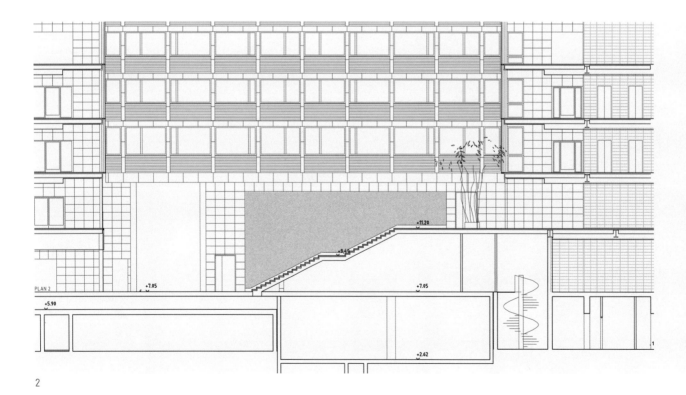

2

4

5

2   Cross section of the access steps with a
    view of the 'plant wall'.
3   The size of the planted area accommodates
    a wide variety of plants without disrupting
    the surface.
4   An exclusive wall covering made from plants
    as part of the interior concept.
5   The wall planting system was installed in a
    wall niche, sunk in flush with the surround-
    ing marble wall cladding. The necessary
    light for the plants is provided by the artifi-
    cial lighting.

3

Roofed patio with garden terrace in the Foothills family home in Pokeno

ARCHITECTURE AND GREEN PLANNING:
Strachan Group Architects
COMPLETION: 2007
LOCATION: Pokeno, Waikato, New Zealand

PLANNING ASSIGNMENT

Weather-protected patio with seating and 'garden' as an extension to the living space and as part of the building's floor plan.

CONTEXT

This large family home lies on the south side of the Bombay Hills on New Zealand's North Island, south of the city of Auckland. In the winter months (from June to August) it is affected by New Zealand's cold weather. The planner's job was to create a protected garden space, so that the inhabitants could sit out on the terrace all year round.

CONCEPT

The Strachan Group Architects architecture firm designed the house and the planting as a single unit. The living and sleeping areas are housed in two separate, low blocks, connected by a roofed patio **2**. The indoor garden is laid out in this connective space: a rectangular bed frames a terrace with wood flooring and seats so that it has a narrow green strip running all around it.

The patio creates a buffer zone between the two blocks, from which it is thermally separated. It has under-floor heating, but this does not need to be switched on, even in the winter, because the greenhouse effect heats up the enclosed courtyard and the concrete floor stores the heat. The patio connects to both the living room and the outer courtyard via large sliding doors **5**. A short wooden staircase leads to a gallery connected to the sleeping area.

A 35 cm gap in the paving creates a continuous planting bed connected to the ground soil **4**. The terrace is covered with local eucalyptus wood *(Eucalyptus pilularis)* and rises 15 cm above the upper edge of the flooring. The concrete subfloor of the patio projects 20 cm over the planting bed on all sides, reducing the open space to a 15 cm strip. The dense mondo grass, also known as fountain grass *(Ophiopogon japonicus)* gives the appearance of welling up from beneath the terrace. →

1   The garden terrace lies in the centre of the family home, unifying indoors and outdoors.

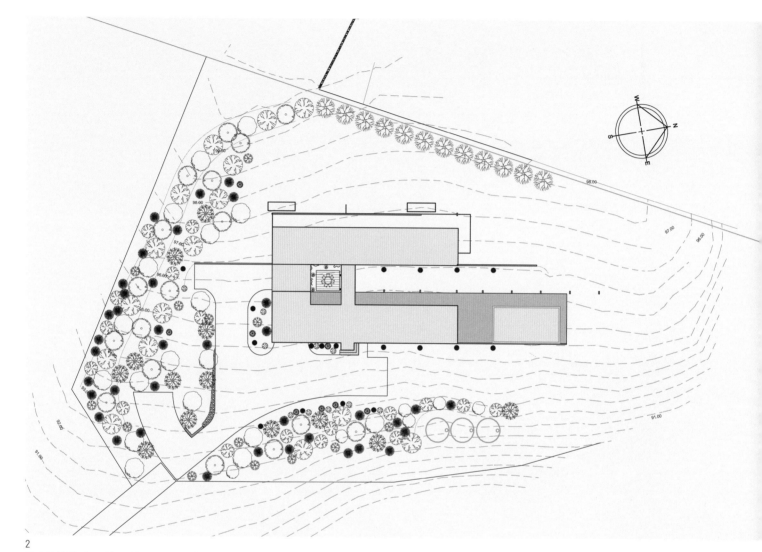

2

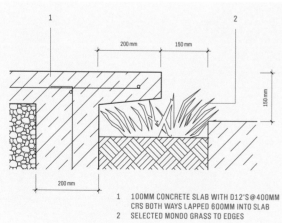

1   100MM CONCRETE SLAB WITH D12'S @ 400MM
    CRS BOTH WAYS LAPPED 600MM INTO SLAB
2   SELECTED MONDO GRASS TO EDGES

2   Site plan and floor plan.
3   Detail of planting bed.
4   The low ground-covering plants in the bed look like a piece of lawn
    inserted around the wooden terrace. The tall plants emphasize the
    protective effect of the niche between the gallery and the wall.
    The glass fibre surface at the side allows light into the garage beyond.
5   The indoor garden extends into the outdoor space (the green strips
    between the two blocks).

3

Taller plants with similar shapes stand amid the ground-covering mondo grass along the sides of the terrace: a multi-trunked Madagascar dragon tree *(Dracaena marginata)*, two king sago palms *(Cycas revoluta)*, two Kentia palms *(Howea forsteriana)* and several bromeliads *(Bromeliaceae)*. The fronded foliage in varying shades of green breaks up the interior and creates a background for the seating **5**.

The planting bed contains local volcanic soil. This soil has a high pore volume, making it suitable for this planting, as there is no danger of waterlogging. To improve the supply of nutrients, a thin layer of humus was added to the soil during planting.

4

5

Loft apartment with indoor garden

ARCHITECTS: planungsgruppe agsn architekten (Theo Boss, Winfried Klimesch)
WITH THE ASSISTANCE OF: Janne Sartorius
INDOOR PLANTING: Strohm Innenbegrünungen
COMPLETION: 2005
LOCATION: Düsseldorf, Germany

PLANNING BRIEF

Convert a former storage space into a loft apartment and improve ventilation/air quality by planting large-leafed plant species.

CONTEXT

The building is an apartment building from 1928. After being partially destroyed during the Second World War, it was rebuilt in 1948. The wooden construction of the roof truss was replaced by a steel girder construction at that time. This steel girder construction was retained during a further conversion from 1972 to 1973 and was deliberately integrated into the April 2005 architectonic concept.

Today, the former storage area is an attractive loft apartment with 132 m² of usable space, including a loggia. The east half of the roof is almost completely glazed, flooding the open room volumes with daylight. The only areas partitioned off by walls are the bathroom and the sleeping space.

CONCEPT

A structure with two plant beds fits between the cooking and dining areas and the living space. The 300×100×50 cm and 120×150×50 centimetre plant beds are clad with light-coloured oak, which matches the floor covering between the beds **7/8**. A pane of translucent glass in the separating wall between the bathtub and the larger of the two plant beds in the living space can be slid to one side so that one can see from the bath into the living space.

The smaller plant bed houses a large rubber tree, or *Ficus elastica* **3**. The slender stem fans out at the top, with the crown taking full advantage of the generous amount of space. The plant's shape and the glossy, dark green leaves make an interesting contrast with the second solitaire plant in the opposite bed: a banana tree, or *Musa* **4**. A small-leafed bougainvillea hybrid climbs up the steel girders of the roof construction. In both plant beds, the solitaire plants are surrounded by ground cover and other plants. Plants with a diverse range of leaf shapes and colours – including, for instance, the long-lived tiger begonia *(Begonia bowerae)* – create an abundant, harmonious overall composition. The abundant leaf surface area also improves air quality. The plants filter the air, bind dust, produce oxygen, improve humidity, and cool the air by transpiration.   →

1   The interior planting improves the quality of life in the loft apartment: it improves the space's climate and introduces a bit of garden into the urban surroundings.

3

4

2   5

6

7

TECHNICAL IMPLEMENTATION

A purely mineral substrate specially developed for interior planting based on green roof requirements was used to pot the plants. The lava and pumice mix keeps the soil aerated, giving the soil good air and water conduction. Clay minerals buffer the basalt salts, and granules of varying sizes provide good root anchorage. The substrate is structurally stable and can keep the plants alive for several decades.

Both plant beds have conduits leading to the building's drainage system, so that the plants can be watered by an automatic irrigation system. If the plants get too dry, moisture detectors in the soil send a signal to the control system, which then releases water from a magnetic valve. The pressure-compensated drip tubes that provide the water are located just beneath the substrate. The plants are fertilized by hand as needed. A product with low levels of ballast salts was used for the planting to prevent a buildup of salts that cannot be absorbed by plants in the soil.

8

2 Floor plan and cross section.
3 Two solitaire trees in two flower beds form a contrasting pair.
   The smaller bed contains a rubber tree *(Ficus elastica)* ...
4 ... and the larger bed contains a banana tree *(Musa)*.
5 Detail of the plant bed: bed construction with sealing and root
   protection film, a drain connected to the building's drains,
   the inspection shaft, drainage, separating film, and substrate.
6 The large, projecting leaves of the banana tree provide natural sun
   protection for the plant bed cladding, which doubles as a seating
   element.
7/8 The two flower beds are an architectonic element that fits
   between the living space and the kitchen, connected by the corridor
   floor covering.

A tree in an Athens apartment

ARCHITECT: Meletitiki – Alexandros N. Tombazis and Associates Architects Ltd.
COMPLETION: 1991
LOCATION: Athens, Greece

PLANNING BRIEF

The planting of a conservatory. Originally a plant bed with various plants. Currently a single tree that fills the whole two-storey volume.

CONTEXT

The residential complex – 17 two-storey terrace houses grouped around a central inner courtyard – was built in 1990/91 **2**. At the start of the project, one of the houses was intended for the architect. Unlike the neighbouring houses, it has a conservatory two storeys high, facing southeast. On the ground floor, the conservatory connects with the living and working space to the north, and the steps up to the first floor. A bridge crosses the airspace on the first floor, connecting the three bedrooms to the stairs. The conservatory's south facade is fully glazed (large windows with glazing bars) and a double door provides access to the terrace. Two window openings in the east facade – a room-sized window with glazing bars on the ground floor and a round window – supplement the intensive sunlight through the south facade. The wall section has a window in the upper storey and an unglazed round opening on the ground floor; daylight reaches the interior of the house through the conservatory.

CONCEPT

The original design involved two fixed-level plant beds connected to the ground: an L-shaped plant bed that runs along the whole width of the east side and along the wall section, separating off the working space, and a second plant bed that is a kind of block construction in the stairwell airspace **3**. Varied, lush, small-leafed vegetation in these beds was intended to provide a touch of green in this light-flooded space. The small *Ficus benjamina* tree was initially planted in the bed near the steps with a 40 cm thick layer of indoor potting compost, with no further aids needed. However, the family later decided to transfer the *Ficus* to the L-shaped plant bed and to have the trunk issuing from a small hole in the floor covering. The tree has since thrived in its new location, with the roots spreading rapidly through the ground under the house, providing the tree with sufficient nutrients and moisture. The *Ficus* bed is not watered or fertilized, but the tree grows so strongly that it has to be cut back two or three times a year.

In 20 years of growing, the tree has taken over the room, and the occupants enjoy the space under the spreading branches. The tree has become one of the building's most striking features.

1   A single large *Ficus* tree is planted in the conservatory.

2

1   ENTRANCE
2   KITCHEN
3   DINING ROOM
4   SUNSPACE
5   OFFICE
6   SITTING ROOM
7   CAR PARK RAMP
8   COURTYARD

4

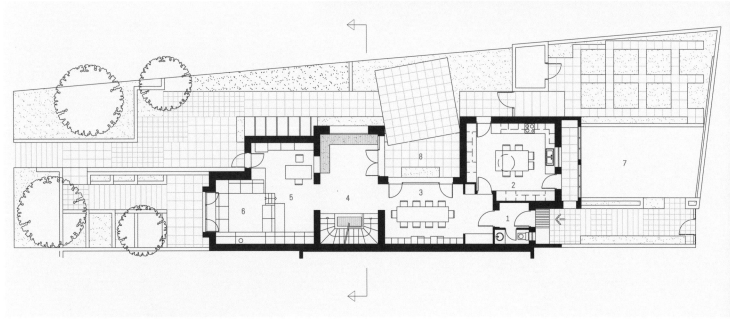

3

5

7

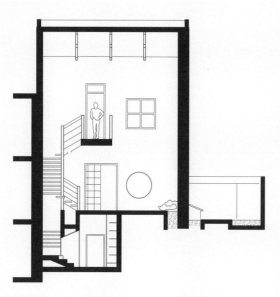

6

2 The interior planting matches the exterior planting, which is
also dominated by solitaire trees.

3 Apartment plan.

4 Exterior view of the building.

5 The original L–shaped and block–shaped plant beds were to be
planted with a wide range of vegetation, which, along with flowering
and climbing plants in pots, would provide a touch of green.

6 A cross section of the conservatory: the planting bed connects
with the ground.

7 The growth form of the *Ficus benjamina* reflects the distribution
of light intensity in the inner space precisely.
The tree turns its crown to the areas of greatest light intensity
– high and to the southeast.

Planting concept for the Seattle Public Library

DESIGN AND GREEN PLANNING:
Inside Outside – Petra Blaisse with
Simao Ferreira, Marieke van den Heuvel,
Mathias Lehner, Peter Niessen,
Floris Schifferli
ARCHITECTS: OMA, New York,
in collaboration with LMN Architects, Seattle
LOCATION: Seattle, Washington, USA
COMPLETION: 2004

PLANNING ASSIGNMENT

Open indoor planting for the Seattle city library, with links to the outdoor space.

CONTEXT

The new city library building was designed by the Dutch architecture firm OMA as a sculptural solitaire building.

The indoor planting is part of the design, which also involved planting the small area of free space around the building on this city site with trees, perennials and various grasses. Due to the facade's folding shape, some of these beds lie beneath the sloped glazing. The 'living room' (main entrance) is several storeys high and has the slanting glass facade as its external shell, which ensures that it receives plenty of sunlight.

The Dutch designer Petra Blaisse and her team at Inside Outside were commissioned to design the landscape. Inside Outside also advised on interior design – acoustics, colour scheme, auditorium curtains and other issues – during the design and completion process, which lasted for over five years.

CONCEPT

Inside Outside planned a planting concept that took advantage of the building's distinctive folded shape and allowed the vegetation from the outdoor space to penetrate into the indoor space by way of inclined surfaces and overlaps. Outdoors, the narrow beds are planted with indigenous trees arranged in groups, framed with perennials and grasses. The small beds under the folds in the glass facade are planted with wild grasses, ferns and perennials. The carpets within the building are a kind of abstract continuation of these. These 'garden carpets' that partially cover the entrance hall and reading floors are printed with enlarged plant structures – small leaves and disorderly grass blades. The 'garden carpets' were intended as an alternative to the plant containers often used in public build-ings. They also dampen noise and make it easier for people to find their way. Their size and large pattern make the furniture look less heavy and more narrow and elegant. →

1 The Seattle library building's shape and glass facade make it look like a crystal. Carpets of perennial and carpets printed with plant motifs, connect the indoors with the outdoors.

There is a single square plant bed in the reading room, on the edge of one of these expansive 'garden carpets' and beneath the inclined roof skin. It is intended to create a connection with the lively green growth outside. The square plant bed's clear geometrical form, emphasized by the wide projections of the framing, creates a harmonious counterpoint to the dynamic lines of the facade grid and the divergent arrangement of the long shelves. The planted area's modern design fits perfectly with the colourful and graphical interior design and with the guidance system for library users. The penetration of the vegetation emphasizes the building shell's transparency and makes the library appear to be part of the outdoor space.

The Inside Outside natural and artificial planting design for the outdoor and indoor areas of the Seattle city library is, once more, a creative and diverse plant design. Even the small indoor bed is a part of the overall design concept, noticed and appreciated by the library's visitors and employees alike.

The conditions in the warm and dry indoor space eventually meant the original vegetation had to be replaced with more low-maintenance species, as several plants had been lost due to insufficient care. The bed is planted with a combination of low perennials, to keep it from obscuring the view into the public reading room and thereby compromising safety. A narrow path was laid through the vegetation to make tending the plants easier. In this closed system, salts that are not absorbed by the plants can gradually accumulate in the substrate. This reduces the vitality of some plants, meaning that they have to be replaced at shorter intervals.

2

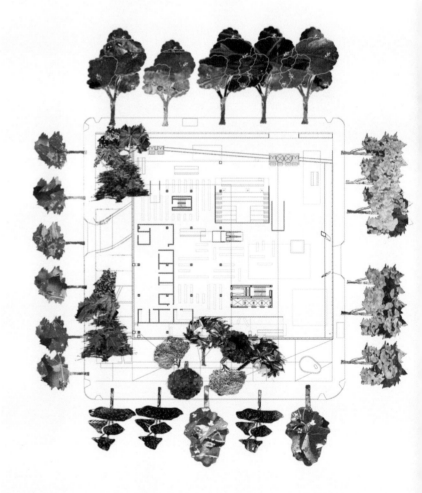

3

4

5   6

2 Exterior view of the building.
3 Floor plan of city library.
4 The indoor planting bed called 'floating
  carpet' is a distinctive feature of the overall
  planning concept.
5 The modern planting design penetrates the
  building's shell. It is continued in the
  indoor space by the 'flying carpet' planting
  bed and by the printed 'garden carpet'.
6 The indoor planting is only separated from
  the outdoor planted bed by a thin glass
  membrane.

Planting concept for the office space at the Combined Traders company

ARCHITECTURE: Marc Koehler Architects
FURNITURE DESIGN: Marc Koehler Architects in collaboration with Made UP interior works
GREEN PLANNING: Marc Koehler Architects in collaboration with Delva Landscape Architects
PROJECT TEAM: Marc Koehler, Kasia Cielibala, Maaike Hawinkels, Kasia Heijerman, Miriam Tocino, Aleksandra Zajac
COMPLETION: 12/2009
LOCATION: Haarlem, the Netherlands

PLANNING ASSIGNMENT

Planting concept as part of an interior design for a large modern office space for ten employees, with different working areas to improve the indoor atmosphere and dampen noise.

CONTEXT

The business is housed in a flexible, roomy and bright workspace with a minimum of obstructions to vision. Employees can work in a concentrated way at individual workstations, but the office also has facilities for teamwork. Employees' work areas are arranged along the outer walls of the main space. The windows are on the gable sides **2** . A continuous table with wavy edges made from corrulite (an MDF slab with a corrugated cardboard core) creates individual workspaces that face towards the walls and are divided spatially by 'archive' islands. The rounded waves can be used for discussions at any time. There is also a small recep-

tion area, a separate conference room that can also be used as a place to relax during breaks **4/5** , and the company management office, which is on an open mezzanine beneath the glazed gable roof. Noise levels are high because of people speaking on the telephone, meaning that sound-dampening measures are needed.

CONCEPT

Several plant containers of different sizes were included in the workspace **8/10** . Large-leafed green plants such as kalanchoe or bamboo palm *(Rhapis excelsa)* function as space-dividers and noise-dampeners. This permanent planting is supplemented by flowering plants and herbs in smaller plant containers, which are closer to the workstations and are intended primarily as decoration. Orchids such as *Phalaenopsis* and mint *(Mentha)* were planted as a finishing touch. Depending on the time of year and preference, these can be supplemented and replaced by hyacinths *(Hyacinthus)*, Indian azaleas *(Rhododendron simsii)* and other flowering plants. The mint is part of the playful side of the planting concept – the leaves can be used to make tea in the small kitchen.   →

---

1   The daylight streaming through the opening onto the mezzanine beneath the glazed gable roof lights up the large office space. Climbing plants and a tall multi-trunked palm emphasize the high, airy nature of the space.

The plant containers are made from PVC tubes 100 to 400 mm in diameter, set into gaps at tabletop level, fixed in place with screws, and with the gap sealed with a silicon joint. The lower end of the PVC tube is closed with a screwed-on lid, and rests on a base on a layer of gravel with the pot plant on top. By removing or adding gravel, the pot height can be adjusted so that the edge of the pot is always beneath the surface of the table top. The plants seem to grow directly out of the surface. It is easy to switch plants, although their development is restricted by the fixed container size.

The worktable planting elements are supplemented by climbing plants: ivy *(Hedera helix)* and mistletoe cacti *(Rhipsalis)* are planted in containers in the mezzanine.

Their tendrils hang down through the gaps in the ceiling into the workspaces **1/9**. Beneath the gable roof, a large umbrella tree (*Schefflera* or *Tupidanthus*) emphasizes the height of the space.

2

3

4

2 The interior combines unadorned formal elements with playful details, such as the swing with climbing plants.
3 A lounge area for informal discussions and breaks was set up in front of the gable–end window.
4/5 A recurring basic geometric shape – the circle – connects the functional elements of the design. Plants placed here and there open up and structure the design.
6 Floor plan.

5

SECTION

1   LARGE PLANTS
2   SMALL PLANTS
3   LOUNGE AREA
4   TRASHCAN
5   ARCHIVE CARROUSEL
6   WORK FIELD
7   ENTRANCE
8   CONFERENCE/LUNCH ROOM

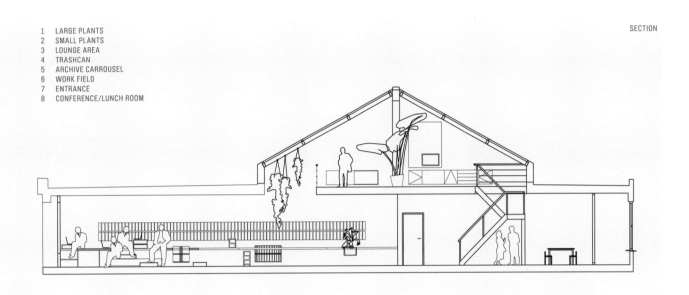

MEZZANINE

OPEN-PLAN OFFICE

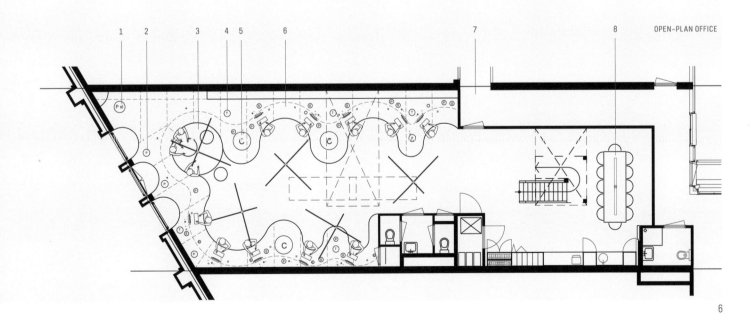

6

7

8

9

7   Marc Koehler Architects designed a flexible, roomy and bright
    workspace with ten workstations and a minimum of obstructions to
    vision. The plants reduce noise and help to divide up the space.
8/10   Plants were chosen for functional reasons: plants with a large
    leaf volume, such as kalanchoe, absorb sound better. Near
    the windows, the light foliage of the bamboo palms lets plenty of
    daylight into the room.
9   The daylight streaming through the opening onto the mezzanine be-
    neath the glazed gable roof lights up the large office space.
11 Cross section detail of plant container.

1   PLANTS
2   SILICONE
3   CORRULITE:
    SPRAY COATED MDF 9 MM
    CORRUGATED CARDBOARD LAYERS
    MDF 9 MM
4   FIXING SCREWS
5   PVC TUBE
6   PEBBLES
7   PVC LID

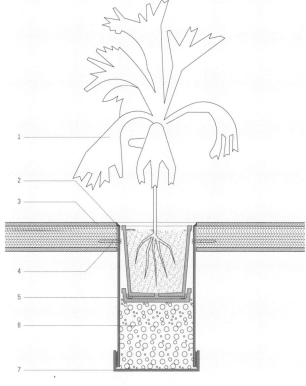

10

11

47

Tree installation in the Chelsea Harbour Design Centre

GREEN PLANNING: Jinny Blom
MANUFACTURE OF PLANT CONTAINERS, STOOLS AND SWANS: Dynamic 3
MODERNIZATION OF INTERIOR: Drinkall Dean Associates
PLANTING WORK AND MAINTENANCE: ISS Waterers
COMPLETION: 2007
LOCATION: London, UK

PLANNING ASSIGNMENT

New planting to rejuvenate three halls in a building from the 1980s.

CONTEXT

The Chelsea Harbour Design Centre is in southwest London, right on the Thames River. Built in the 1980s, it comprises three large four-storey cylinders with an octagonal floor plan, interconnected and capped by glass domes. The Design Centre, which is open to the public, offers office space and showrooms for furniture and object designs; the building also contains a hotel, a restaurant, a café and a fitness club.

Before the redesign, the courtyard-like atria directly under the glass domes in each cylinder were cold, draughty and unappealing, and were rarely used. As part of the renovation of the interior elements by the architecture firm Din Associates, the garden designer Jinny Blom was commissioned by the board of directors of the Design Centre to improve the atria. The quality of the spaces was to be enhanced and their design brought into line with the high-level aesthetics 1 expected by the design firms and their visitors.

CONCEPT

Before commencing the design process, the planting planner commissioned a study to measure the light levels and temperatures in the spaces. The age of the building infrastructure makes it difficult to control the interior temperature. During the building renovation, light-sensitive transparencies had been applied to the domes to diffuse the glare of direct sunlight. Access openings to the atria are also restricted. All these factors were taken into account during planning and plant selection. The greatest challenge, however, was the low bearing load of the ground storey ceiling, above the underground garage. This clearly ruled out large plant beds, or traditional containers made from steel or stone. To create a climate favourable to plants, the automatic sliding doors were replaced with revolving doors, with the aim of reducing the wind tunnel effect. →

1   Each storey offers a different view of the trees. From above, the main effect arises from the homogeneous texture and colour of the small-leafed tree crowns against the white background.

For the two outer atria, Jinny Blom developed a unique installation of large plant containers made of Jesmonite, a composite material made from plaster and synthetic resin. The containers are planted with large trees with tall trunks. The middle atrium, which has a sculptural spiral staircase climbing up the centre **4**, was not given any plants. The organic shapes of the plant containers, and the low seats made of the same material, are the connecting elements for the three atria **6**.

The surfaces of the white containers and low seats are smooth, soft and matte, enhancing haptic perception. The plantings in the two outer courtyards are restricted to a single species of tree, so that the vegetation will not compete with the remarkable shapes and materials but instead be part of a harmoniously composed picture. Three Chinese fig trees *(Ficus panda)* with compact dark green spherical crowns on top of multiple trunks flourish in the warmer south courtyard **5**.

In the north courtyard, the light and airy crowns of the black olive trees *(Bucida buceras)* from South Florida, which rise to varying heights, emphasize the height of the space **3/14**. The uppermost twigs touch the lower ends of the rods and swans suspended in the glass domes. These swans were originally intended as a temporary installation to give the revitalization project a touch of whimsy. They became so popular that they were allowed to continue flying through the airy heights.

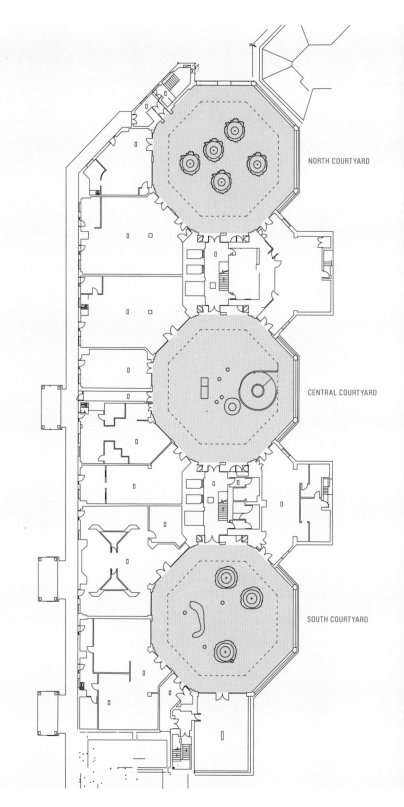

NORTH COURTYARD

CENTRAL COURTYARD

SOUTH COURTYARD

2 Floor plan of the halls with plant installations.
3–5 The three north courtyards: north courtyard, central courtyard
     (without any plants), south courtyard.
6 View of the north courtyard: the mobile stools, made from the
    same material as the plant containers, have similar but individual
    organic forms.

2

3

4

5

6

Trees about 4 to 5 m high were provided by a special-ist garden supplier from the Netherlands. On location, they were planted in the containers, using a special-ized substrate intended for woody plants grown in-doors. This substrate has a stable structure and a high pore volume that aids ventilation and water storage. The completed project required no special measures; just professional maintenance checks.

The design won the Platinum BALI Award for In-terior Landscaping 2008. The redesign and planting has completely transformed the three atria. They have become popular, and the project's originality and high design quality have supplied the symbolic and com-municative function requested by the client.

7

8

9

10

11

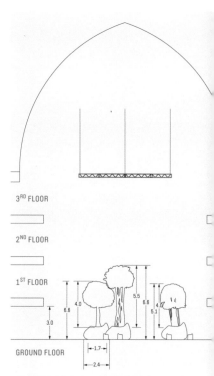

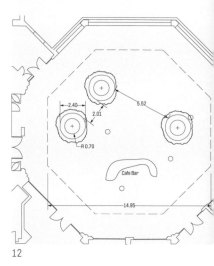

12

7–9 The shapes of the plant containers were developed using computer and clay models and then crafted in Jesmonite, a lightweight compound material made from plaster and artificial resin. Particular attention was paid to the soft, smooth surface.

10/11 The weighty solitaire plants were placed in the plant containers onsite, which were covered to protect their surfaces.

12 Floor plan and cross section of the south hall.

13 Floor plan and cross section of the north hall.

14/15 The shapes and sizes of the plant containers give the large trees sufficient root space and stability, while the organic shapes and materials look striking and classy.

16 For transport, the plants were given various kinds of protection, such as wrapping the stem and covering the substrate, to protect them from damage from physical impacts, direct sunlight, cold and drafts.

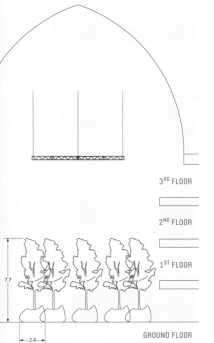

3RD FLOOR

2ND FLOOR

1ST FLOOR

7.7

2.4

GROUND FLOOR

14

3.11

4.04

3.09

2.4

1.61

2.07

2.2

1.41

2.72

14.95

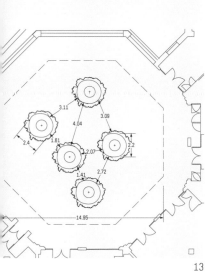

13

15

16

Indoor gardens in the ESO Hotel Desert

ARCHITECT: Auer+Weber+Assozierte
PROJECT MANAGEMENT: Philipp Auer,
Dominik Schenkirz
STAFF: Robert Giessl, Michael Krüger,
Charles Martin
GREEN PLANNING: Gesswein
Landschaftsarchitekten, Ostfildern
COMPLETION: 2002
LOCATION: Atacama Desert, Chile

PLANNING BRIEF

Large roofed garden for recreation and leisure, also designed to increase humidity in the accommodations of the ESO scientists in the dry Chilean desert.

CONTEXT

The European Organization for Astronomical Research in the Southern Hemisphere (abbreviated to ESO) operates a Very Large Telescope (VLT) on the top of Mount Cerro Paranal in the Atacama Desert in northern Chile. This astronomical device consists of four single telescopes, the mirrors of which can be adjusted to work together to achieve very high resolution. The desert location at an altitude of 2600 m is a long way from interference factors caused by human population centres, such as light, atmospheric pollution and dust; the coastal city of Antofogasta is 120 km away.

Conditions are extreme in the desert: the sun shines 360 days per year; winds are often very strong; precipitation is less than 10 mm per year; and the relative humidity is only 5 to 10%. About 150 scientists conduct research here for periods of one to two weeks; they need facilities that include glare-free workstations and a climatically pleasant retreat where they can relax and recover. And of course, the building

must not emit any light pollution at night, so that work with the telescope is not impaired.

The design by the Auer+Weber+Assozierte practice provides 120 rooms, office space, a restaurant and leisure facilities; it meets strict technical demands in terms of furniture, equipment, and earthquake safety.

The form of the building relates to the empty, bleak landscape: the building is rather like a retaining wall, and spans a shallow trough in the terrain. It exploits the geography of the location in a manner borrowed from Land Art, works of art by Richard Serra, or cliffdwellings. The only element of the building that rises above the accessible flat roof is the shallow dome over the entrance hall, which houses a large indoor garden **7/9** . Like all the other public areas, it is sunk into the ground and lit only from above. The curve of the dome is a subtle allusion to the telescope's concave mirror.

The entire residence was built of exposed concrete, cast in situ, coloured with iron oxide pigments. The reddish shading blends with the colours of the desert, and the rough concrete surfaces also impact upon the interior.

CONCEPT

The garden rotunda forms the entrance hall for the building. It is accessed via external ramps cut into the terrain on level -2, and a porch-like air lock **2** . On entering the garden, the light changes gently from dazzling to diffuse, while the humidity rises rapidly from the outdoor norm of 5 or 10% to a moist 65%. →

---

1   The hotel entrance hall's garden, with its lush foliage, contrasts with the sparsely planted desert landscape outside.

The air is humidified by means of fine water misting at the entrance, plus the natural evaporation from the swimming pool and the plants, and spreads from the garden into all the public area and access zones. The offices and the restaurant, which has views of the garden, are on level -2. The leisure and recreation areas, including the swimming pool, are on level -4.

The intensively planted tropical garden in the rotunda serves as a climate well and recreation area. These functions are also performed by a second garden, a rectangular inner courtyard planted with palm trees on level -2, lit by skylights **5/11** .

TECHNICAL IMPLEMENTATION

The planting in the rotunda extends to two linked rising planted areas connected to the soil, supported by a limited number of retaining walls; they are 345 m² and 210 m² in size respectively, and a gravel path runs through them. The slanting planted areas have direct access to the natural soil. The subsoil was dug and raked to a depth of 40 cm before the planting substrate was added, in order to increase permeability. The deeper planting troughs for the trees are linked by a drainage hose to prevent accumulation of moisture.

A separate space for gardening tools, care products and spare parts for the automatically controlled watering system was provided close to the swimming pool.

As well as providing natural climatization for the garden, the high humidity prevents the timber from drying out and makes it possible to use this natural building material without difficulty; it also emphasizes the oasis effect of the interior.   →

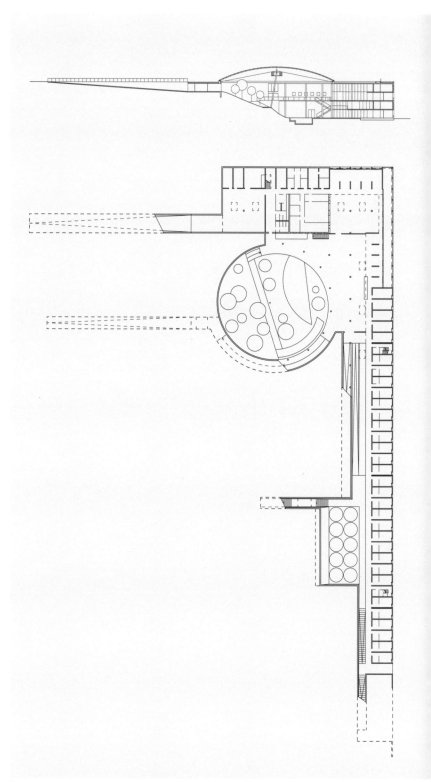

2   Cross section and floor plan of the hotel.
    The only planted areas inside the hotel are the circular
    entrance hall and the rectangular inner courtyard.
3   Floor plan of rotunda.
4   Cross section of rotunda.
5   Floor plan of patio.
6   Detail of patio tree pit.

2

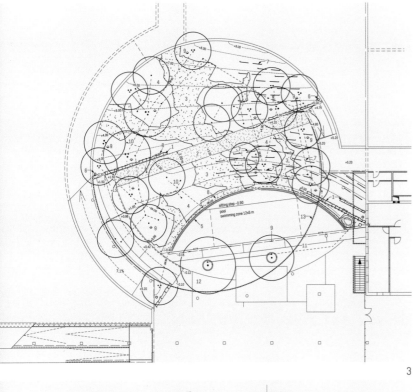

3

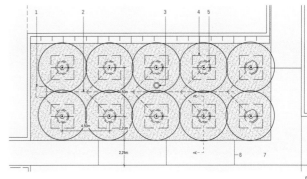

5

1   UNDERFLOOR DRAIN PIT 1×1×1 M
     FILLED WITH GRAVEL 32/63
2   DRAIN PIPE
3   PIT HYDRANT
4   FLAT GRID WITH GRAVEL
     (SEE SECTION AA)
5   IRRIGATION SET
6   EXPANSION JOINT
7   IN SITU CONCRETE

1   RETAINING WALL
2   GRAVEL WALK
3   PLANT AREA: COVERED WITH GRAVEL AND
     CRUSHED STONES
4   PLANT AREAS: GROUND COVERS
5   DRAINAGE CHANNEL
6   PIT HYDRANT
7   SHEARING RESISTANCE:
     UNDERFLOOR WOODEN BOARDS
8   DRAIN PIPE
9   ILLUMINATION: POOL PROJECTORS,
     GROUND SPOT LIGHTS
10   FOG-SYSTEM: PIPE AND NOZZLE
11   IN SITU CONCRETE
12   GRAVEL CONCRETE
13   FRONT EDGE CEILING

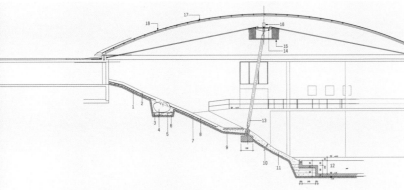

4

1   SUBGRADE PREPARED 40 CM BELOW
     SURFACE
     EXISTING SOIL DUG AND
     FORKED FOR WATER PERMEABILITY
2   WATER PIPE FOG SYSTEM
3   SOIL SEPARATING FLEECE
4   FILLING OF TREE PIT WITH MIXTURE: 50%
     SUBSOIL, 50% GRAVEL 2/16
5   DRAINAGE COURSE 2/32 MM
6   DRAINAGE OF THE TREE PIT BY DRAIN PIPE
     DN 100 CONNECTED TO NEXT TREE PIT
7   SOIL SEPARATING FLEECE AND ROOTING
     WEB UNDERNEATH PLANT AREAS
8   30 CM PLANT SUBSTRATUM
9   GRAVEL WALK: 3 CM COVERING LAYER
     GRAVEL CHIPS 3/8, 12 CM COMPENSATING
     COURSE 0/16, SAME MATERIAL AS COVER,
     15 CM WEARING COURSE 0/32,

10   SHEARING RESISTANCE UNDERFLOOR
     WOODEN BOARDS, 2×30×300 CM,
     FIXED BY PEGS, 60 CM
11   STONES AND GRAVEL 8/16
12   POOL
13   HINGED STEEL COLUMN Ø 270 MM
14   DOME BLACK-OUT SYSTEM
15   TEXTILE
16   MOTOR
17   STEEL SUB CONSTRUCTION
18   DOME ROOFING: HOLLOW POLYCARBONATE
     SLABS

6

1   IN SITU CONCRETE SMOOTH FINISH REINFORCED, 15 CM
2   GRAVEL AREA: 3 CM COVERING LAYER GRAVEL CHIPS 3/8,
     12 CM COMPENSATING COURSE 0/16, SAME MATERIAL
     AS COVER, 15 CM WEARING COURSE 0/32
3   TREE IRRIGATION SET CONSISTING OF RING
     SHAPED DRAIN PIPE DN 80 WITH ALUMINIUM CAP
     INTEGRATED IN FLAT GRID, IRRIGATION PIPE LAID
     ON TOP OF ROOT BALL
4   FLAT GRID QUADRATIC, MESH WIDTH 30X30, COVERED WITH
     GRAVEL CHIPS 3/8, DIMENSION 2,20 M × 2,20 M
5   30 CM PLANTING SUBSTRATUM CONSISTING OF:
     60% LAVA GRANULATE 2/6 MM, 20% COMPOST SOIL,
     10% SAND 0/2 MM, 10% BARK HUMUS
6   FILLING OF TREE PIT WITH MIXTURE:
     50% SUBSOIL, 50% GRAVEL 2/16
7   SOIL SEPARATING FLEECE
8   DRAINAGE COURSE 2/32 MM, DRAINAGE OF TREE
     PIT BY DRAIN PIPE DN 100 CONNECTED TO DRAIN PIT

The dome over the garden is a section from a sphere 35 m in diameter, with its apex at 3.73 m. The bars on the grid are square cavity profiles arranged in two layers. Polycarbonate hollow panels 2.5 cm thick are fastened to the steel substructure with terminal strips. The adjustable blinds under the domed roof are not there to protect the garden from the sun, but to reduce light levels and avoid light pollution: the radial textile curtain is run out in the evening and closes the domed roof off completely.

The exotic plants have developed better than expected since completion in 2002: this is mainly the result of intensive sunlight in combination with high humidity. The location conditions are like those in a greenhouse, and the banana shrubs (*Musa*) in particular often have to be cut back. Two pests have become widespread, however: mealybugs *(Pseudococcus spp)*, which attack mainly palms and bananas, and the tomato leaf miner *(Tuta absoluta)*, which attacks lower shrubs and bushes. The struggle with different pesticides suitable for interior use is a constant trial of strength and one of the principal jobs for the gardener who looks after the planting, as the watering is controlled automatically; so far the problem has not been resolved.

7

7   The dome rises above the level of the accessible roof.
8   The sun shines for 360 days a year in the desert, so that the plants
    flourish as they would in a greenhouse, given the humidity level
    under the dome, which is raised to 65%.
9   The garden landscape in the rotunda was modelled from excavated
    material from the building. The large planted areas connected
    to the natural rise from the swimming pool on level –4 to the
    entrance on level –2.
10 The garden at night with lowered manipulators.
11 The rectangular patio is also lit only from above; it helps to raise
    humidity in this part of the building and provides seating niches
    under palms.

8

9

10

11

Tropical garden in the roofed patio of the Postmedia building

GREEN PLANNING (REDESIGN AND EXECUTION):
Oriole Landscaping Ltd.
LOCATION: Toronto, Ontario, Canada
COMPLETION: 10/2008

PLANNING ASSIGNMENT

Renovation of a 20-year-old tropical garden on the roofed patio of a newspaper headquarters.

CONTEXT

At the end of the 1980s, Butterfly Landscapes company planted this roofed inner courtyard in the Postmedia Network building (then the Can-West building) in Toronto, headquarters of the daily newspaper, the *National Post*. After 20 years, the planting needed to be replaced and renewed. The newspaper company commissioned the Canadian landscape architecture firm Oriole Landscaping to redesign the planted inner courtyard, give it new walls and plants, and install an irrigation system. The redesign – including the masonry, plastering and planting work – was carried out while the newspaper carried on with business as usual.

The roofed inner courtyard, over 310 m², has an elongated octagonal floor plan and is connected to the upper storeys by two open stairways that cross the airspace. Galleries with open metal parapets provide varied views of the plants **2**. It is lighted solely through the glass roof; large areas of the inner courtyard receive direct sunlight throughout the day. The offices on the ground floor are separated from the in-

ner courtyard by expansive windows, but their inhabitants can see directly into the courtyard and receive plentiful sunlight. The garden is kept at room temperature all year round.

CONCEPT

The aim of the redesign was to create a bright and lushly planted recreational and connective space, with the summery atmosphere of a Mediterranean plaza. First, the path system was altered: a broad, paved path now runs diagonally across the space from the lobby **3/7**. Three circles of varied sizes project from the path into the two plant beds at the sides, creating semicircular enclaves with space for tables and stools. The paving complements the circular shapes in the flooring and modifies the linear paths. The third, almost round, planting bed frames the lower flight of the steps leading up to the first storey **4**.

The round bed directs the paths towards the cafeteria and the washrooms, while screening the entrances to both areas so that they cannot be seen from the recreational parts of the garden.   →

1   In the Postmedia Network building's protected recreational and entrance courtyard, the seating fits into semicircular bays.

The plant beds are all surrounded by stone walls 40 cm thick and about 50 cm high, all made from the same 'Brussels Block' shaped tumbled blocks **6/8**. The slightly projecting top of the wall is light grey in colour, while the pattern of stones below is enlivened by different shades: light beige, orange and red-brown.

Seven large plants dating from the original planting project were retained and integrated into the new design. Large, with broad crowns, they take advantage of and enhance the high airspace, but also fit into the scale of the storeys and of the plot as a whole. They make their mark on the lush subtropical scene, and are enhanced by the new smaller plants – an assortment of perennials and bushes. The assortment of perennials deliberately incorporates many different leaf shapes, colours and textures, in order to emphasize the garden's lushness and variety. Some of the species chosen have unusual flowers, such as the bird of paradise flower or the ginger variety *Zingiber collinsii*, with its eye-catching light-and-dark patterned foliage.

The new smaller plants were chosen by Oriole Landscaping, in the following species and quantities:

2

Chinese evergreen *(Aglaonema 'Mary Ann')*, 12 plants

Chinese evergreen *(Aglaonema 'Peacock')*, 3 plants

Codiaeum 'Petra', 30 plants

Lilyturf *(Liriope muscari)*, 45 plants

Philodendron *(Philodendron 'Imperial Green')*, 10 plants

Philodendron *(Philodendron 'Imperial Red')*, 5 plants

Philodendron *(Philodendron 'Xanadu')*, 9 plants

Snake plant *(Sansevieria 'Black Coral')*, 35 plants

Giant Bird of Paradise flower *(Strelitzia nicolai)*, 1 plant

Cardboard palm/cycad *(Zamia furfuracea)*, 3 plants

'Golden Tree' *(Zamioculcas zamiifolia)*, 25 plants

Ginger *(Zingiber collinsii)*, 3 plants

Hollow, freestanding lamps that look rather like street lamps stand in the planting beds, helping to give the garden the appearance of a public Mediterranean plaza **4**.

3

4

5

6

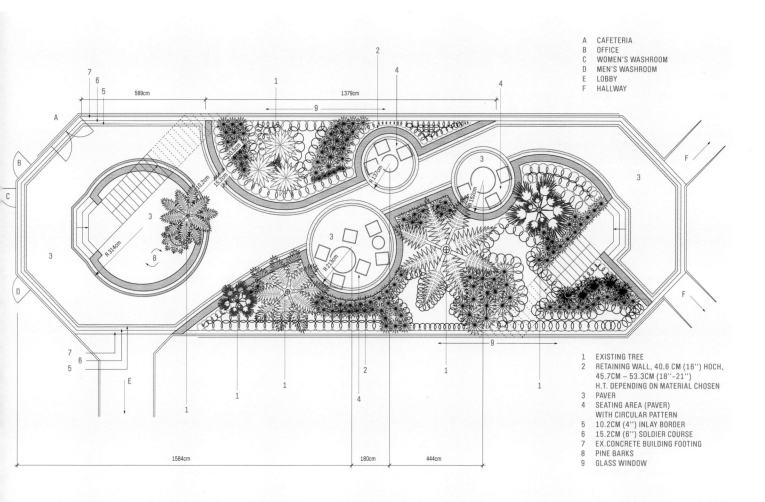

A CAFETERIA
B OFFICE
C WOMEN'S WASHROOM
D MEN'S WASHROOM
E LOBBY
F HALLWAY

1 EXISTING TREE
2 RETAINING WALL, 40.6 CM (16") HOCH,
  45.7CM – 53.3CM (18"–21")
  H.T. DEPENDING ON MATERIAL CHOSEN
3 PAVER
4 SEATING AREA (PAVER)
  WITH CIRCULAR PATTERN
5 10.2CM (4") INLAY BORDER
6 15.2CM (6") SOLDIER COURSE
7 EX.CONCRETE BUILDING FOOTING
8 PINE BARKS
9 GLASS WINDOW

7

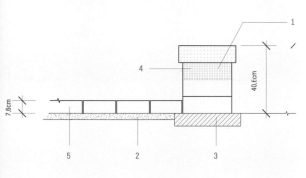

1 BRUSSELS BLOCK
  10.2 CM × 20.3 CM × 30.4 CM
2 MORTAR LEVELLING
3 BEDDING SAND
4 HIGHLIGHT COURSE
5 SANDSTONE OR DESERT SAND (PAVER)

8

2 The inner courtyard, which is kept at room temperature all year round, is lit entirely
  from above, providing the adjacent offices with daylight.
3 The new paths criss-cross the elongated, octagonal courtyard diagonally.
4 From the round plant bed, this stair ascends to the first upper storey.
5 Large parts of the garden receive direct sunlight throughout the day, so additional
  artificial lighting is not needed.
6 The light-coloured shaped stones of the 50 cm walls and the floor covering reflect the light.
7 Floor plan of patio with garden.
8 Detail stone wall.

Planted atrium in the St. Pölten retirement and care home

ARCHITECT: Georg W. Reinberg
PLANTING PLANNING: Anna Detzlhofer
COLLEAGUES: Heidelinde Holzinger,
Heinz Vockenberger
COMPLETION: 8/2000
LOCATION: St. Pölten, Austria

PLANNING BRIEF

Planting the central atrium as a recreational space for residents of the St. Pölten retirement and care home.

CONTEXT

In the centre of the home's compact structure is an atrium surrounded by galleries **1**. This houses a ground-floor venue for events where residents meet up and socialize. The pergolas provide a number of lines of sight and views. Narrow bridges cross the air space, offering quick access to all rooms and a variety of walks through the garden space. The air space also plays a role in the building's energy and ventilation concept **6**. A mechanical ventilation system provides a constant, controlled supply of fresh air without creating drafts. In summer, the incoming air can be cooled by solar collectors. The exhaust air is sucked out of the wet rooms, and in winter its energy heats the incoming air in a heat recovery system.

The glass roof allows daylight to penetrate deep into the building's interior, bringing with it the weather, the time of the day, and the changing seasons.

For another thing, the massive straight steel supports of the subconstruction reduce the transparency. To reduce this effect, the supporting structure has been covered with mirrors **3**.

CONCEPT

The green space concept involves planting in the central atrium, as well as outside the building, along various paths and in planted areas. Climbing plants climb up vertical wires stretched between stainless steel beams. The beams are anchored in large flower beds in the ground storey and first storey. Immediately beneath the glass roof, the wires are anchored to suspended mountings set to the side.

The chestnut vine, or lizard plant *(Tetrastigma voinierianum)*, is ideal for this location. This climbing plant comes from Tonkin in Vietnam and is found all over Southeast Asia. It grows in spurts, and can grow several m in a year. It can be cut back as needed.

This kind of planting is very lively and emphasizes the atrium's verticality. The tall plants can be seen from all storeys. The planting remains narrow, and does not restrict freedom of movement or views through the airspace.

1   Climbing plants project through the atrium vertically on almost invisible wires.

2 The atrium shortly after completion.
  The planting is still 'young'.
3 The mirrored concrete supports reflect
  daylight into the narrow inner courtyard.
4 Floor plan of retirement home.
5 Longitudinal and transverse cross section
  of the atrium.
6 Energy concept.
7 Planting plan
8 The planting plan can be seen clearly in
  this freshly planted bed.

2

3

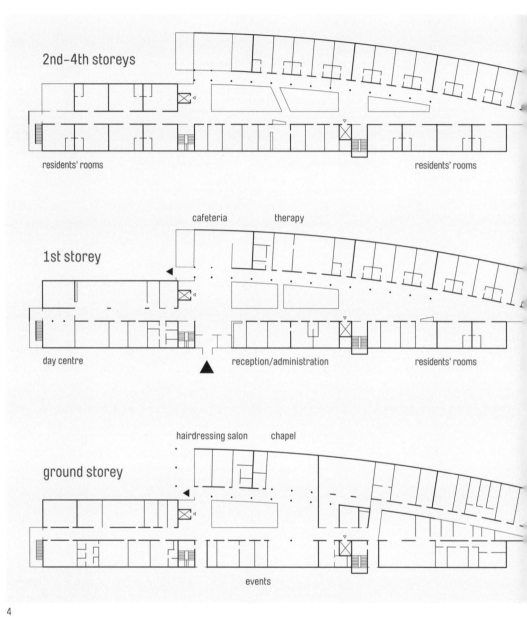

2nd–4th storeys

residents' rooms   residents' rooms

cafeteria   therapy

1st storey

day centre   ▲   reception/administration   residents' rooms

hairdressing salon   chapel

ground storey

events

4

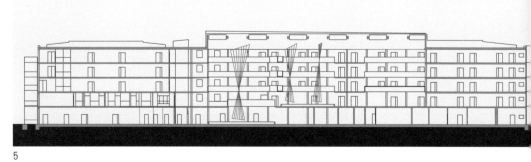

5

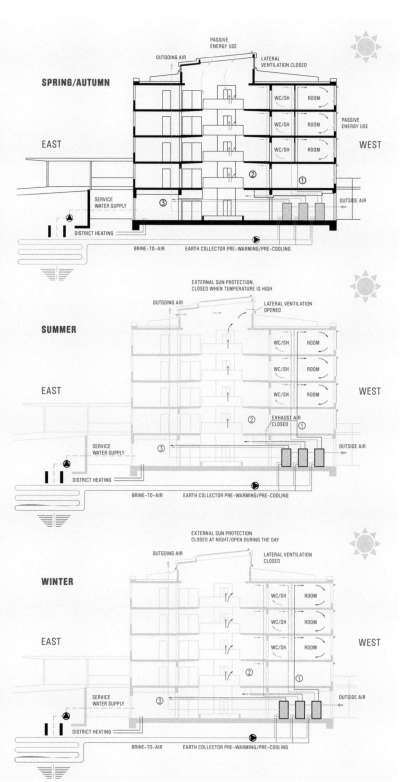

SPRING/AUTUMN

PASSIVE ENERGY USE

OUTGOING AIR

LATERAL VENTILATION CLOSED

EAST

WEST

WC/SH ROOM

WC/SH ROOM

WC/SH ROOM

PASSIVE ENERGY USE

SERVICE WATER SUPPLY

OUTSIDE AIR

DISTRICT HEATING

BRINE-TO-AIR   EARTH COLLECTOR PRE-WARMING/PRE-COOLING

SUMMER

EXTERNAL SUN PROTECTION, CLOSED WHEN TEMPERATURE IS HIGH

OUTGOING AIR

LATERAL VENTILATION OPENED

EAST

WEST

WC/SH ROOM

WC/SH ROOM

WC/SH ROOM

EXHAUST AIR CLOSED

SERVICE WATER SUPPLY

OUTSIDE AIR

DISTRICT HEATING

BRINE-TO-AIR   EARTH COLLECTOR PRE-WARMING/PRE-COOLING

WINTER

EXTERNAL SUN PROTECTION CLOSED AT NIGHT/OPEN DURING THE DAY

OUTGOING AIR

LATERAL VENTILATION CLOSED

EAST

WEST

WC/SH ROOM

WC/SH ROOM

WC/SH ROOM

SERVICE WATER SUPPLY

OUTSIDE AIR

DISTRICT HEATING

BRINE-TO-AIR   EARTH COLLECTOR PRE-WARMING/PRE-COOLING

6

EXHAUST AIR
OUTSIDE AIR
OUTGOING AIR
DISTRICT HEATING F
DISTRICT HEATING F
COLD WATER
COLD FLOW
COLD REFLUX

PUMP

VENTILATION SYSTEM

A A ROOM LAYOUT
B B GENERAL LAYOUT
C C KITCHEN LAYOUT

a	CRETAN BRAKE FERN – *PTERIS CRETICA*	C	SPIDER PLANT – *CHLOROPHYTUM COMOSUM*
r	REX BEGONIA – *REX-BEGONIA*	A	CAST-IRON PLANT – *ASPIDISTRA ELATIOR*
e	SHIELD FERN –	C	BUSH LILY – *CLIVIA MINATA*
	POLYSTICHUM AURICULATUM	D	PALM LILY – *CORDYLINE TERMINALIS*
n	BUTTON FERN – *PELLEA ROTUNDIFOLIA*	O	LIZARD PLANT –
s	FITTONIA VERSCHAFFELTII		*TETRASTIGMA VOINIERIANUM*
	(SYN. FITTONIA ALBIVENIS)		
l	CLIMBING FIG – *FICUS PUMILA*		

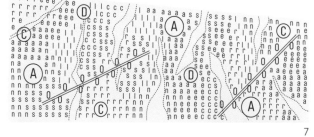

7

8

Planted patio, Giardino delle Ninfee

PLANTING PLANNING: Tamassociati/Agrisophia, Simona Ventura

ART: Silvia Zagni, Monica Macchia

GARDEN CONSTRUCTION AND PLANTING: Giovanni Vannacci

COMPLETION: 02/2006

LOCATION: Bologna, Italy

PLANNING BRIEF

Redesign of a previously unused patio in a vocational college, turning it into a garden, with no access.

CONTEXT

The vocational construction college building from the 1970s was expanded at the beginning of the 1990s. The space between the two buildings was turned into an open patio in order to provide natural light for the classrooms and offices. However, the patio was never completed and was not useable. Its asphalt paving and bare walls presented a desolate picture.

The college's leadership wanted the patio to be redesigned as a visually appealing planted inner courtyard. The idea was to create a new central point for the building, a shady secret garden that could only be discovered and viewed from the interior of the buildings.

CONCEPT

Landscape architect Simona Ventura's first design suggestion involved a bamboo field and a watercourse with water lilies. This design proved to be inadvisable for two reasons: an analysis of the predominant climate and sunlight incidence on site showed that there was not enough sunlight for water lilies and that bamboo would grow too tall. In the end, the planner decided to incorporate bamboo and water lilies into the garden design as artistic objects rather than as plants.

The rectangular inner courtyard's surface is divided into areas for plant beds, water, and a wooden terrace at one end, using various rectangular basic shapes that emphasize the longitudinal direction. The straight watercourse bisects two thirds of the courtyard, but is set off-centre. In combination with the planting style, this asymmetrical division makes the courtyard look natural rather than formal.

The gable wall opposite the wooden terrace is penetrated by a single small window, but it has a clear vertical termination in the form of a ledge. The artist Monica Macchia painted the whole expanse of the wall with a fresco showing a bamboo meadow that looks like a view of the countryside from a distance. In the lower middle part of the wall, large-leafed plants mark the transition to the inner courtyard: below, the watercourse issues down a cascade made of piled-up natural stone slabs. It runs through the yard in a straight line and empties into a square pond in which white water lilies appear to float. These are also artificial: Silvia Zagni created flowers and leaves – and an original spherical lamp – from white porcelain. The water lilies are attached to the bottom of the pond with bent copper wires.   →

1   The patio of the vocational college can be viewed from all sides and from the upper storey, but cannot be entered.

The edging of the watercourse and the pond is made of copper – a metal that develops its own patina over time. The rectilinear division, the artificial elements, and the unusual presence of copper all fit into a natural and harmonious garden image thanks to the planting in the beds on the long side. Low-growing *Pittosporum nano*, *Sarcococca hookeriana*, boxleaf honeysuckle (*Lonicera nitida*), ground-covering bamboo (*Pleioblastus pygmaeus*) and hardy David Bisset bamboo (*Phyllostachys bissetii*) were chosen for the local conditions in the shady courtyard, which receives no direct sunlight. The courtyard is not terraced or inclined longitudinally, and the water course has only a minimal gradient. The slight terracing of the longest and narrowest bed, and the density and lushness of the different planted habitat types create relief, depth and tension.

A conventional planting soil, consisting of 45% siliceous sand, 35% peat moss, and 20% fine sandy loam, was used as the substrate. The large expanses of water affect the inner courtyard's climate, which has proven to be favourable for the selected plants; since completion, the plants have been growing exceptionally well.

The lighting provided by the original ceramic lamp in the centre of the long side, and by the spotlights in the beds, in the water feature, and along the wooden terrace, shows the new garden off to best advantage in the evenings. Despite its small scale, the design, which can also be seen from the windows of the upper storeys, offers a great variety of lines of sight and striking features. The garden radiates peace and quiet, but the constant movement of the water ensures it is also dynamic.

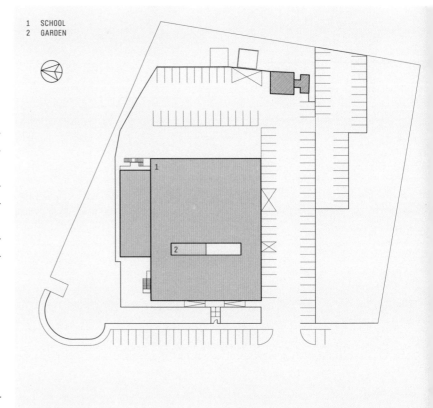

1   SCHOOL
2   GARDEN

2

2   Site plan
3   Floor plan with a planting plan. The vegetation is restricted to six different species with similar colouring, leaf size, and growth density. The following species were planted in the four separate beds in the following densities:
   – David Bisset bamboo *(Phyllostachys bissetii)*, 3 plants per m^2
   – Ground–covering bamboo *(Pleioblastus pygmaeus)*, 8 plants per m^2
   – Boxleaf honeysuckle *(Lonicera nitida)*, 4 plants per m^2
   – Japanese maple *(Acer palmatum)*, 1 plant per m^2
   – *Pittosporum nano*, 4 plants per m^2
   – *Sarcococca hookeriana*, 3 plants per m^2
4   Cross section aa

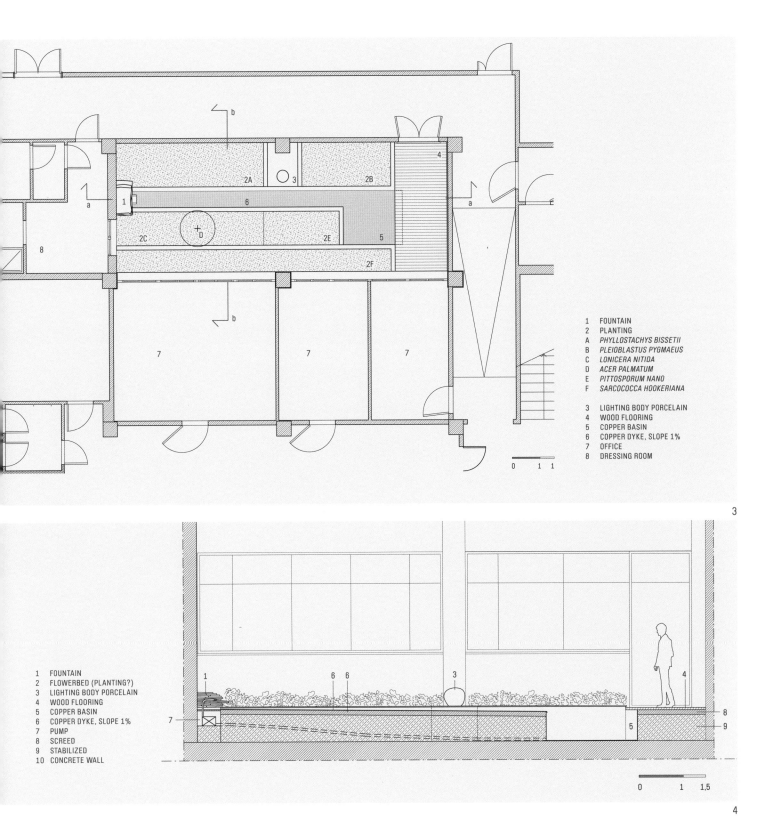

1 FOUNTAIN
2 PLANTING
A *PHYLLOSTACHYS BISSETII*
B *PLEIOBLASTUS PYGMAEUS*
C *LONICERA NITIDA*
D *ACER PALMATUM*
E *PITTOSPORUM NANO*
F *SARCOCOCCA HOOKERIANA*

3 LIGHTING BODY PORCELAIN
4 WOOD FLOORING
5 COPPER BASIN
6 COPPER DYKE, SLOPE 1%
7 OFFICE
8 DRESSING ROOM

0   1   1

3

1   FOUNTAIN
2   FLOWERBED (PLANTING?)
3   LIGHTING BODY PORCELAIN
4   WOOD FLOORING
5   COPPER BASIN
6   COPPER DYKE, SLOPE 1%
7   PUMP
8   SCREED
9   STABILIZED
10 CONCRETE WALL

0   1   1,5

4

71

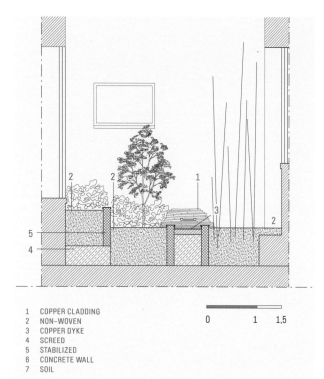

1   COPPER CLADDING
2   NON-WOVEN
3   COPPER DYKE
4   SCREED
5   STABILIZED
6   CONCRETE WALL
7   SOIL

0   1   1,5

5

6

9

7

8

10

11

5   Cross section bb
6   Before the redesign, the empty courtyard was a desolate sight.
7   The artist Monica Macchia paints a bamboo meadow,
    providing a 'natural' view
8   The completed patio harmoniously combines plants, water,
    painting and art.
9   Design sketch for the wall fresco, with red paint on the
    concrete supports to highlight the garden space.
10 Real water lilies would not thrive in this location due to
    insufficient sunlight.
11 The white ceramic flowers and leaves are a striking feature
    of the quadratic pond at the edge of the watercourse.
12 The completed garden: the arrangement of the beds, the different
    plant species, and their planting densities are clearly defined.

12

Loft apartment with garden courtyard in London

GARDEN DESIGNER: Chris Maton, Olivebay
COMPLETION: 2009
LOCATION: London, UK

PLANNING ASSIGNMENT

A green space on the roof: planning of a small apartment with an open garden courtyard that can be sealed off.

CONTEXT

A penthouse apartment in an exclusive residential area in the London district of Chelsea has a large (9 × 15 m) previously unused roof terrace. This was to be turned into a planted space.

After analysing the roof storey's bearing load and whether it could support the new storey and the planting elements, large steel girders were added to the roof to strengthen it.

CONCEPT

The Olivebay garden design firm initially designed a pure roof garden, but due to the size and the potential of the available space, the firm later proposed building a complete little apartment with an enclosed garden courtyard and a sun terrace with wooden decking **2**.

The courtyard was designed and executed as a fluid extension of the living space, enclosed by three walls and open to the sky **3**. The same materials were used as for the interior. The walls are plastered in white, there are wooden shutters in front of the windows, and the floor is paved with light-coloured limestone. Mediterranean species dominate the selection

of plants: low boxwood hedges (*Buxus sempervivens*), lavender *(Lavandula angustifolia 'Hidcote')*, figs on an espalier (*Ficus carica*), and giant African lilies (*Agapanthus umbellatus ovatus*).

In the middle of the line of sight from the living area, through the garden and the folding wood door over the sun terrace, is an eye-catching olive tree (*Olea europaea*), with rock roses *(Cistus pulverulentus Sunset)* planted below. Lavender and low box hedge triangles provide some depth outside the windows without destroying the view. The delicate sprays of several Lindheimer's clockweed plants *(Gaura lindheimeri)* and hostas *(Hemerocallis)* rise above the lavender and box, relieving the regularity of the side planting.

All the plants are planted in unobtrusive steel planting troughs about 60 cm high, arranged along the walls to leave enough space to move around easily. The smooth, light-grey surfaces of the containers, gently reflect the light, and create a homogeneous background for the colours and textures of the plants. The substrate is a special lightweight mix for roof gardens, containing compost. →

1   Room-high walls with door and window openings surround the roof garden, which can be reached through a sliding glass door.

Several regularly spaced cables are stretched over the dining table. Over time, as requested by the client, they will be overgrown with wisteria and jasmine *(Jasminum officinale)*, forming a green roof over the dining table. The garden is illuminated in the evening: spotlights in the beds highlight individual plants, and indirect lighting on the underside of the plant troughs creates a comfortable atmosphere.

The difficulty of transporting the building materials and the plants to roof level, five storeys up, was solved by the use of a crane winch.

2   Floor plan with planting plan.
3   Cross section of garden courtyard with terraces.
4   The garden is accessed from the apartment's living space through the sliding glass door.
5   View of the garden from the living room. The symmetrical arrangement of the plants on either side of the folding-leaf door creates a balanced composition, with a range of different leaf and flower shapes that frame the space optically.
6   The selection of plants in the 60 cm planters emphasizes differences of height: small plants at 30 cm in height, including boxwood hedges, lavender and phormiums; then figs, African lilies and the olive tree at eye level; with wisteria and jasmine acting as a green roof.
7   Directly above the wisteria and jasmine trellises, the garden courtyard's open roof can be sealed off using a watertight awning.

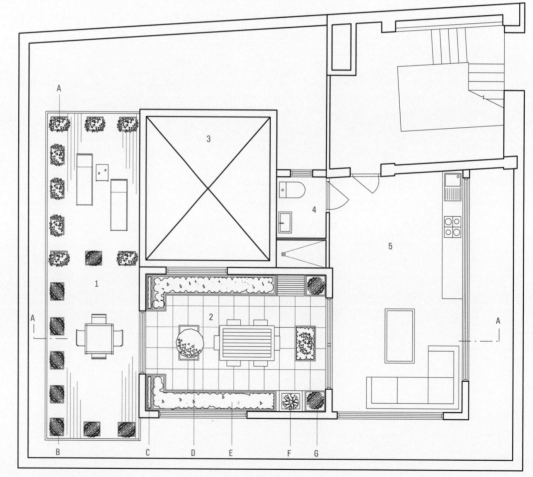

1   DECKED SUN TERRACE
2   OUTDOOR WALLED DINING AREA
3   EXISTING SKYLIGHT
4   WET ROOM
5   KITCHEN/LOUNGE

A   GOLDEN BAMBOO – *PHYLLOSTACHYS AUREA*
B   FEATHER GRASS – *STIPA TENUISSIMA*
C   FIG TREE – *FICUS CARICA*
D   OLIVE TREE – *OLEA EUROPEA*
E   BEECH TREE AND LAVENDER –
    BUXUS & LAVANDULA
F   SOFT TREE FERN – *DICKSONIA ANTARCTICA*
G   STRAWBERRY TREE – *ARBUTUS UNEDO*

2

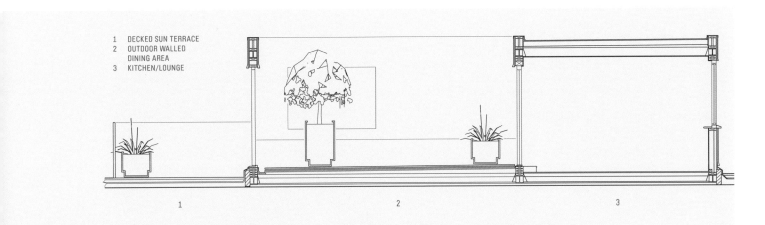

1 DECKED SUN TERRACE
2 OUTDOOR WALLED
  DINING AREA
3 KITCHEN/LOUNGE

1

2

3

3

5

4

6

7

Glass Bubble greenhouse

ARCHITECT AND GREENPLANNING:
GORA ART&LANDSCAPE, Monika Gora
WITH THE ASSISTANCE OF:
Mårten Setterblad, Jens Linnet
LOCATION: Malmö, Sweden
COMPLETION: 2006

PLANNING BRIEF

Greenhouse with exotic conservatory as a recreational space for residents of a retirement home.

CONTEXT

On a rather inhospitable site close to Malmö harbour, in the inner courtyard of a U-shaped residential retirement complex, landscape architect Monika Gora has created a two-part urban landscape design. The trees and plants to the rear of the courtyard and in the neighbouring plaza call to mind the native plant life of northern Sweden. These plants can withstand the salty air and the frequent gales on the exposed shoreline and are happy in shallow beds of barren soil – the site is on reclaimed land created by piling up soil. By contrast, exotic plants flourish in the greenhouse, which can be used all year round.

CONCEPT

The greenhouse is at the entrance of the courtyard facing the sea. Its organic shape is very different from the starkly linear architecture that surrounds it. This greenhouse shields the courtyard and its irregularly shaped planting beds, and appears to invite the residents of the retirement home and their visitors of out of the urban surroundings and the indoor environment and into the natural world. At night and during the dark winter season, the glass sculpture lights up its surroundings like a lantern. The paving under foot, both inside and outside, is a type of Norwegian slate called 'Otta Högseter'. The colour of the slate ranges from greenish black to rusty orange, due to its high iron content. This paving connects the two contrasting garden worlds, which are only separated by a thin glass membrane.

The glass structure, which will finally be 22 m long, 10.5 m high and 7.5 m wide, and lets the maximum amount of light into the interior, was developed with the aid of three-dimensional digital models. The two layers of glass (16 mm thick in total, with a low iron content that makes them particularly clear and transparent) have a static function. The glass lies over the steel rib arches like a transparent skin, with no additional vertical support struts. The use of curved panes was rejected at the outset of the project due to the cost. Instead, the round shape was implemented using flat panes of glass. Triangular panes were also ruled out, due to the increased number of struts they would require, and the consequent reduction in transparency.

The structure's double arches were cut with a laser. The glass panes are fixed in place with 200 retainers ('spiders') connected to the arches. The manufacturing and construction process demanded a high degree of precision; the shape and position of each holder is unique and every pane had to be fitted into place individually.   →

1   In the darkness, the Glass Bubble radiates a warm light, turning the greenhouse into a beacon.

The garden within is lush and exotic: forms, colours, fragrances, fruits and a water feature appeal to all five senses. The planting includes citrus fruits, camellias and magnolias → PLANT LIST **P. 82.** The edging for the beds was handcrafted from Norwegian slate to look like traditional stone walls. They line the winding path that the visitor can wander along, making discoveries and lingering in the miniature landscape.

The automated climate-control technology prevents the temperature from falling below freezing in winter. In summer, the inside temperature is consistently lower than the outside temperature. Ventilation flaps near the ground on both sides can be opened manually as needed **14** . The plant beds contain drip tubes for direct irrigation, and six vapour jets mounted higher up can be used to raise the humidity. Metal halogen and LED lamps were installed to supplement the inadequate sunlight in the winter.

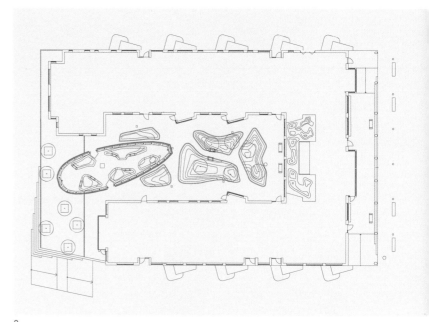

2

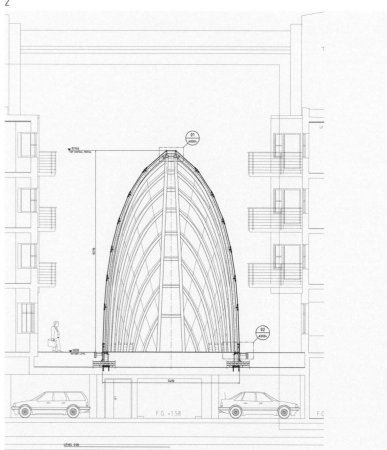

2 Site plan.
3 Cross section.
4 Floor plan of Glass Bubble and garden.
5/6 Detail of glass membrane.
7 Ventilation system

3

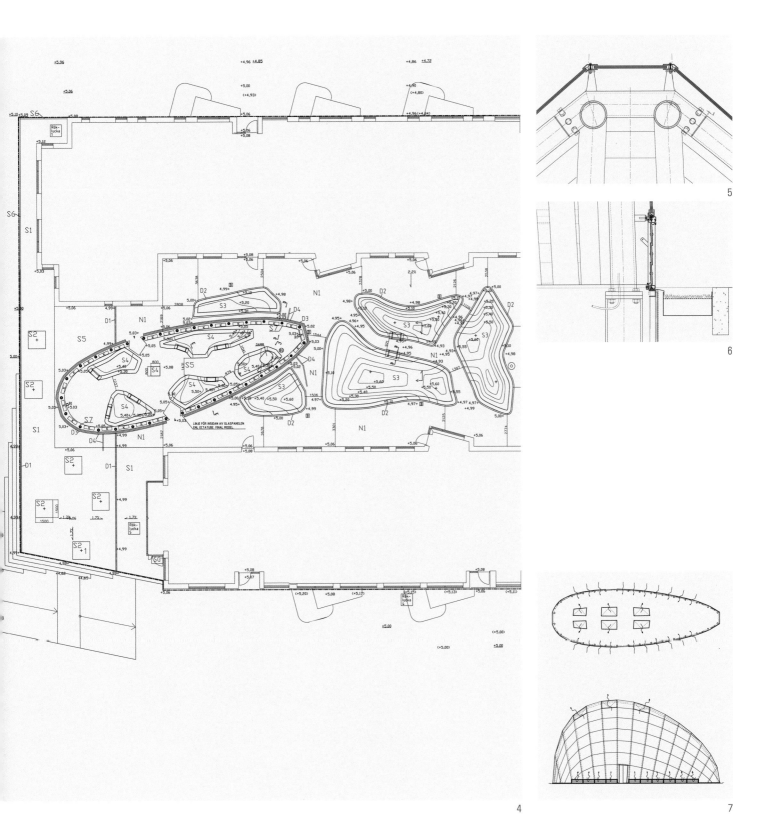

4

5

6

7

The following plants were used:

Herbaceous perennials and ferns
Adiantum pedatum
Adiantum venustum
Asarum europaeum
Asarum maximum
Asarum splendens
Asplenium trichomanes
Apslenium bulbiferum
Cathea cooperii
Cyrtonium falcatum
Danae racemosa
Davallia mariesii
Helleborus corsicus
Helleborus x sternii
Ophiogon japonicus 'Minor'
Ophiogon planiscapus
Ophiogon planiscapus 'Nigescens'
Pellaea rotundifolia
Uncinia egmontiana

Geophytes
Arisaema candidissimum
Arisaema ciliatum var. liubaense
Arisaema concinnum
Cyclamen cilicium 'Album'
Cyclamen coum 'Album'
Cyclamen graecum 'Album'
Cyclamen hederifolium 'Album'
Cyclamen persicum

Woody plants
Cameliia japonica 'Mathotiana Alba'
Cameliia japonica 'Swan Lake'
Cameliia japonica
Citrus x limon
Choisya 'Aztec Pearl'
Choisya ternata
Cycas revoluta
Embothrium coccineum 'Inca Flame'
Fatsia japonica
Magnolia grandiflora
Magnolia grandiflora
'Gallisonnière Nana'
Nandina domestica 'Firepower'
Nandina domestica 'Richmond'
Trachycarpus fortunei

Climbing plants
Clematis armandii
Hedera helix ssp. canariensis
Lapageria rosea
Passiflora x exoniensis
Tropaelum speciosum
Trachelospermum jasminoides

Water plants
Nymphaea tetragona
Equisetum hyemale
Thelypteris palustris
Zantedeschia aethiopica

8

9

10

8 At the courtyard entrance, the transparent Glass Bubble appears to grow out of the ground, in stark contrast to its hard, linear surroundings.

9 The identical paving connects the two very different indoor and outdoor garden worlds, separated only by a thin glass membrane.

10 Amid the tall, dense vegetation, seating provides places to gather. The sheltering greenhouse can be visited by residents of the home in all kinds of weather.

11 Simple wooden benches are integrated into the elevated bed edgings made from vari-coloured slate.

12 The rounded area at the front of the Glass Bubble is free of plants and offers a view of the sea across the open Scania plaza.

13 Automated climate-control technology opens and closes the roof ventilation flaps.

14 The woody plants, palms, herbaceous perennials and ground cover are densely planted, creating spatial boundaries that allow the garden to be discovered step by step. Flowers create touches of colour that change throughout the year.

12

11

13

14

Planted atrium in the Covent Garden building

ARCHITECTURE AND GREEN PLANNING:
Art&Build, in collaboration with
Montois Partners
GARDEN CONSTRUCTION: Anygreen
COMPLETION: 2007
LOCATION: Brussels, Belgium

PLANNING ASSIGNMENT

Planted atrium between two office buildings. An recreational space in the city core that compensates for the complex's rainwater-impervious surfaces, and processes collected waste water through natural plant filters.

CONTEXT

Art&Build collaborated with Montois Partners to build the Covent Garden complex in the northerly district of Brussels, adjoining the railway station and a botanical garden. A garden with an 1,100 m² glass roof connects the two autonomous office buildings: a tower 100 m high with an oval floor plan, and a nine-storey angled building 2–4.

The striking high-rise architecture gives the company an identity within the commercial North Station district, while the lower building creates a transition to the existing buildings and to the neighbouring botanical gardens.

The indoor garden is at access level and can be entered from the street; it is open to the public. The height of this four-storey planted atrium, with its wide openings and transparent entrance facades, create lines of sight beneath the high-rise building, leading out of the complex and into the city.

CONCEPT

The large indoor garden, which remains above 18 °C all year round, is a large inner-city recreational area for office employees and the general public that also fulfils the requirement to offset the rainwater-impervious surfaces. The garden design's shapes and materials suit the angular, clear and efficient architecture. In expansive, curved flower beds with low ground cover plants, large trees of different growth types stand in a loose arrangement. They give the appearance of a light deciduous woodland, in contrast with the regularly arranged round, gleaming stainless steel containers and their flourishing tall trees with dense round crowns. This row of trees in containers runs along the line of sight from the main entrance, under the tower, and towards the city, extending the planting to the foot of the oval tower 3. The short length of the containers and beds stresses the expansiveness of the planted space, while the trees emphasize the height of the space and take full advantage of it. The paths and bed edging are light-coloured stone, with a few corner seats near the stainless steel containers. The garden contains the following species: black olive (*Bucida buceras*, 4 m/5 m), Indian laurel fig (*Ficus nitida*, 6/7/8 m), weeping fig (*Ficus benjamina*, 4 m), *Ficus longifolia* (6 m), small umbrella tree (*Schefflera arboricola),* peace lily (*Spathiphyllum wallisii),* lilyturf (*Liriope muscari)* and Chinese evergreen (*Aglaonema 'Silver Queen').*

→

1   The atrium garden is a connective element between the two
    sections of the Covent Garden office complex.

Covent Garden is the first office building in Brussels to be equipped with an 'Eco Machine' system for collecting and purifying waste water so that it can be immediately reused. The building's waste water is purified using anaerobic and biological filters before finally being processed in plant filters so that the water can be reused within the building: to flush the toilets, to clean the building, and to water the plants in the atrium garden.

The natural plant filter consists of several low rectangular basins, arranged in a cascade along the curved facade of the office tower. The basins are densely planted with swamp plants. Their low height and unobtrusive shape keeps them from competing with the tall plants in the beds and containers and ensures that they do not affect the view of the atrium from the offices.

Large spotlights illuminate the trees from below, emphasizing their vertical thrust. These are part of an artificial illumination system that produces at least 1000 lux, allowing the plants to flourish. Round mirrors beneath the atrium roof reflect both the sunlight and artificial light into the various areas of the complex.

2 Covent Garden consists of an oval tower 100 m high and a nine-storey angled building, linked together by the planted atrium.
3 The planted atrium, which is primarily lit from above, is four storeys high: an ideal height for the various tree species.
4 The floor plan shows the extent of the open areas and the lines of sight through the building.

2

3

10   0

10

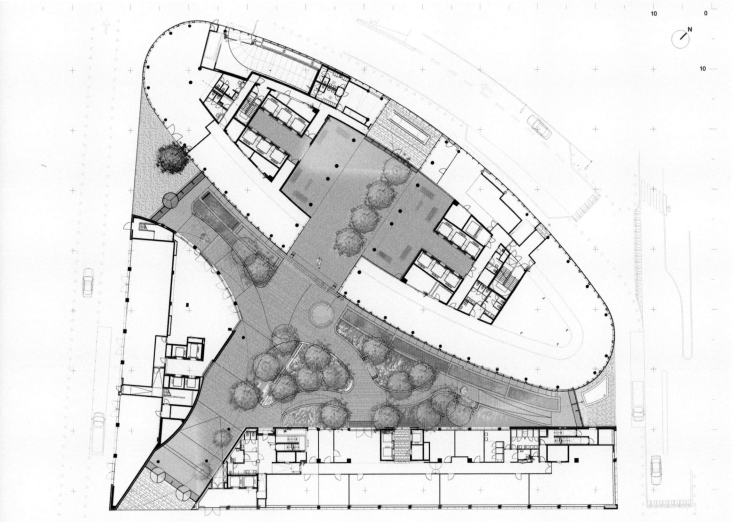

4

5   A view looking up at the three office block
    towers through the glass roof of the atrium.
6   People in the surrounding office spaces have
    a view of the planted area. Those above the
    fifth storey can see it through the glass roof.
7   LED lamps illuminate the paths.
8   View of the atrium garden from above.

5

6

7

8

Devonian Gardens indoor gardens

PROJECT MANAGEMENT AND GREEN PLANNING:
Janet Rosenberg + Associates,
Landscape Architecture / Urban Design
ARCHITECTS AND PROJECT TEAM:
Eleven Eleven Architecture (architecture);
Halcrow Yolles, Hidi Rae (technical planning);
Eclairage Public (light design);
BTY (cost optimization);
Dan Euser (water systems planning)
COMPLETION: 2011
LOCATION: Calgary, Alberta, Canada

PLANNING ASSIGNMENT

Redesign of an indoor park from the 1970s on the roof of a shopping centre.

CONTEXT

The 'Devonian Gardens' indoor park in Calgary was built in 1977 by J. H. Cook Architects and Engineers, sponsored by the Devonian Group of Charitable Foundations and Calford Properties. This 10,000 m² park is located on the roof of a shopping centre in the downtown core, 45 m above street level. This is the largest roofed garden in Canada, and it has become an iconic feature of Calgary, known worldwide and attracting many visitors. The central area of the city has changed over the past 20 years, however, and the formerly sunny garden is now shaded by the surrounding buildings. The ageing infrastructure also makes it harder to maintain the complex and increases operating costs.

The city of Calgary commissioned the landscape architect and urban planning firm Janet Rosenberg + Associates to redesign the whole complex. Due to the complicated nature of the project, the firm developed the new sustainable concept through an elaborate planning process, in close collaboration with the city, and with a multidisciplinary team of specialists. The aim of the design was to revive the complex and restore it to its role as an exceptional attraction known far beyond the city. A spatial programme was developed that would be attractive to visitors and could be used flexibly for commercial purposes. Parts of the infrastructure and building systems also had to be altered and renewed. All the glazing and all the insulation, mechanical features and electrical systems had already been replaced, which had meant clearing away the whole of the original garden. The garden is set to reopen in 2011.

CONCEPT

The new spatial programme includes a variety of open use areas, separated by plants, expanses of water, changes in level, and the use of different materials. The use areas include a children's play area, a restaurant with an herb garden, an exhibition space for garden shows, a round lounge with trees, a large wooden terrace, and an events area. Broad paths with varied designs incorporating slopes, bridges, stairs and other elements run through the garden and enable people to stroll through the garden and discover it step by step. Enclosed spaces for washrooms, building systems, offices, personnel and storage were arranged within the floor plan to optimize the cost-effective management of the complex. →

1   The green plan involves tall trees with low ground cover plants in the inner area and an opaque screen of plants around the edges. The different use areas – including the children's play area to the northwest – are separated without making the park look less expansive.

The garden is intended to be used all year round, so it is kept at room temperature – around 20 °C. The garden is heated by the air exiting the four-storey shopping centre; ventilation openings in the sides of the glass facades can be opened to cool it. The vegetation is primarily subtropical.

The original glazing was not thermally decoupled. It has now been replaced with thermally decoupled double glazing. A non-tearing PVB film between the two frames absorbs almost all damaging UV radiation. A coating (PPG Solarban 60) filters out up to 62% of the longwave infrared radiation, while letting through 70% of shortwave visual light. This allows the maximum of daylight into the inner space while preventing it from heating up and avoiding the buildup of condensation.

The light conditions were analysed with reference to the planting. Measurements were taken on site and the amounts of daylight received by the different parts of the garden, which are heavily shadowed by the neighbouring buildings, were assessed using computer models. Due to the reflective surface of the glass facades, a relatively large amount of sunlight is reflected into the garden. The daylight alone was not enough to keep the plants healthy, so it is supplemented by artificial lighting.

2

3

2   The park landscape is gently modelled, and most of the beds connect directly with the paving, with no edging. Below the slanted glass facade are several planting areas. These increase leaf volume and can be seen from outside → SEE ALSO 7 .

3   A large pond with a water feature dominates the northeast quadrant, which is a quiet, relaxing recreational zone with paths for strolling and with mobile seating.

4   The central venue terrace can be used for events at any time. Large mobile plant containers hold seasonal plants; these can be rearranged as needed to provide additional highlights, or removed to make more space.

5   Large hanging lamps set off the venue terrace and highlight the space and the plants at night.

4

5

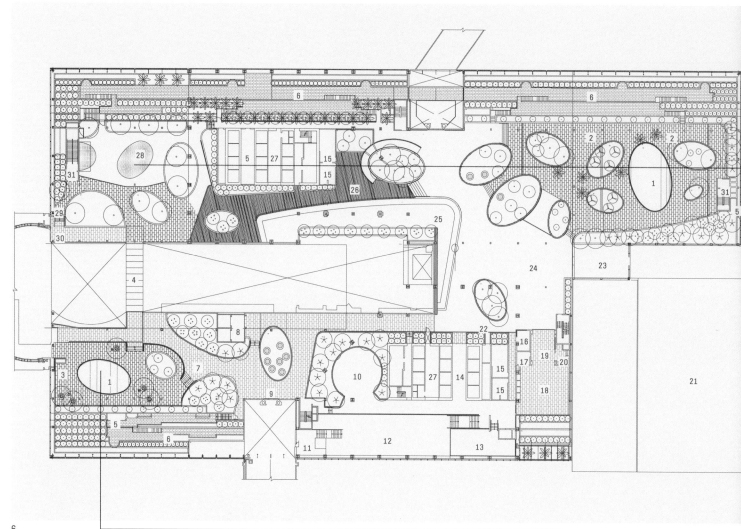

6

1	KOI POND	19	EVENT SERVICE ROOM
2	SEATING AREA	20	STORAGE AREA
3	SOUTH-WEST GARDEN ENTRANCE	21	OFFICE AREA
4	PEDESTRIAN BRIDGE	22	MOVEABLE POTS WITH SEASONAL
5	FOUNTAIN MECHANICAL ROOM		PLANTING
6	TERRACE WALKWAY	23	HORTICULTURAL STAGING AREA
7	GARDEN PATH	24	EVENTS TERRACE
8	FREIGHT ELEVATORS	25	CENTRAL KOI POND WITH WATER SPOUT
9	SOUTH ELEVATOR ENTRANCE		FEATURE
10	FUTURE LOUNGE AREA	26	IPE DECK
11	LOWER RESTAURANT TERRACE	27	BUILDING CORE
12	RESTAURANT TERRACE	28	CHILDREN'S PLAYGROUND
13	KITCHEN GARDEN	29	DEVONIAN GARDENS INFORMATION BOOTH
14	RESTAURANT ENTRANCE HALLWAY	30	NORTH-WEST GARDEN ENTRANCE
15	RESTROOM	31	ENTRY/EXIT STAIR
16	OFFICE		
17	WATER CLOSET		
18	AMENITY AREA		

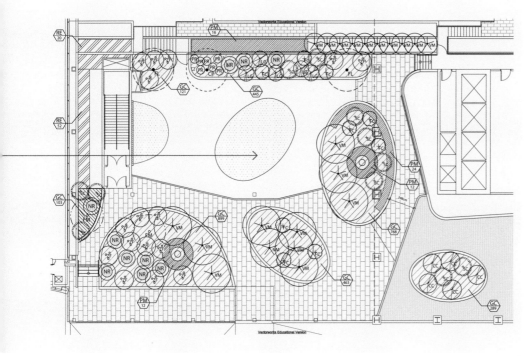

6-8 Cross sections and planting plan

PALMS
VM MANILA PONYTAIL PALM –
    NOLINA RECURVATA / BEAUCARNEA RECURVATA
CC QUEEN SAGO – *CYCAS CIRCINALIS*
LG VANUATU FAN PALM – *LICUALA GRANDIS*

DECIDUOUS TREES
FL FIDDLE-LEAF FIG – *FICUS LYRATA*
FM AMSTEL KING BANANA-LEAF FIG –
    FICUS MACLELLANDII ‚AMSTEL KING'
CP PEACOCK FLOWER, PRIDE OF BARBADOS –
    CAESALPINIA PULCHERRIMA

SMALL PALMS
PR MINIATURE DATE PALM – *PHOENIX ROEBELENII*
ZF CARDBOARD CYCAD – *ZAMIA FURFURACEA*
RE BROADLEAF LADY PALM – *RHAPIS EXCELSA*
SC AUSTRALIAN TREE FERN –
    SPHAEROPTERIS / CYATHEA COOPERI

SHRUBS
PM KUSAMAKI, INUMAKI – *PODOCARPUS MACROPHYLLA*
FC TALL, PILLAR-LIKE RUBBER TREE – *FICUS COLUMNAR*

GROUND-COVERING PLANTS
GC VARIOUS

7

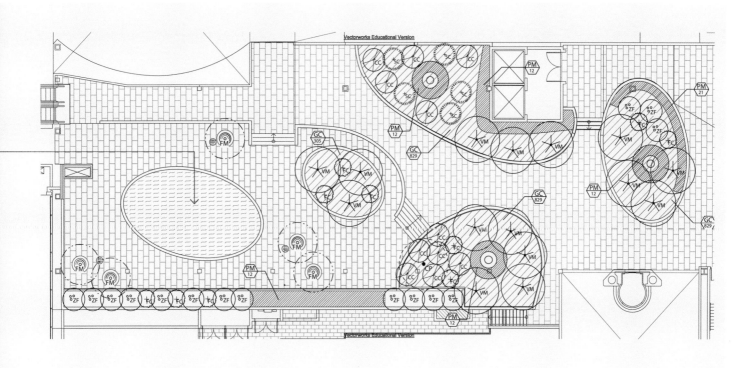

8

95

9

10

9–11 Cross sections

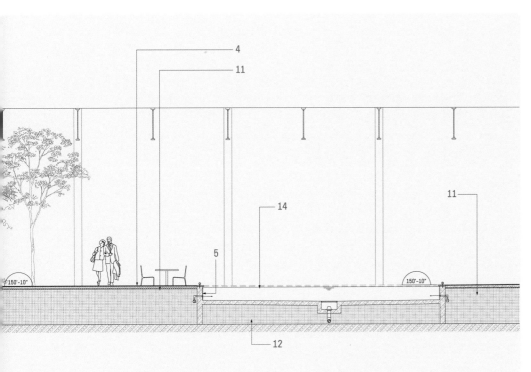

1   EXISTING CONCRETE FLOOR SLAB
2   CONCRETE PLANTER WALL FACADE TO BE TILE/STEEL/
    PLASTIC APPLIED TYPE FINISH
3   STONE COPING
4   TILE PAVERS ON MOTARD BED/CONCRETE SLAB
5   8'' DRAINAGE COURSE (EXPANDED SHALE)
6   AERATION/CLEAN OUT 4'' DIA PVC W/PERFORATED
    AND REMOVABLE DRAIN CAP. TYP.
7   FILTER CLOTH
8   PLANTING VOLUME 18'' MIN. – 36'' MAX. DEPTH.
9   PLANTER DRAIN
10 INSULATION FILL AS REQUIRED TO
    MAINTAIN MAX. 36'' SOIL DEPTH.
11 STRUCTURAL FLOOR
12 SUB FLOOR
13 MOSAIC TILE TYP.
14 KOI POND
15 EXTEND OF EIGHT ELEVATOR BEYOND

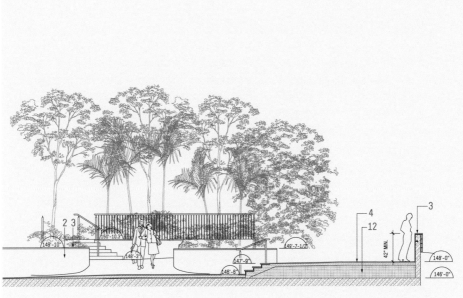

Themed gardens in the atria of the Lufthansa Aviation Center

ARCHITECTS: ingenhoven architects, Düsseldorf
GREEN PLANNING: WKM Landschaftsarchitekten, Klaus Klein, Rolf Maas
ADVICE ON CHOICE OF PLANTS:
Maria Sansoni-Köchel/Flora Mediterranea
COMPLETION: 2005
LOCATION: Frankfurt am Main, Germany

PLANNING ASSIGNMENT

Planting for nine atria to serve as climatic and noise-reducing buffer zones for the Lufthansa administration building. The planting concept is intended to be part of the company's image and to symbolize the airline's global connections.

CONTEXT

Lufthansa's administration building with planted atria is located at Frankfurt's airport, a transport hub between the A3 motorway, the airport ring road, a feeder road, and the ICE railway line. It is in a central – and noisy – location.

The company was impressed by the 'double comb structure' building designed by the architecture firm ingenhoven architects, which alternates office sections with large planted atrium halls.

The glazed building shell allows the atria to be seen into from outside. Plenty of daylight reaches the inner courtyards (and the offices and meeting rooms) through the paraglider-like, transparent roof, which is a cantilevered glass and gridwork shell construction.

It is glazed with white glass, which lets the part of the light spectrum used in photosynthesis pass through with very little loss.

CONCEPT

WKM Landschaftsarchitekten were involved in the green planning for the atria from the beginning. To symbolize the openness of the company and its role in bringing people together, 'Gardens of the Continents' was chosen as the design concept. Design themes from the five continents in the nine atria symbolize the airline's global connections. However, the various landscape images are highly abstract, consciously avoiding the ambience of a botanical garden. Each garden is composed of a small number of design elements: plants (trees, bushes, low-growing plants), minerals (stones, rocks, sand), and, in some cases, water. These individual landscape images are unified by an identical flooring of white stone chips. →

1 The green atria of Lufthansa's new administration building enhance the company's image.

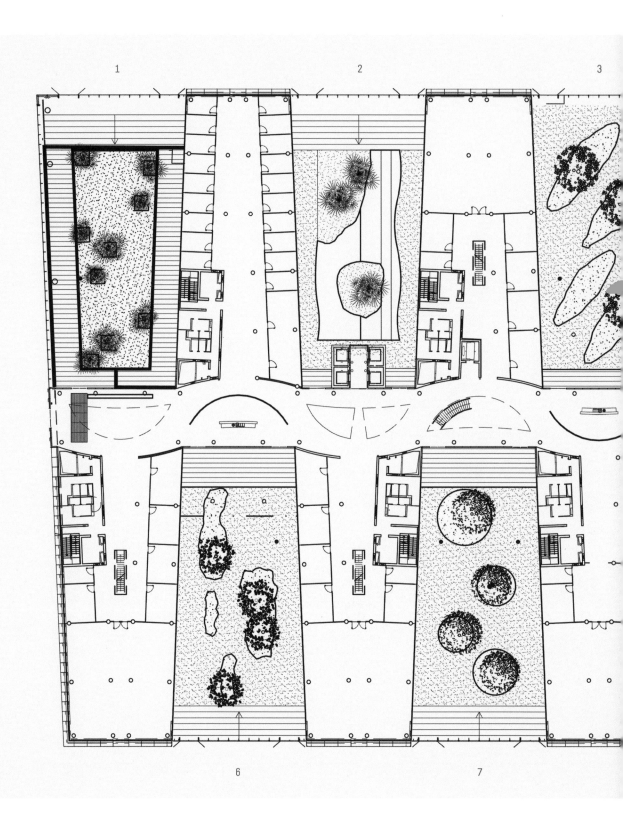

2

Concrete tiles under the stone chips allow telescopic work platforms (or scissor lifts) to be set up to clean the facades and glass. It was a design requirement that the design of the atria and the planting beds allow unrestricted access and use for these telescopic platforms in all the halls.

The atria are unheated greenhouses where the temperature can fall as low as -2 °C. The summer temperature may rise very high. Modern, innovative sun and glare protection is used to shield the workspaces from the negative impact of the sun, and ventilation control in the atria guarantees a comfortable indoor climate even when the outdoor temperatures are high. Based on daylight calculations by the light planner, and climate simulations by the building systems planner, plants originating in Mediterranean or subtropical climates were chosen. The green planner recommended the use of light sources that emit plenty of light in wavelengths useful to photosynthesis, providing the plants with more than enough rather than too little light.

An intensive mineral-organic substrate was used for all the gardens. This mixture has good ventilation and structural stability and does not become fatigued or turn to mud. Plants are fertilized according to their individual needs during planting and care.

3

1 Themed garden Beach

In the themed garden entitled 'Beach', California is symbolized by sun, wind and palm trees, creating the abstract *Sunshine Boulevard* landscape image. The concept is restricted to two materials: light-coloured sand and irregularly arranged palms *(Washingtonia robusta)*. A volleyball net can be set up on the sand. The light planning is part of the concept, with the artificial lighting seeming to imitate strong sunlight. Additional effect lighting from below shows the atrium to best effect in the evening. Due to its position on the periphery, this landscape image is particularly highly visible from outside the complex. The striking outlines of the palms, with their tall, slender trunks and large fan-shaped fronds, can be seen from a considerable distance.

2   Floor plan and planting plan.
3   The atria are easily visible from passing vehicles.
4   The corner position and alignment of this atrium allows plenty of
    daylight into this particular hall.

4

2 Themed garden Lago

The abstract 'Lago Maggiore' landscape image, with its Chinese windmill palms (*Trachycarpus fortunei*), camellias (*Camellia japonica*), sweet osmanthus (*Osmanthus fragrans*), water, coarse gravel and dark natural stone rocks, is a symbol of the south and of the yearning of northern Europeans for the Italian coast. An island and a peninsula are slightly elevated and planted with tall dense vegetation that slopes down to the water. Although the Chinese windmill palm is not native to Europe, it is the first palm one encounters in any great numbers on a journey from northern to southern Europe. The winter-flowering plants, the heavily scented osmanthus and the camellias, express the yearning for spring. Dark stone chips and rocks create a clear outline around the water surface and reinforce the abstract nature of the landscape image by contrasting starkly with the surrounding white stone chips. The use of the same dark stone for the floor of the pool also reinforces the reflective effect. After dark, lighting the palms from below creates the mood of a warm summer's night at sea. The stone chips and rocks for the pond were put in place only after the planting had been fully completed **5/6**.

5

1 HIGH QUALITY CHIPPINGS
2 BASE COURSE 0/45 MM
3 PIPE FOR DRIP IRRIGATION
4 PLANT SUBSTRATE
5 FILTER FLEECE
6 DRAINAGE COURSE, E.G. LAVA 8/11 MM
7 PROTECTION COURSE
8 ROOF SUPERSTRUCTURE AS PER BUILDING PHYSICS
9 COVERING (QUARRY STONE, CRUSHED STONE, CHIPPINGS)
10 SEAL (FLEECE, FOIL, FLEECE)
11 GRAVEL AND SAND FILLER MIXTURE
12 SUPPORT POINT CONCRETE C 20/25

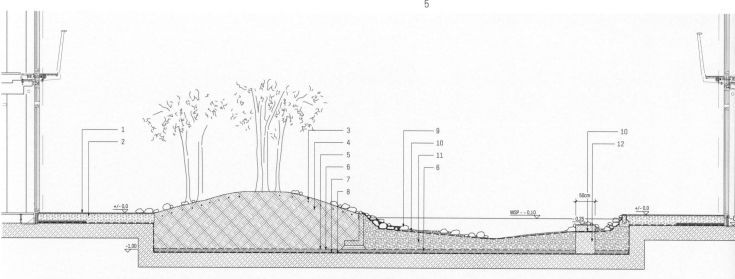

6

1 CHUSAN PALM – *TRACHYCARPUS FORTUNEI*
2 CAMELIA – *CAMELLIA JAPONICA*
3 OSMANTHUS – *OSMANTHUS BURKWOODII*
4 SWEET OSMANTHUS – *OSMANTHUS FRAGANS*
5 FALSE OLIVE – *PHILLYREA ANGUSTIFOLIA*
6 UNDERPLANTING WITH 'MONROE WHITE' LILYTURF
  (*LIRIOPE MUSCARI* 'MONROE WHITE')
7 INSPECTION SHAFT OVER OUTLET
8 MAGNET VALVES
9 IRRIGATION PIPES
10 SERVICE WATER DELIVERY
11 SHAFT APPROX. 300×100 CM FOR WATER
   TECHNOLOGY FILTER PLANT
12 REINFORCED CONCRETE SUPPORT POINT 100×70 CM
13 CONCRETE SLABS UNDER CHIPPINGS 90×60 CM
   (STANDING AREA FOR FAÇADE CLEANING CHERRY
   PICKER)
14 UNDER WATER LAMPS
15 BUILT IN GROUND LAMPS
16 STAINLESS STEEL COLUMN WITH CONTROL UNIT
   FOR AUTOMATIC IRRIGATION

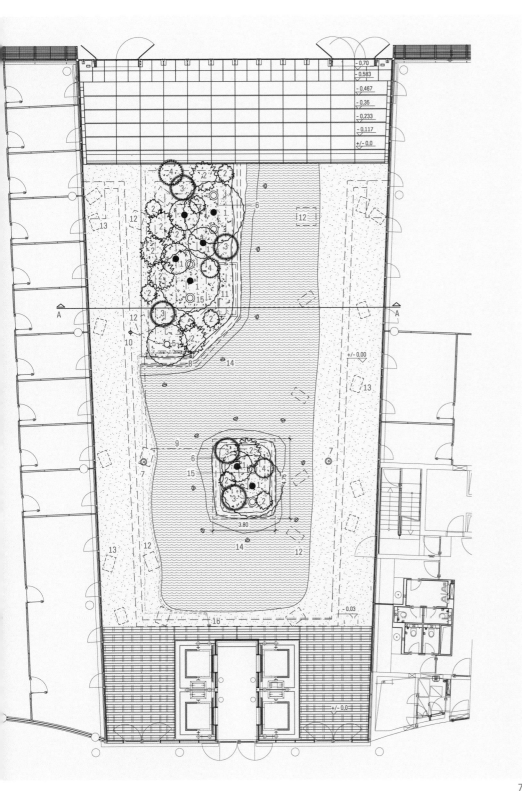

5 After the buildings were completed, the plants were put in place. The pond was then laid out. A covering protected the hall's floor, which was ultimately paved with white stone chips.

6/7 Lago cross section and planting plan

7

3 Themed garden Tea

The 'Tea' themed garden represents the scenic landscape of 'tea plantations in the highlands of Malaysia'. The evergreen leaves symbolize the lush green of this warm, moist climate. As in a plantation, solitaire trees shade the tea bushes, with camphor trees (*Cinnamomum camphora*) and cheesewoods (*Pittosporum*) standing in for real tea bushes. The dense, amorphous shapes of the hedges, some of which reach eye level, are maintained 'by the constant plucking of leaves, just as they would be in a real plantation'.

8 In the Tea themed garden, dense cheese-wood hedges symbolize tea – true tea plants do not grow well indoors.

9 From a distance, the outlines of the dense, dark green vegetation set the tone. Closer to, the texture, fragrance and colour of the leaves and flowers become apparent.

10 The leaves of the low bamboo and the ground cover plants are similar in colour and texture.

11 In the Cape themed garden, the Bird of Paradise plant grows on black stone islands framed by white chipped stone.

8

9

10

11

4 Themed garden Camellia

The abstract 'camellia forest' landscape image uses the camellia, which symbolizes impermanence, and the fragrant-leafed camphor tree (*Cinnamomum camphora*), which is typically planted near temples. The dense and lush evergreen camellias (*Camellia sasanqua* or *japonica*), with their autumn and winter flowers, represent change. The design emphasizes the various heights of different plants in the dense planting – woody plants, shrubs and low-growing herbaceous plants (*Ophiopogon* or mondo grass and *Liriope* 'Monroe White'). The narrow range of colours in the delicately textured foliage emphasizes the density, unity and harmony of the composition.

5 Themed garden Zen

The 'Islands in the Sea of Japan' Zen garden imitation is a simplification of the Zen Buddhism icon standing for simplicity, serenity and meditation. A species of bamboo (*Bambusa vulgaris* 'Striata') that is lower-growing than the type used in the *Bambus* hall grows in amorphous, gently mounded beds along with low, dense ground cover planting (*Liriope* 'Monroe White'). The leaves of the two different types of plant are similar in their colour and texture, making the straight lines of the light-coloured, densely planted bamboo stems stand out more, and emphasizing the vertical. In this hall, the white stone chips underfoot are raked into waves to represent water.

6 Themed garden Cape

The 'Cape' landscape image is embodied by two island groups with plants set in black stone: lush landscapes with several species in the northern section, and smaller islands to the south planted with only Bird of Paradise flowers *(Strelitzia reginae)*. The materials used were black stone with flowering perennials and woody plants.

7 Themed garden Outback

The fourth atrium, named 'Outback', is a dry, harsh natural landscape image. Large Australian silver oaks (*Grevillea robusta*) stand within geometrically exact circles of low-piled ochre-coloured natural stone coarse gravel. These circular elevations are similar in style to Aboriginal paintings. The tall, slender growth and the irregular shape of the oaks both emphasize the height of the six-storey hall and give a natural, 'windswept' appearance. The silvery foliage suggests heat. The loose planting of the New Zealand flax (*Phormium tenax*) that serves as ground cover acts as a counterpoint to the severity of the geometrical flower beds. The pointed leaves symbolize the inhospitable nature of this hot landscape. For effect lighting, spotlights are concealed in the coarse gravel to light the trees from below. Flexible seating is included: the white colour and simple design of these chairs fits into the abstract composition. In pictures, the seats help the viewer to gain an impression of scale and of the size of the trees.

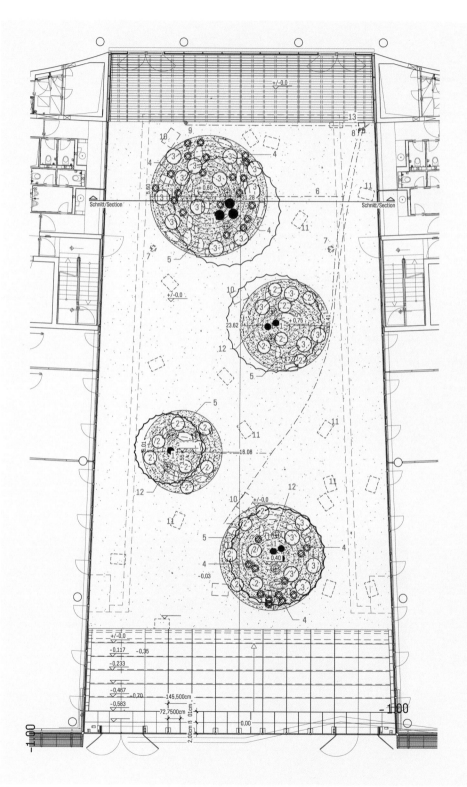

12/13 Planting plan and cross section

14/15 This plant and coloured gravel
composition and the shapes of the beds were
inspired by the hot, dry Australian outback.

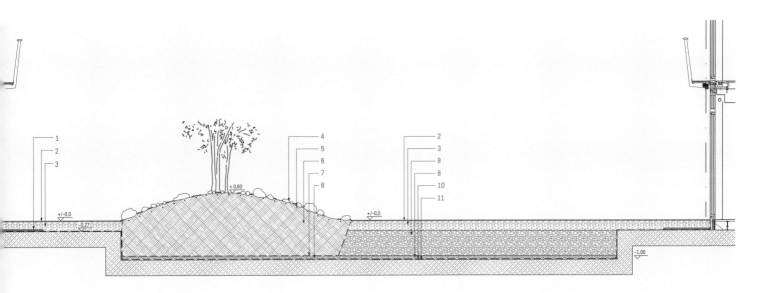

13

← 1 SOUTHERN SILKY OAK - *GREVILLEA ROBUSTA* -
GROWTH HEIGHT 8 M + 2 M, DIAMETER 5 M + 1 M
2 NEW ZEALAND FLAX
3 NEW ZEALAND PITTOSPORUM
4 COPROSMA SPECIES
5 PLANTED AREA COVER WITH CHIPPINGS/
CRUSHED STONE/QUARRY STONE
6 IRRIGATION PIPES
7 INSPECTION SHAFT ABOVE OUTLET
8 MAGNET VALVES
9 SERVICE WATER DELIVERY
10/11 CONCRETE SLABS UNDER CHIPPINGS 90×60 CM
(STANDING AREA FOR FACADE CLEANING
CHERRY PICKER)
12 BUILT IN GROUND LAMP
13 STAINLESS STEEL COLUMN WITH AUTOMATIC
IRRIGATION CONTROL UNIT

1 INSULATION
2 CHIPPINGS 8/11 MM
3 BASE COURSE 0/45 MM, WITH EXTRA 0/22 MM
4 COVERING FOR PLANTED AREAS
(QUARRY STONE, CRUSHED STONE, CHIPPINGS)
5 PIPE FOR DRIP IRRIGATION
6 PLANT SUBSTRATE
7 FILTER FLEECE
8 DRAINAGE COURSE, E.G. LAVA 8/11 MM
9 GRAVEL AND SAND FILLER MIXTURE 0/32 MM
10 PROTECTION COURSE
11 ROOF SUPERSTRUCTURE AS PER
BUILDING PHYSICS

14

15

8 Themed garden Oasis

In the 'Oasis' landscape image, the fronded date palms (*Phoenix dactylifera*) symbolize the 'classic' palm (in contrast to the fan-shaped palms in the 'Beach' and 'Lago' atria). The scent of the common myrtle (*Myrtus communis*) stands for the 'unexpected salvation' represented by oases in the desert. The myrtles are cut into block shapes and planted in quadratic and rectangular beds that express the love for geometric forms often seen in the Arabian region. The beds are slightly elevated to accommodate the palms' root balls, which can reach up to 150 cm in height. The edging is white concrete, to reinforce the impression of 'blinding desert sunlight'. It is shaped to provide seating.

Like most of the plants in this scenic landscape, the date palms were purchased from specialists in southern Europe. An initial visit to assess quality, size and availability was conducted 2.5 years before the actual planting. Transporting the palms, which are heavy and up to 14 m in height, was a logistical challenge. The plants are sensitive – especially the crown or 'heart' of the palm, from which the leaves spring. The palms were planted using machinery, with the bed edging covered for protection. The palms were anchored with cables for stability.

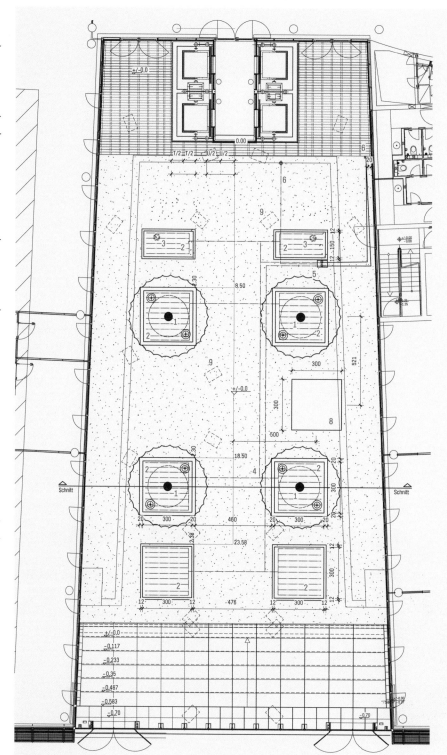

16

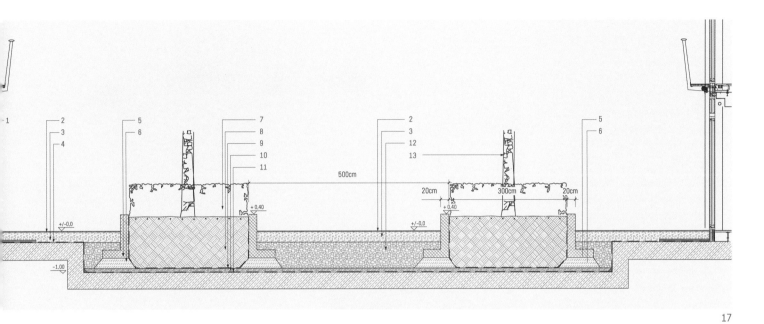

17

1 INSULATION
2 CHIPPINGS 8/11 MM
3 BASE COURSE 0/45 MM
4 ROOF SUPERSTRUCTURE AS PER BUILDING PHYSICS
5 PREFABRICATED CONCRETE SECTION
6 B15 CONCRETE (CURRENT IDENTIFICATION: C12/15)
7 MYRTLE/TRUE MYRTLE – *MYRTUS COMMUNIS*
8 PLANT SUBSTRATE
9 FILTER FLEECE
10 DRAINAGE COURSE, E.G. LAVA 8/11 MM
11 PROTECTION COURSE
12 GRAVEL AND SAND FILLER MIXTURE 0/32 MM
13 TRUE DATE PALM – *PHOENIX DACTYLIFERA* – GROWTH
   HEIGHT 14 M + 0 M, DIAMETER 4 M + 1.5 M

1 TRUE DATE PALM – *PHOENIX DACTYLIFERA* –
   GROWTH HEIGHT 14 M + 0 M, DIAMETER 4 M + 1.5 M
2 TRUE MYRTLE – *MYRTUS COMMUNIS* – EXTENSIVE
3 INSPECTION SHAFT ABOVE OUTLET
4 IRRIGATION PIPES
5 MAGNET VALVES
6 SERVICE WATER DELIVERY
7 STAINLESS STEEL COLUMN WITH AUTOMATIC
   IRRIGATION CONTROL UNIT
8 LOCATION FOR ART OBJECT
9 CONCRETE SLABS UNDER CHIPPINGS 90×60 CM
   (STANDING AREA FOR FACADE CLEANING CHERRY
   PICKER)

16/17 Planting plan and cross section
18 The artwork in the Oasis themed garden is
    one of several works by a total of seven
    artists on display in various places within
    the Lufthansa Aviation Center.

18

111

9 Themed garden Bamboo

In the 'Bamboo' themed garden, the impression of a Chinese bamboo forest is created, using typical Chinese landscape features – the light, swaying bamboo that is so ubiquitous in Asian life, combined with water and islands. The primary materials were bamboo (*Phyllostachys pubescens*) and water. In Asia, bamboo serves as a building material, a food plant, a weapon, and many other things; the 'bamboo' character also stands for elasticity, perseverance and stubbornness. The gentle movements of the majestic stalks with their delicate leaves are reflected in the water, creating varied light and shade effects.

19 In the Bamboo themed garden, *Phyllostachys pubescens* grows in continuous rows parallel to narrow, flat ponds.

19

20 The illuminated atria communicate
   by day and by night.

20

Atrium hall in the Alltours headquarters

PLANTING PLANNING:
WKM Landschaftsarchitekten,
Klaus Klein, Rolf Maas
COMPLETION: 2002
LOCATON: Duisburg, Germany

PLANNING BRIEF

Planting and landscape design for an atrium hall for the new Alltours travel company headquarters in Duisburg as a flexible space and pictorial presentation of the 'holiday' concept.

CONTEXT

The planted atrium hall, the plaza in the Alltours Flugreisen GmbH company headquarters by the inner harbour in Duisburg, forms a link between two five-storey wings of the building. This new office block accommodates over 450 employees, a bistro and a restaurant. The atrium hall with stage makes it possible to stage events for up to 400 people. The restaurant is open to the public, but the plaza itself is not. The views of the tropical landscape design in the atrium from the outside, and of the restaurant, make passersby and clients curious, and are part of the firm's corporate communication and image [1].

Connecting bridges cut through the air space in the conservatory, linking the various levels of the two office wings. The dominant material in the facades on the hall side and the bridges is wood, combined with light-coloured concrete sections and steel girders. The hall floor is paved with concrete slabs, the matte surfaces of which reflect the bright light without glare. The glazed hall is unheated, so the indoor planting is designed as if for a cold house in which the winter temperature does not fall below 5 °C because of waste heat from the adjacent offices. The large areas of glass admit sufficient daylight and direct sunlight into the interior, so the plants need no artificial light [6].

CONCEPT

The design concept for the indoor landscape is based on the movement of a river that flows longitudinally through the hall from the outer areas, which are planted with trees. Two watercourses, with different depths of up to 150 cm, breaking up floor paving as gaps with an irregular outline, give the impression of flowing through the building in the subsoil. A flat bridge and stepping stones make it possible to cross the larger of the two streams on the long side of the hall.

The plant beds are set in gaps in the paving and meet the paving without a distinct edge. It was not possible to build a basement because of the proximity of the harbour, so the plant beds could be built in contact with the natural soil [7]. A large number of rocks, some of them piled up, form a relief between the plants and along the water; some of the stones form part of the moving water feature [4].   →

1   The atrium hall between the two five–storey wings of the building
    is a flexible space designed to convey the idea of 'holiday'.

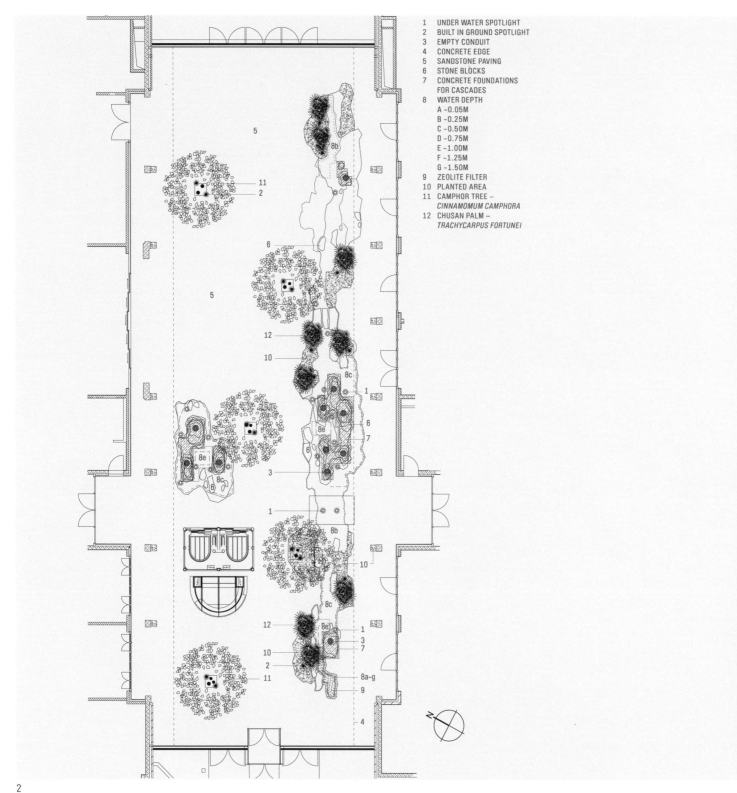

1 UNDER WATER SPOTLIGHT
2 BUILT IN GROUND SPOTLIGHT
3 EMPTY CONDUIT
4 CONCRETE EDGE
5 SANDSTONE PAVING
6 STONE BLOCKS
7 CONCRETE FOUNDATIONS
  FOR CASCADES
8 WATER DEPTH
  A –0.05M
  B –0.25M
  C –0.50M
  D –0.75M
  E –1.00M
  F –1.25M
  G –1.50M
9 ZEOLITE FILTER
10 PLANTED AREA
11 CAMPHOR TREE –
   CINNAMOMUM CAMPHORA
12 CHUSAN PALM –
   TRACHYCARPUS FORTUNEI

2

2 Floor plan.
3 The flowing water seams to
   'break through' the soil.

3

The selection of plants for this location in the cold house is a varied mixture of Mediterranean and sub-tropical species. After all the building work was completed and the ground cleaned, it was possible to plant the following species and quantities in mineral-organic intensive substrate, fertilized as needed during planting on site.

TREES
- Chusan palm *(Trachycarpus fortunei),* 11 items, height 200–800 cm
- Camphor tree *(Cinnamomum camphora),* 5 items, height 500–700 cm

SHRUBS
- Giant Bird of Paradise tree *(Strelitzia nicolai),* 2 items, height 100–150 cm
- Crane flower *(Strelitzia reginae),* 2 items, height 80–100 cm
- Laurestine *(Viburnum tinus)* 5 items, height 60–175 cm
- Mastic tree *(Pistacia lentiscus),* 2 items, height 60–150 cm
- Mock orange *(Murraya paniculata),* 3 items, height 60–150 cm

GROUND COVER
- Lilac Beauty lilyturf *(Liriope muscari 'Lilac Beauty'),* 240 items
- Black mondo grass *(Ophiopogon planiscapus),* 400 items

CLIMBING PLANTS
- Chestnut vine *(Tetrastigma voinierianum),* 5 items
- Jasmine *(Jasminum officinale),* 7 items
- Bower vine *(Pandorea jasminoides 'Alba'),* 5 items

AQUATIC PLANTS
- European water chestnut *(Trapa natans),* 25 items
- Frogbit *(Hydrocharis morsus-ranae),* 20 items
- Water soldier *(Stratiotes aloides),* 20 items

BULBS
- White crinum *(Crinum powellii 'Album'),* 15 items

4

5

6

7

4   Some of the natural rocks are piled up as natural stones in the
    water feature cascade.
5   The balustrades on the galleries and walkways make perfect, stable
    plant support structures. The rapidly growing chestnut vine can be
    cut back if necessary as part of the maintenance programme.
6   The lavish tropical planting in the plaza conveys the company's marked
    awareness of quality to the outside world through the glass facade,
    and stimulates customers' curiosity.
7   The new building has no basement, which made it possible to set up
    the planted areas with direct contact to the natural soil, so the massive
    plants can extend their roots under the floor slab.

Two planted atria for the Alterra laboratory and administration buildings

ARCHITECT: Stefan Behnisch
LANDSCAPE WITH: Copijn Garden and Landscape Architects, Michael Singer (artist)
GARDEN CONSTRUCTION: Copijn Realisation
COMPLETION: 1998
LOCATION: Wageningen, the Netherlands

PLANNING ASSIGNMENT

Constructing a new institute building – a European pilot project for ecological construction – with intensive natural planting in two atria to save energy and create a comfortable indoor climate for employees.

CONTEXT

The laboratory and administration building for the Institut für Forst- und Naturforschung (IBN) – now Alterra – was a European ecological building pilot project in connection with the 1992 Rio de Janeiro summit. Among other things, the sustainability strategy involved minimizing carbon dioxide emissions and energy use for heating and lighting, and using ecological materials containing no pollutants, preferably sourced locally.

In order to prove that sustainable construction was possible without unusually high investment costs, the project partners also had to keep to a standard budget.

CONCEPT

At first glance, the site appeared unsuitable for this kind of project, because it was formerly agricultural land, and had been overfertilized and leached of nutrients. The setting up of 'gardens' with dry walls, embankments, groves, hedges, avenues, ponds, swamps and canals created new habitats for flora and fauna where ecosystems could gradually regenerate. The building itself was not supposed to dominate the rural surroundings – the idea was for it to grow out of the landscape. Two of the gardens are planted atria with a planted area of about 18 × 60 m and a height of 12 m, fitted laterally into the three-winged building **3**. Their position makes it possible for all the workspaces to be directly connected with the inner or outer gardens. The outer facades of the two atria face south. Like the roof, they are made from mass-produced, non-insulated standard greenhouse glass. The saving made by using this glass is estimated at 75%. The unheated atria are crucial to the building's climate concept, acting as a thermal buffer and a shade provider and improving the climates in the adjacent offices, which they also supply with sunlight.   →

1   The highly natural atrium garden connects the indoor and outdoor space.

2

3

2   The two atria fit into the building's structure, between the office blocks.

3   The lush plants and the pond actively help to cool the indoor garden and the nearby offices.

4   The plants are taken primarily from the mild climates of southern Ireland and northern Spain. They have a high resistance to pests.

5   The structure of the 'gardens' runs through the building: the planted atria are a part of the landscape planning.

4

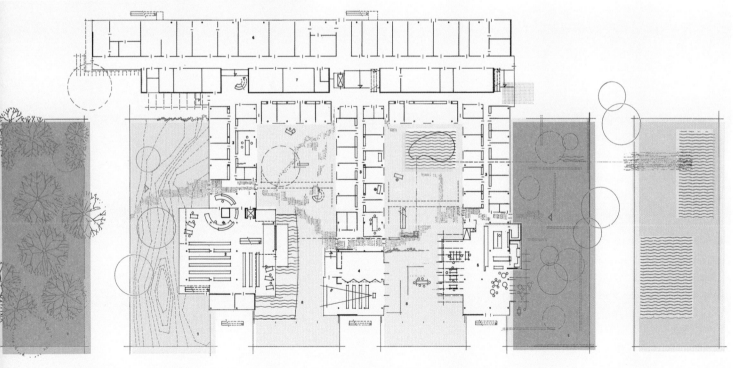

5

The temperature in these sheltered gardens is generally between 15 °C and 25 °C, with extremes of 0 °C and 30 °C, meaning that the changes of the season can be felt within the building. In winter, the atria function as a thermal buffer. The building's inner facades were built economically, and the offices are supplied with warm air from the sheltered gardens. Employees can open tilting and sliding windows as needed.

Sunlight falling on the atria creates a passive energy gain. Energy efficiency is even better in the winter, when the internal blinds, which are used at other times to provide shade, can be closed at night to provide additional insulation.

The Dutch firm Copijn Garden and Landscape Architects was commissioned to design the indoor gardens – jointly with the American artist Michael Singer, who also created some artworks for the atria and the concrete floors, also of the ponds. The ponds, plant beds and paths are laid out as 'naturally' as possible, to match the indoor climate. The beds are connected to the soil, so that the large plants can take in moisture from the groundwater to a depth of 2 m. Rainwater from the roof is collected in an outdoor pond and used to water the garden. The water is first pumped into the large basin in the west atrium, where it is buffered and warmed, and then channelled into the smaller, warmer pond in the east atrium, which feeds into the automatic irrigation system.

The atrium is planted like an outdoor garden, with a layer of herbaceous plants and bushes. Prominent ground cover plants include lilyturf (*Liriope muscari*), climbing fig (*Ficus repens*) and ferns. Bushes include cheesewoods (*Pittosporum*), camellias (*Camellia*) and viburnum (*Viburnum*). Only a few low trees were used. A few climbing plants scale the handrails of the spiral staircases and galleries of the upper storeys: passion flowers (*Passiflora*), jasmine (*Jasminum officinale*), clematis (*Clematis*) and roses (*Rosa*). No special substrate was used for the planting in the atrium. Instead, the nutrient-rich sandy soil was treated slightly to improve it's structure further.

The institute building is a perfect example of the successful integration of indoor gardens into a building. The annual energy saving on heating, cooling,

6   In summer the atria are naturally ventilated by leaving the windows constantly open, permitting transverse ventilation.

7   Energy concept for the building.

8   Internal roller blinds with a special thermal coating shade the glass roof in summer, and are closed at night to provide additional thermal protection in winter. They are a standard mass-produced model normally used in tomato cultivation.

9   The natural filter systems of the ponds are self-cleaning, with high water quality.

6

GREENHOUSE   MASS

TEMP

TIME

DAY
SHADE AND VENTILATE GREENHOUSES.
THERMAL MASS ABSORBS HEAT.

NIGHT
HEAT FROM MASS
DRAWN OFF

7

8

9

ventilation and lighting is considerable, and the use of natural materials, such as native woods, proved to be a good choice. The planting design has developed very well over 12 years, with 80% of the original plants continuing to flourish. They have been supplemented by a few new species.

The atrium gardens are popular with the institute's employees because they ensure a healthy atmosphere in the offices and are good places to meet, hold discussions, and relax during breaks. The ponds contain fish, frogs and other life, and numerous animals have migrated into this new habitat through the almost constantly open ventilation flaps. Birds, butterflies, microbes and insects have discovered a new habitat within the gardens.

10

11

13

14

10 A few trees serve as highlights, emphasize architectonic
   boundaries, or create a frame for special places.
11 The workspaces have direct views of the gardens and receive
   abundant daylight through the large glazed apertures.
   The lighting situation is further improved by the reflective expanses
   of water and the light-coloured flooring of the atria.
   The office facades have an additional layer of sun and glare
   protection, some elements of which can be individually adjusted
   by employees.
12 The planting is like an outdoor garden, with a layer of small
   herbaceous plants and bushes.
13 Dense planting with generally low perennials and bushes and
   largely open paths create a 'natural' garden.
14 The inner facades look like outer facades. The planted atrium feels
   like an outdoor space, despite the 12 m high glazed roof.

12

Indoor planting for the Genzyme Center office building

ARCHITECTS: Behnisch Architekten
PLANTING PLAN FOR THE INDOOR GARDEN:
planungsgruppe agsn architekten gmbh,
Jürgen Frantz, in LOG ID
ADVICE: Büro Happold
LIGHT ADVICE: Bartenbach LichtLabor
COMPLETION: 10/2003
LOCATION: Cambridge, Massachusetts, USA

PLANNING ASSIGNMENT

Sixteen different indoor gardens to complement the overall design concept for a sustainable office building, with particular emphasis on daylight quality.

CONTEXT

The Genzyme Center is the new headquarters of the Genzyme Corporation biotechnology company, located in Cambridge, Massachusetts, USA. Behnisch Architekten won the competition with a design that did not concentrate on the outer appearance of the building, but instead prioritized the indoor space – both its climate and the provision of daylight for the workspaces. They took a unified approach; their plan included the building shell, the airspace, the atrium, decentralized technology, daylight systems, photovoltaics, garden systems, rainwater utilization systems, and efficient energy use. In 2005, the building was awarded the LEED Platinum Certificate – the highest category of the prestigious American sustainable architecture certification system.

CONCEPT

The gardens in the central atrium, which runs up through 12 storeys of the building, improve the indoor air quality by absorbing carbon dioxide and giving off oxygen, and by binding dust, increasing air humidity, filtering out pollution, and cooling the air by transpiration and shading. The 16 different garden spaces are also intended to enhance the building aesthetically and to be actively used by employees – for discussions and for relaxation, for instance.

The central atrium is the most important element in the daylight strategy. On the roof, 7 heliostat mirrors that follow the position of the sun catch the light and redirect it into the lower storeys via fixed mirrors, without creating glare or overheating the atrium. A 'chandelier' made from 768 prism panes and a controlled 'light wall' of aluminium slats reflect the natural light down into the depths of the surrounding rooms.

The chandelier prisms move in the rising draught, and the resulting sunlight patterns, which change with the position of the sun, enliven the atrium gardens. The slatted blinds on the inner facades that reflect natural light into the offices in the upper areas are automatically controlled, but can also be regulated individually. →

1   Plenty of daylight reaches the gardens and the partially open,
    partially enclosed workspaces via the atria and the glass facades.

To increase sunlight reflection further, the balustrades are made from aluminium, and expanses of water are incorporated into the entrance area design as part of the planting layout.

The indoor gardens create a wide variety of different spaces within the variously shaped storey floor plans. The atrium connects all areas of the building and promotes communication between employees. Some of the gardens can be seen from outside, through the building's transparent shell. →

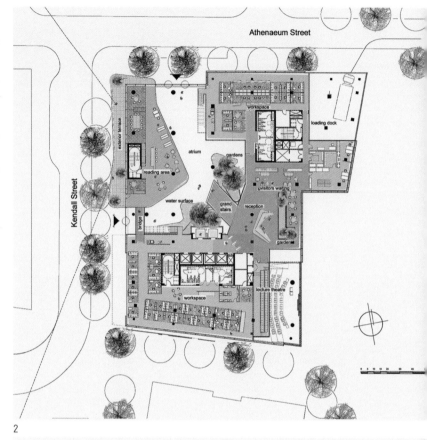

2

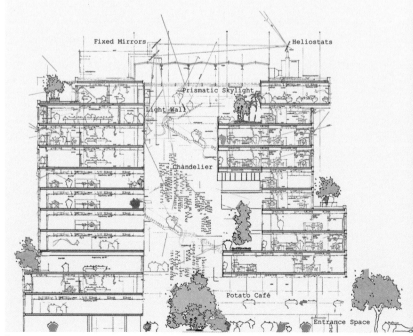

2 Plan of the ground floor.
3/4 Longitudinal and transverse cross section, showing the position of the gardens around the central atrium.
5 Cross section showing how daylight enters the atrium via the movable and fixed mirrors, the 'light wall' and the 'chandeliers'.
6 Sketch for planting concept.

3

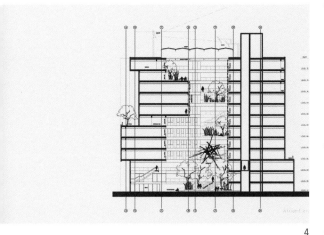

4

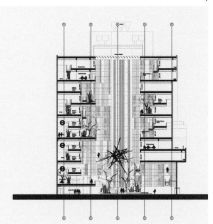

5

6

The permanently warm indoor climate creates ideal conditions for a selection of tropical plants. Plants from different regions are grouped in the individual gardens, simulating a journey around the world:

ATRIUM
Tropical Forest theme with *Ficus longifolia 'Alii'*. This species is reminiscent of bamboo. The tree is easy to maintain.

LEVEL 2
Welcome Garden with *Ficus retusa* from Southeast Asia. The tree has a particularly sculptural appearance.

LEVEL 4
Umbrella Tree Garden with *Schefflera actinophylla* from Australia; a very strong and resistant tree with a wide, overhanging crown; and *Clusia rosea*: the oval leaves have an unusual leather-like surface composition.

LEVEL 5
Rose Apple Garden with *Syzygium samarangense* from Southeast Asia; a bush with a pyramidal crown, very delicate blossoms, and fragrant, edible fruits.

LEVEL 6–1
Japanese Teahouse Garden with *Cinnamomum camphora*; a large tree with light-green, fragrant leaves; and *Phoenix roebelenii* the only species of palm to be used in this project, and a symbol of vitality.

LEVEL 6–2
Buddhist Meditation Garden with *Podocarpus macrophyllus*: a slow-growing tree with a dense crown and strap-shaped leaves, often grown as a bonsai tree.

LEVEL 8–1
Bird of Paradise Garden with *Strelitzia*; in winter, its orange and blue flowers are particularly eye-catching.

LEVEL 8–2
African Fig Garden with *Ficus lyrata*. The shape of the leaves gives the fiddle-leaf fig its name. It is a large, ornamental tree.

LEVEL 9
African Pine Garden; the east African mountain pine looks like a green curtain.

LEVEL 11–1
South American Guava Garden with *Psidium guajava* and other species from Florida and the Caribbean. Guava trees produce edible fruit.

LEVEL 11–2
Inga Garden with *Inga edulis*; a small to medium-sized tree with long seed pods and edible fruit that tastes like ice cream; along with *Heliconia stricta 'Firebird'* to represent the rainforest.

LEVEL 11–3
Black Olive Garden with *Bucida buceras* and *Coccoloba uvifera*, both chosen for the characteristic shape and colour of their leaves. →

The gardens are laid out in beds fitted into gaps in the ceiling of each storey and surrounded with raised edging. The edgings increase the substrate layer depth, ensuring that even large woody plants have sufficient root space. The edgings keep substrate from leaving the plant beds and also provide simple seating. Each bed has an automated irrigation system. A hygrometer measures the degree of moisture in the substrate, opening a magnetic valve as needed. Drip tubes are laid in the beds. After being tested, these are concealed in the soil. To prevent waterlogging, each bed is provided with drainage and a connection to the building's drain system. Each bed also has a control shaft with an alarm system. If water escapes, this alarm emits an optical or acoustic signal and cuts off the water supply. To make maintenance easier, space is provided near the gardens on each level for implements, fertilizers, and work clothes for the gardeners.

The building has received various awards for the overall design concept, and in a statistical study commissioned by Genzyme Corporation, over 70% of employees claimed to feel more alert, more productive, and more in touch with their colleagues in the new building. Almost all employees considered that the view of the garden and being able to walk in the garden contributed to their well-being. The numbers of people calling in sick had also fallen.

7

8

7   Model photo: the design prioritizes the indoor daylight quality and climate. Some of the plants can be seen from outside the building through the glass facade.
8   The broad steps in the entrance area are flanked by large plant beds. The pools in front of them reflect the sunlight directed into the ground storey.
9   The glass roof is shaded by prisms, allowing only indirect sunlight into the interior, to prevent the atrium from overheating.
10 The planted bed adjacent to the facade allows the indoor planting to be seen from outside the building.

9

10

133

'Gardens in the Sky' in the Fusionopolis complex

ARCHITECT: Kurokawa Architects
PLANTING PLANNING:
Symbios Design (Oculus Landscape Architecture and urban design and Terragram Pty Ltd)
HORTICULTURE: Horti-Flora Services Pte Ltd
WATERING AND WATER FEATURES:
Landscape Engineering Pte Ltd
ROOF PLANTING SYSTEM: Zinco Singapore Pte Ltd
CLIENT: Jurong Town Corporation (JTC)
COMPLETION: 2008
LOCATION: Singapore

PLANNING BRIEF

Devising 'Gardens in the Sky' for the Fusionopolis project as open and closed green spaces with different volumes, designs and functions.

CONTEXT

The One North urban development project is to come into being over an area of about 200 hectares in Singapore. The aim is to create an autonomous town that is complete in itself, where an appropriate number of creative scientific, research and technology companies and some humanities experts are to be housed. Japanese architect Kisho Kurokawa designed the 'Fusionopolis' complex in this context, in the form of three connected towers with vertical zoning. Energy is generated and organic waste is recycled in this multifunctional complex with apartments, offices, and public and commercial spaces. Over 10,000 m² of garden areas form a large public complex at street level and advance upwards through the various levels.

CONCEPT

The original plan intended the gardens to be vertical elements linking the individual levels like stitches **2**. But this concept was diluted in the course of the project, and now simply passes through the 15 main gardens as a symbolic thread. These provide a high-quality passive recreation area for residents, neighbours and visitors.

From the environmental point of view, the plants function as insulation and climate buffers, to prevent the building from becoming too hot; they absorb carbon dioxide and give off oxygen, and also filter pollutants out of the air.

Every garden concept addresses ideas of size, location, function and the volume of the space. Design elements created especially for this project, such as water features, plant containers, or seating, reinforce the individuality of the gardens. The connecting elements in the gardens include an emphasis on verticals, a restricted range of materials for the floor coverings, the choice of plants, and the expanses of water. Tall trees anchored in the subsoil, and a wide range of creepers and climbers, are used to emphasize the vertical as a means of linking the levels. →

1   Sealed plant beds, with creepers as ground cover, float in the water in the gardens on level 5.

TECHNICAL IMPLEMENTATION

It emerged during the realization phase that the cross-beams in the loadbearing structure had to be reinforced. This affected the depth of the plant beds and water features, so most of the gardens had to be modified. As maintaining and tending the gardens had to be conducted safely and at a reasonable price, direct access was planned from the outset to the trellises, some of which were very high, and to the facades; fixing devices for cleaning gondolas were also planned.

Other factors influencing the implementation of the design were: the need to collect and drain off precipitation and provide distribution boxes in the gardens, and placing facilities intended to perform a particular function on other floors, which meant that some visitor flow could be diverted. Direct sunlight, air circulation and rainfall were considered at the overall conception stage and when choosing plants for each garden. The substrate used for the roof garden is characterized by high structural stability and porosity. It resists erosion by wind and water, is fireproof, free of pests, weeds or disease, and stores moisture. Plants that did not develop well were moved or replaced by different species in the course of the completion and maintenance processes. The reason for this was usually increased air movement or the diversion of moving air by the building volume.

The following selection presents five different garden areas as examples:

Satellite Garden | level 11

The 'Satellite Garden' sits at a connecting point between two towers and can be accessed from both sides. Mobile 'satellites' are placed on a homogeneous paved floor criss-crossed by lighter stripes. The 'satellites' are made of orange fibreglass and can be placed flexibly to structure the space **4**. Planting in the form of raised beds on the floor containing palms (*Chrysalidocarpus lutescens*) and ground cover (*Philodendron 'Moonlight'*), and peripheral planting with climbers (*Tristellateia australasiae*), growing upwards on wire cables stretched between the floor and the ceiling, is restricted to the outer edges of the space. The climbers winding upwards are picked out by floodlights after dark.

Garden of Contemplation | level 16

The name 'Garden of Contemplation' refers to the peace and simplicity of this area, which is reminiscent of a Japanese Zen garden in its choice of materials. A narrow aquarium with aquatic plants and fish extends along the long side of this garden **8**. The floor is largely covered with grey tiles. Low, bushy palms (*Chamaedorea elegans*) and bright green ground cover (*Pilea nummulariifolia, Ophiopogon japonicus*) grow in a long bed with irregular angles. A stone seat and a second, rectangular, plant bed complete the arrangement.

2   Sketch of the original concept.
3   Complex of buildings.
4   Ground plan of satellite garden.
5   *Tristellateia australasiae*, planted in rows, climb
    upwards on taut wires at the edge of the space.
6   These mobile elements are on castors
    and can be moved to restructure the space
    as needed.
7   Ground plan for Garden of Contemplation.
8   This garden is like a Japanese Zen garden composed
    from the elements stone, water and plants,
    and a stone bench is provided for contemplation.
9   Green Stage ground plan.

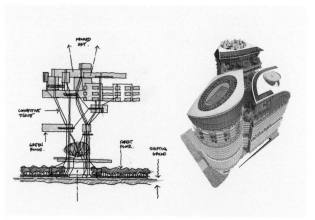

2   3

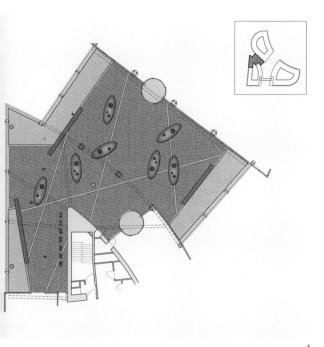

4

5

6

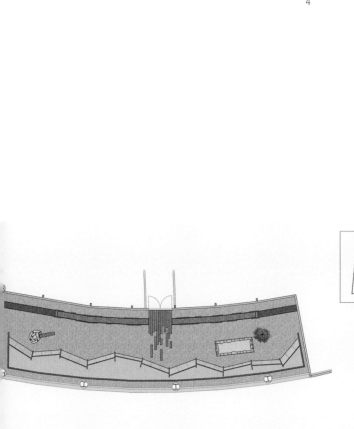

7

8

Green Stage | level 18

Viewers experience the 'Green Stage' from the floors opposite in the neighbouring tower through the white grid of the open facade structure. It creates a theatrical effect: an undulating structure made up of metal and wire mesh provides a backdrop on the rear wall; nature is the performer. The metal waves of various lengths, with some tops thrusting out into the space, are reminiscent of the drama of the steep cliffs found in Thailand, Vietnam or Malaysia. The wire mesh provides a climbing support for various creepers and climbers (*Epipremnum aureum, Philodendron erubescens 'Gold', Monstera obliqua, Monstera deliciosa*), graded according to their leaf size from the bottom (small) to the top (large). On the ground, the waves continue in the form of mounds with low, dense vegetation (*Aglaonema* 'Silver Queen', *Anthurium spp, Ophiopogon japonicus, Philodendron* 'Xanadu', *Selaginella spp.*). The red benches in synthetic resin also take up this shallow undulating form.

Labyrinth of Lians | level 20

Rapidly growing climbers (*Thunbergia laurifolia*) wind their way upwards on linear arrangements of steel cables between floor and ceiling, effectively forming green curtains in this high, narrow space called the 'Labyrinth of Lians'. The colour orange, which runs through the garden areas as a linking motif, is used here as an eye-catching accent colour to line a round pool. Simple seating is built into the rows of climbing plants.

10 Labyrinth of Lians ground plan.
11 Nature provides a performance on the 'Green Stage', which can be viewed through the grid in the open facade structure in the tower opposite.
12 The fast-growing climber *Thunbergia laurifolia* brings greenery to this narrow, accessible space, where occasional simple seats have been built into the rows.
13 This linear arrangement of climbing plants winding their way upwards creates green room dividers that filter the incident light in the adjacent rooms.

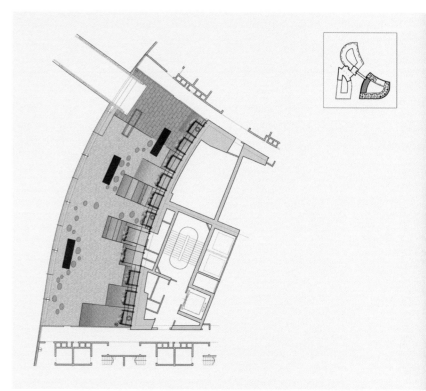

9

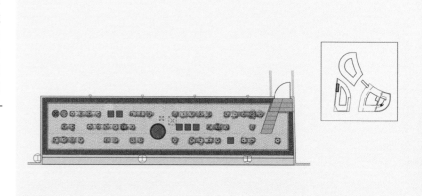

10

11

12

13

Garden of Seven Wells | level 23

Seven different wells of water and a zigzag path characterize this garden, which is open to clients of the neighbouring fitness club. The paths, with their differently textured paving, are also intended to direct visitors into other garden areas. The trees (*Pisonia alba*) along the outer sides can also be seen from a distance from the outside. Spatial depth is created by emphasizing different heights and more intricate planting from the outer edge towards the fitness club, making the U-shaped garden look bigger than it is. The following species were planted in this garden: **TREE:** *Schefflera actinophylla;* shrubs: *Dracaena sanderiana, Rhapis excelsa;* **CLIMBERS:** *Tristellateia australasiae;* **GROUND COVER:** *Philodendron scandens, Aglaonema* 'Silver Queen', *Anthurium andraeanum, Anthurium* 'Dwarf Red', *Spathiphyllum cannifolium, Spathiphyllum wallisii, Asplenium nidus, Aglaonema* 'Peacock', *Liriope spicata, Polyscias fruticosa, Neomarica gracilis* .

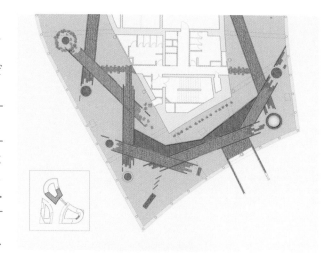

14

16

15

14 Garden of Seven Wells ground plan.
15 This climbing aid using stretched wire cables is at the top left-hand end of the U-shaped ground plan and completely encloses a round well within its conical shape.
16/17 The open-crowned trees along the outer sides and the more intricate plantings towards the core of the building give this narrow space a sense of depth.

17

General basic planning

2

Ideally, planning for a building intended to include interior green areas should involve close consultation between client, architect, a specialist planner for the internal green areas, and, where necessary, other specialist planners. This is to develop an overall concept that can bring the context, the architecture, and the green space together as a coherent whole. Close co-operation of this kind is absolutely essential if the planting programme is part of the building climatization system.

Interior planting is a planning item that can be implemented in a wide variety of ways. A carefully planned concept creates optimum conditions for the plant habitats and forms the basis for effective functioning over the longer term.

Since the planned use determines the internal climate, particularly in terms of temperature, and this in turn affects the possible choice of plants, all possible options should be carefully analysed from the outset. This means that even at the building planning stage the right conditions can be created for the necessary amount of light, maximum and minimum temperatures, and humidity.

Planning is concerned in the first place with determining the function, location, size, shape, and orientation of the green areas. But the choice of materials for the glazing, floors, bed edging or plant containers, as well as questions relating to statically viable weight, including when the substrate is saturated, must all be considered as early as possible in the planning process. In addition, the client should be kept informed in detail about follow-up costs for care and maintenance. Setting up automated watering and climatization systems means higher investment costs, but reduces long-term care and maintenance requirements. Retrofitting is usually expensive, and in some cases even impossible. So this fundamental decision should be taken before building starts wherever possible.

If green areas are planned later, all the important building details, such as permissible floor loads or light transmission values for glazing, have to be compiled. The aim then becomes to be able to define and plan architectural changes to improve the spatial situation of the climatic conditions for locating the plants as early as possible. This might include remodelling door and window apertures, in order to ensure the required air change rate, to avoid draughts, or even to offer maximum access, as trees and other large solitaire plants can often be transported and planted only by using hoists.

For example, when planting the atriums at the Chelsea Harbour Design Centre → **p.48** the low load-bearing capacity of the floors had to be taken into consideration and an unwelcome wind tunnel effect tackled; this was done by making the plant containers of particularly light material and by replacing the sliding doors with revolving ones.

Another important aspect of planning is that use has to be limited during the building and planting phase, so it is important that all those involved agree on detailed scheduling in good time.

Subsequent changes of use that affect the internal climate must be agreed upon with the planner, both for new plans and for establishing green areas at a later stage. For example, if heating is later supplied to a cool glass extension so that the space can be used all year round, the location factors change so radically that many of the original plants will not flourish in the long run.

Function

The decision to plant inside a building is seldom taken as a measure to be considered in isolation, but is part of a concept responding to a variety of needs. Here the symbolic effect of the plants is very important, as well as their physical and chemical ones. Symbolic in this context refers to the human need for nature and the enhancement of well-being, and physical and chemical to the effect of plants on the quality of the air in the space and the sound insulation function.

CREATIVE AND COMMUNICATIVE EFFECTS

Even a small green area, if it is skilfully presented, can be an attraction, as a result of its silhouette, colour, size and characteristics. Sightlines in a particular space or the building in general can be created, shifted or emphasized, without overloading the interior or reducing the impact of the architecture. Planting sets off the interior furnishings, and even when it takes up additional space does not diminish or cramp the space, but enhances it. Generally speaking, it is possible to consider structures of any kind, whether they are horizontal, vertical, straight, diagonal, placed at particular points, or designed as a natural-looking undulating space. The garden can dominate the space, be a complementing element, or be completely subordinate to the architectural form. The still relatively new vertical planting approach offers a great deal of creative scope, even for spaces that do not at first sight seem suitable for long-term planting. This approach uses green walls with closed, automated systems that are extremely easy to maintain and can, if necessary, survive mainly on artificial light.

Using plants is a powerful communication tool. For one thing, it signals a general interest in the environment, and can also play a part in a company's corporate identity. Planting that is visible from the outside often does double duty in this way, in that it does not merely appeal to workers and visitors inside the building, but also highlights corporate culture from a distance. In the Lufthansa Aviation Center → **p. 98** and the Alltours headquarters → **p. 114**, for example, the planting in the atrium halls was arranged so as to be readily visible from the outside, making the company's values and products accessible to potential clients. In the Tryg insurance building **1/2** AND → **p. 16** the tree metaphor in the canteen underscores how the merged insurance companies are growing together and flourishing jointly; the tree structure is artificial, but the planting in the vertical wall systems is natural.

1/2 The vertical planting in the canteen of the Tryg insurance building in Copenhagen symbolizes development, harmony, balance and growth, in the sense of the corporate culture growing together, and joint economic growth as a profit–making enterprise.
3 In the Beaumont Hospital, the tall trees in the atrium offer protection from the heat of the sun. They are natural copies of visual and design functions.
4 Many patients' rooms look out over the light-flooded atrium and the green area; thus patients who are confined to bed can benefit from the positive visual effect of the plants.
5 An area with an imaginative design inspired by a popular children's book has been set up especially for children in the Beaumont Hospital.

1

2

SYMBOLIC, PHYSICAL AND CHEMICAL EFFECTS

In our present environment, which is predominantly urban and thus distant from nature, the human need for nature and natural life is often not met. Having something living around the home, at work, or in buildings where we spend even a short time, improves our experience of the space. The living quality of the plants creates a feeling of familiarity and comfort, and enhances well-being. Studies have shown that productivity increases in workplaces with green areas, and stress is reduced. It was shown at Washington State University that the number of errors made when solving a problem remained constant, but response speeds were higher when there were plants in the space.[1] Many companies that commission interior planting are expressly aiming to enhance the well-being of their employees. An internal study has shown that workers in the Genzyme Center office building → p. 128 have a strong sense of increased concentration, productivity, well-being and community feeling, and at the same time the rate of absenteeism through illness has been reduced by 5%.

This positive effect made by plants has also been used successfully in medical institutions through interior and exterior planning. They help the patients, some of whom are seriously ill, to regain their dignity and self-esteem, and they reduce the stress felt by relatives and nursing staff. It was shown that the visual impact alone – just looking at the plants – speeds up convalescence for patients, and they need fewer painkillers.[2] The design for two planted spaces in the Beaumont Hospital **3–5** in Royal Oak, Michigan, USA by the Grissim, Metz, Andriese practice relies on this effect: a planted atrium with lots of comfortable seating for adult patients and a very imaginative and colourful adjacent room for children – both furnished entirely with artificial plants, because natural plants and soil substrate are not permitted in this hospital for reasons of hygiene. Particular attention does have to be paid to certain requirements relating to permitted materials in medical facilities. Natural plants can often be used only in a kind of hydroculture, to rule out health risks from germs in the soil substrate.

But green areas also hold a powerful attraction for people in commercial buildings. For example, people prefer protected seating, framed by plants or placed under trees, to free-standing benches in exposed locations.

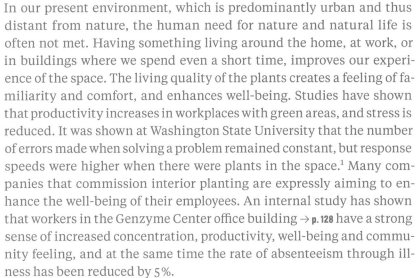

3

4

5

1   Lohr, Virginia: *Indoor Plants Increase Worker Productivity*, Washington State University
2   Ulrich, Roger S.: *Health Benefits of Gardens in Hospitals, Center for Health Systems and Design*, Colleges of Architecture and Medicine, Texas A & M University, USA, Paper for conference, Plants for People, International Exhibition Floriade, Holland, 2002

In addition, plants have a measurable positive effect both physically and chemically, improving comfort and health through air purification, humidification, and sound insulation. If the planted interior is part of a building's energy concept, savings can also be made in heating, ventilation and climatization.

Humidity and air quality in the space

Plants grow through photosynthesis. In order to do so, they absorb CO_2 (carbon dioxide) from the air through their foliage and emit O_2 (oxygen). They take in water and nutrients through their roots, and some of the water then evaporates (transpires) through their leaf pores. This transpiration produces evaporative cooling and increases air humidity. The higher the humidity in a space, the more dust is laid; people find higher humidity pleasant, especially in office spaces with many elements that dry the air out (computers, printers, carpeting, paper). Most people are familiar with the effects of evaporative cooling from the effect felt in urban parks on hot days: temperature differences, which can be clearly felt, are usually around 3–4 °C, and can be as much as 6 °C in the shade of a large tree.

Plants also filter pollutants out of the air in the photosynthesis cycle; they include volatile organic compounds (VOCs), carbon-based materials that evaporate easily or are in gaseous form even at room temperature. This filter effect was first proved in 1989 in a much-quoted NASA experiment concentrating on formaldehyde, trichloroethylene and benzene. Formaldehyde is a colourless gas contained in tobacco smoke, among other things, and it evaporates from many insulation and chipboard products used for interior furnishings.

Like other air pollutants, it triggers allergic reactions and is damaging to health, with effects ranging from irritation of nose, throat, lungs and eyes, via headaches and rashes, to changes in genetic makeup. These VOCs are used, among other things, as solvents, plasticizers, or stabilizers in paint, and in ink, coatings, lubricants, adhesives, carpets, and many other everyday products. Maximum permissible values are met in many cases for individual substances, but the interior climate can be unpleasant or even harmful if a number of factors come together. This phenomenon is known as 'sick building syndrome'.

Vital plants grown not just above ground level, but also in the root area. They can absorb pollutants from the air through both their leaves and their roots, then convert these substances and break them down through metabolic processes. Series of experiments have identified various species that are proven to break down certain pollutants and are particularly suitable for air purification. Special forms of air purification were also proven to be taking place; for example, it was shown that devil's ivy *(Epipremnum pinnatum aureum)* does not eliminate nicotine, but stores it in its leaves.[1]

Pollutants can also be filtered out of the substrate by microbiological breakdown.[2] But bacteria and roots can also live in symbiosis in the soil in liquid substrates. Their reaction products are nutrients for the symbiotic partner in each case, which means that the bacteria also survive periods in which there are no pollutants in the air. Increased ventilation for the substrate enhances filtering performance and, as a rule, hydrocultures filter more effectively than soil substrates.

1 Kerstjen, Karl-Heinz: 'Funktion und Wirkung von Innenraumbegrünungen', in: *Handbuch Innenraumbegrünung,* ed. Renate Veth, Braunschweig: Thalacker Medien, 1998

2 Tarran, J., Fraser, T., Burchett, M.: 'Use of Living Pot-Plants to cleanse Indoor Air – Research Review', in: *Proceedings of Sixth International Conference on Indoor Air Quality, Ventilation & Energy Conservation in Buildings – Sustainable Built Environment,* 28–31 Oct 2007, Sendai, Japan, Volume III, 249–256, 2007

6 Plants that breakdown Formaldehyd*

Areca palm	*Chrysalidocarpus lutescens*
Bamboo palm	*Chamaedorea seifrizii*
Banana	*Musa oriana*
Chinese evergreen	*Aglaonema commutatum*
Corn plant	*Dracaena fragrans*
Croton	*Codiaeum variegatum, pictum*
Devil's ivy/pothos	*Epipremnum aureum, pinnatum, Scindapsus aureus*
Dieffenbachia	*Dieffenbachia maculata*
Dwarf umbrella tree	*Schefflera arboricola*
Fiddle-leaf fig	*Ficus lyrata*
Geranium aralia	*Polyscias guilfoylei*
Gerbera	*Gerbera jamesonii*
Goosefoot plant	*Syngonium podophyllum*
Grape ivy, oak-leaf ivy	*Cissus rhombifolia*
Heartleaf philodendron	*Philodendron scandens*
House lime	*Sparmannia africana*
Ivy	*Hedera helix*
Kentia palm	*Howea forsteriana*
Lacy Tree philodendron	*Philodendron selloum*
Lady palm	*Rhapis excelsa*
Lemon lime	*Dracaena deremensis*
Lobster claw	*Heliconia rostrata*
Madgascar dragon tree	*Dracaena marginata*
Mother-in-law's tongue	*Sansevieria trifasciata, laurentii*
Peace lily	*Spathiphyllum 'Mauna Loa', Spathiphyllum clevelandii*
Philodendron	*Philodendron oxycardium*
Silver Queen Chinese evergreen	*Aglaonema modestum*
Spider plant	*Chlorophytum comosum, Chlorophytum elatum*
Spineless yucca	*Yucca elephantipes*
Sword fern	*Nephrolepis exaltata*
True aloe	*Aloe vera*
Weeping fig	*Ficus benjamina*

*   After Weidner, M., Teixeira da Silva, J. A.: *Potential and limitations of ornamental plants for indoor-air purification, Floriculture, Ornamental and Plant Biotechnology,* Volume IV, Global Science Books, UK, 54–63, 2006, and Wolverton B.C., Johnson, A., Bounds, K.: *Interior landscape plants for indoor air pollution abatement,* Final Report, NASA, USA, 1989

Besides the filter effect, interior planting can minimize the necessity of installing or switching on air conditioning. Air conditioning plants often circulate air that is very dry or even polluted by germs through buildings, and are viewed critically by many people. Natural climatization by the buffer effect of the building, evaporative cooling from flourishing vegetation, or well adjusted ventilation systems can also work as individual factors or combine to improve the quality of the interior air. Large leaf areas can also alleviate unpleasant odours, in medical facilities, for example, or overlay them with the pleasant odour of soil and aromas reminiscent of the air in a greenhouse.

But there are limits to the purifying and humidifying effect of plants. Too much dust blocks leaf pores and the leaves will sometimes need to be rinsed regularly. Chemicals in the space, such as chlorine in swimming pools, or from recently used material such as paint, adhesives or floor coverings, can strain plants to the extent that they die.

Noise reduction

Plants have another physical quality that can be used positively inside buildings: their capacity for noise reduction. Here it is not just the leaves that are significant: the mass of the plant containers and the substrate plays a part as well. Noise reduction is affected by the arrangement of the vegetation: several groupings distributed around the space reduce sound to a greater extent than rows or a concentration of plants in the middle of the space. For example, a lot of telephone calls are made in the open plan office Combined Traders **9/10** AND → **p.42** and the planting integrated into the modern interior furnishings serves mainly to reduce noise levels. In the Tryg insurance building canteen **11** AND → **p.16**, noise reduction by the planted wall is further reinforced by concealed sound-absorbing panels fitted inside the planted structure.

7

———— Pollutants in
the air

———— Active
plant filter

———— Purified air
given off
again

8

7/8 The ANDREA air filter developed by French designer Mathieu
Lehanneur with Harvard professor David Edwards can be set up as
a mobile interior unit. A quiet fan draws air into the container,
where the plant absorbs pollutants through its leaves, roots and
the bacteria active in the substrate. The purified air is released
back into the room.

9/10 Wall planting by the café tree in the Tryg insurance building
reduces noise levels in the canteen.

11 Plants are used for sound reduction in the Combined Traders office
by Marc Koehler Architects.

9

10

11

Context

Each design emerges in its own specific context. Interior planting is often part of a building with an overall design that considers a certain context, such as the topography of the site, or special historical features. The interior planting planner then considers both the building's relationship with the exterior space and how the interior that is to be planted relates to the architecture of the building.

Climate data should also be gathered as early as possible, or measured on the spot. Temperature and light intensity are subject to strong seasonal fluctuations in most locations, which means that multiple measurements are necessary over a long period in order to assemble the data required for planning the planting. Shading by neighbouring buildings or high trees, especially when the sun is low in the sky, can have an adverse effect to which the design must respond appropriately.

Context analysis makes it possible for planners to make a deliberate decision to adapt the design to the conditions and structures of the surrounding area, taking up individual aspects or presenting a contrast with an individual design.

If the planting is intended to be visible from the outside, then sightlines, the transparency or reflecting quality of the facade, and the size, contour lines and colours of the plants are important conceptual considerations. Pedestrians looking at the garden designed by Breimann & Brunn Landschaftsarchitekten 12, for example, are aware of the large plants in the planted rooms at different heights as they walk past and from distance. The plants are even presented well at night, with the aid of carefully placed lighting. The building, through the planting, thus communicates with observers outside on the autobahn even when it is closed or not being used.

Another example is the green wall in the ING Direct café in downtown Vancouver 13. It catches the eye of passersby in the street and serves as an advertisement for the ING Direct Bank, which offers a café with ATMs and bank advisers for their customers.

The planner can forge links with the context by using shapes, materials, or colours from the architecture or the exterior space when planting outside

12

13

14

15

16

17

18

19

the building. Flowerbeds that seem to pass through the skin of the building from the outside to the inside (or vice versa) make it look more transparent and tie it into its surroundings. The Japanese garden in the One Kowloon office building **15** is based on the principles of Zen Buddhism, continuing down from the upper floors into the lobby and from there across the floor covering, through the glass facade and out to the partially roofed exterior.

The square flowerbed in the public library in Seattle **14** AND → **p. 38** adopts the angular formal language of inner city architecture. In contrast, the natural-looking vegetation in the Alterra laboratory and office building **16** AND → **p. 120** ties the building into the rural outdoor space, meaning that the varied and luxuriant planting in the atrium comes close to representing an intensification of the outdoor space, which is less intensively planted and more extensive. The transparent envelope of the green space in the Lufthansa Aviation Center **17/18** AND → **p. 98** and in the Alltours travel company headquarters **19** AND → **p. 114** relate the planning to the surrounding area, while the abstract design for Lufthansa and the exotic one for Alltours embody individuality and take the company's character into account.

12 The planted interiors at the DWS Investment GmbH office complex (Frankfurt am Main, Germany) communicate with passers-by day and night, as the size, outlines and colour of the vegetation are visible from a distance as well.

13 The vertical garden serves as a poster advertising the ING Direct Bank in its building in downtown Vancouver.

14 The straight lines of the flowerbed in the library interior in central Seattle take up the architectural language of the surrounding area.

15 Unframed glazing separates the designed exterior from the interior space in the Ono Kowloon office building in Hong Kong. The Japanese garden continues seamlessly through the facade.

16 The Alterra laboratory and office building is set in a rural area of Holland. The natural-looking planting in the two atrium halls integrates the building into its surroundings.

17/18 The transparent envelope of the Lufthansa Aviation Center in Frankfurt am Main forges links with the surrounding area, while the abstract character of the planting expresses the individuality of the building – and the company.

19 The tropical garden in the Alltours building in Duisburg can be seen from the outside and promotes sales of the company product: holidays.

Creating space

The planted interior breaks down into used areas and rest zones, planted areas and, especially in the case of larger plants, technical maintenance areas, with established guidelines for volumes, proportions and boundaries. Outdoor space is created mainly by vertical demarcations, e.g. plants, soil modelling, or built elements, while interior planting is quite often composed from vertical and horizontal elements that respond to the limitations imposed by the enclosing building envelope. Interior plantings will also tend to be viewed from close up, and often from different (height) perspectives 21/22 .

Lavish internal planting offers more scope than spatially restricted gardens in terms of the definition of space through the shape, size, and height of the flowerbeds; the vegetation; and the used spaces and pathways. Even so, it is also possible to harness the nature of the planting and design to present even small complexes in a way that is spatially exciting if the planners work with contrasts such as constriction and spaciousness, or closed and open sections. It is often enough simply to indicate these elements that help to create space: for example, by using slender hanging plants or low woody plants that protect a seating niche without completely blocking the view. Several vertical elements can also combine to form a boundary: a young olive tree in a 50 cm high plant container closes the space in front of the exit to this private London sun terrace 26 AND → p.74 with its framing walls; the tall, narrow trunk does not restrict the eye-level sightlines.

The connection between space and proportion, that is, the extent of the planned planting or the height to which the plants grow, is a crucial planning parameter. Intricate, horizontally emphasized planting in a large, high spatial volume can make just as bad an impression as a large woody plant that threatens to impinge upon the built spatial boundaries.

20

21

22

23

24

25

20/21 The atrium planting in the Design Centre in London's Chelsea Harbour can be experienced on a variety of levels: from the upper storeys the installation looks very graphic, while on the ground floor level the white plant tubs designed especially for the project and the verticality of the trees are the dominant factors.

22/23 The elements of space, light and planting make a different impression on each floor of the residential and nursing home in St. Pölten, near Vienna, and offer a constantly changing backdrop for the residents' lives over the course of days and weeks.

24/25 The design concept for the planting of the 'Plaza' at the Alltours headquarters is best understood when viewed from the upper floors. At ground level the complex seems very spacious because of the different plant characteristics.

26 The olive tree in a plant container marks the boundary of the dining area without blocking the view of the town roofs.

26

BOUNDARIES

The enclosed area around the interior establishes the maximum line for the boundaries of any interior planting. This means that the bed borders represent firm boundaries that can be either at ground level or raised. These can follow and emphasize the lines of the interior or be free forms, creating new links within the space. Paths around or through the beds can adapt to the topographical modelling or create or reinforce scenic sightlines. The shape of the very narrow bed, largely planted with ground cover plants, in the private house called 'Foothills' **27** AND → **p. 26** is a special case here: these clearly defined areas are not intended to be walked on, but crossed, in order to get to the seating on the terrace.

Groups of plants or other design elements, such as water, can structure and order the space within a bed. Different planting density above or below the viewer's eye level – with deciduous woody plants, tall trees, trimmed shrubs as a hedge, for example, or herbaceous plants defining the space – can establish the transparency and texture of these borders. In the atrium of the Covent Garden office complex **29** AND → **p. 84**, the height of the clearly defined bed areas and the planting under the herbaceous perennials is limited to under 1 m. The lower edge of the treetops is at or lower than eye level, which means that the structure within the beds remains filigree. When indoor gardens cannot be entered, the vegetation can be provided with clearly defined borders, as in the case of the atria planted with *Cycas revoluta* in the DWS Investment GmbH office complex in Frankfurt am Main, Germany **30/43**.

27

28

29

APERTURES

Access points and facade apertures have to be appropriately dimensioned and kept free from obstructions, as they are usually very important in terms of ventilation. Plant growth has to be taken into account as well, so that protruding branches will not block ventilator flaps, for example. Structures protruding into the interior, plants at the edge of a bed or growing out beyond it, ventilation or shading systems that block access make it more difficult to clean windows and tend the planted areas and so generate higher maintenance tasks. There is also a danger that plants can be snapped off or trodden on, or damaged by cleaning products or the placing of ladders, towers or other equipment if there is not adequate room for movement or stabilization of the ground.

30

31

27 Staggered spatial boundaries are created in the private house 'Foothills' in New Zealand in the niche adjacent to the staircase by means of beds abutting the floor covering and framing a slightly raised terrace.
28 This bed inside the Can-West building in Toronto, like all the other planted areas, is separated from the traffic areas by a stone wall 50 cm high. The non-transparent windows of the adjacent offices form an enclosure rising through the full height of the space, but its severity is relieved by the reflection of the vegetation.
29 Borders and facades create boundaries for the planted areas in the Covent Garden office complex in Brussels. Single trees in large, low plant containers create a broken boundary along the wide passageway below the two parts of the building.
30 The two storey atria at the DWS Investment GmbH have a transparent glass border on all sides, so that the transition from exterior to interior seems fluent.
31 The limited area of the 'Glass Bubble' conservatory creates a powerful experience: the densely planted beds come close to the transparent skin of the building, but the paths through the plot are curved.

VERTICAL LINKS

Climbing or hanging plants and high trees empha-size verticals. They draw the eye upwards, make a major impact in terms of structure, and can link several storeys together. The vegetation can be planted as solitaires, groups or rows. Detail creates a distinctive atmosphere: a single palm combined with low accompanying planting makes a different impact on a high space than a bamboo grove, for example, or a curtain made up of climbing plants with or without a trellis, growing from top to bottom or bottom to top. In the Fusionopolis building → **p. 134**, differently designed green areas penetrate and link the floors of the high-rise building and many of the climbers and creepers grow along unique structures designed for the space in which they are used.

Green walls can also be installed in narrow spaces to link and enhance corridors, access points or staircases visually. Two examples are the 'Plant Wall' in a Swedish law firm **32** AND → **p. 22** and the green cladding of the lift shaft in the white access corridor of the Tryg insurance building in Copenhagen **33** AND → **p. 16**.

32

33

34

35

32 The green wall along the access stairs in the Mannheimer Swartling law firm in Stockholm emphazises the vertical qualit of the stairwell.

33 The tall, round lift shaft is made into a key design element by planting in a lobby in the Tryg insurance building in Copenhagen.

34/35 Two visionary designs by American artist Robert Cannon are used to emphasize the height of a foyer.

36 Wooden terrace, water feature, beds, planting, and the fresco structure the space in the foreground, middle ground and background of the 'Giardino delle Ninfee' in the inner courtyard of a school building in Bologna.

37 The horizontally graded foreground, middle ground and background are grouped very tightly around the water feature in the Alltours head-quarters.

38 The different heights of the stone and vegetation design elements in this garden in the Fusionopolis building lend great depth to the narrow space but do not impede sightlines to the exterior space.

HORIZONTAL LINKS

Paths through a planted interior garden or the layering of elements in foreground, middle ground or background create horizontal links and hence spatial depth. Carefully controlled sightlines along a planted row or looking towards water, as in the Alterra project → **p. 120**, give a sense of these links and emphasize individual spatial situations. One clear example of a horizontal composition in an interior garden is the 'Giardino delle Ninfee' in Bologna, Italy, a planted open inner courtyard in a school building → **p. 68**: the arrangement of the beds and areas of water and the height of the vegetation was matched to the distance from which the garden is viewed. There is no access to the courtyard; it can only be seen through the windows surrounding it. The terraced structure is particularly clear on the long sightline down the length of the garden **36** : the starting point for viewers is a little wooden terrace at ground level, slightly raised above a still pool. A stream and a stone cascade are framed by terraced vegetation on both sides, leaving the windows free. The end point and spatial border is a fresco taking up the full height and width of the wall on the ground floor.

The planting at the Alltours headquarters **37** AND → **p. 114** and in the garden of contemplation in the Fusionopolis building **38** AND → **p. 134** both also acquire spatial depth through horizontal graduation. The planting in the Alltours atrium can be seen from all sides, and the horizontal links are stressed to differing degrees. In the garden of contemplation, the design gradually develops in height from the access point at ground level to the height of the palms against the vertical boundary of the space.

36

37

38

GROUPING

The custom-built plant containers for the trees in the Chelsea Harbour design → **p. 48** harmonize in terms of material, shape, and colour, and are reflected in the stools that are another part of the design. This means that the overall design is linked through the three atrium courtyards, even though the middle courtyard is not planted.

Arranging individual plants as a group creates a spatial situation that is influenced by the group in different ways:

— A solitaire is not, strictly speaking, a group, but it dominates the space and defines it in that way **40**.
— Pairs communicate with each other, create an arc of tension, or form a frame **41**.
— Rows establish a direction, form boundaries, and can create a harmonious background **42/43**.
— Irregular groups **44** and
— Regular grouping (grids) can link parts of a building, define areas, and give more depth to a space **45**.

Ground cover and other low accompanying planting can create a three-dimensional effect as groups; planting in beds always looks more natural than planting in containers. Even areas or patterns formed by densely planted vegetation with homogeneous leaf structure, colour and shape emphasize the horizontal plane, or the vertical plane in the case of planted walls **46**. This homogeneity can calm a design and also look lavish. Detecting an abstract structure can enhance the architectural effect of a space, especially from a distance. The density of the planting and the grouping of the individual plant species makes wall planting into a graphic pattern **47**. The homogeneous low underplanting emphasizes the width of the space in the Covent Garden atrium hall **48/49**.

39

40

41

43

44

45

46

47

39 This two-storey-high ficus in a private house in Greece dominates the space but still looks filigree.

40 A rubber plant and a banana tree in two separate beds form a frame in the loft apartment and establish a clear spatial distinction between the entrance area and the living space → **p. 30.**

41 Bamboo plants are often deployed in rows or as a grove, for example, in the Bamboo Hall of the Lufthansa Aviation Center.

42 The bamboo rows in Covent Garden accompany pathways through the atrium and emphasize sightlines.

43 The irregularly grouped bamboos in the Zen Hall at the Lufthansa Aviation Center define the space and have a strong physical presence.

44 The grid planting with *Cyclas revoluta* palms in the DWS Investment GmbH defines the space and gives it depth, while the fine homogeneous underplanting holds the group together.

45 The green wall in the Morris House by Fytogreen emphasizes the area and the vertical quality.

46 The various plant species grouped according to the planting plan draw a graphic pattern on the large interior wall of the 'Anthropologie' shop in London.

47 The dense and homogeneous perennial planting in the Covent Garden atrium in Brussels gives the effect of a coherent, extensive area.

Perception

FORM, STRUCTURE, HABIT

Plants are perceived according to their form, structure, and habit; in other words, their characteristic growth form. This form is determined by an outline, and emerges from the different parts of a plant, particularly when they are densely planted. It can easily be shown graphically as being derived from basic geometrical forms in the case of compact shapes. All characteristically shaped plants – not just woody ones – make a graphic or architectural impact and create structure within a space.

It is easiest to recognize the characteristic growth form of a plant – its habit – without its foliage, and plants are drawn this way for classification purposes. The natural habit develops when the location corresponds with the plant's needs. Many plants that do not get enough light or nutrients become stunted, and do not flower, or they develop very long shoots in the direction of the light source.

Simplification in presentation, and classification in form and habit type, makes it easier to compare different species and to decide which is best suited to which spatial situation. Here it should be borne in mind that form and habit tend to make an impact from a distance, but the effects of colour and texture dominate from closer up.

One special case is trimming, which is not appropriate for all plants. Well-known examples are the box tree *(Buxus sempervivens)* and holly *(Ilex aquifolium)*, which can be trimmed into a variety of geometrical shapes as hedges or solitaires; even the olive *(Olea europaea)* is rarely left in its natural habit, but rather shaped in a typical way by cutting back the individual trees. These readily understood geometrical forms make a powerful contribution to structuring a space, as edging, for instance, which can also emphasize different heights. Woody plants that have been trimmed into a paticular shape are often arranged in rows or repeating patterns. Their clear, ordered effect does not break up an architectural structure with straight lines, but reinforces it. In other situations combinations of contrasts are an interesting means of creating tension: a tall, narrow tree emphasizing the vertical on the curved edge of a path, or a delicately structured palm in front of an austerely linear glass facade CHAPTER GROUPING → **p. 158.**

Form types of trees

BALL-SHAPED
ACER PLATANOIDES 'GLOBOSUM' (NORWAY MAPLE)
COMPACT SMALL TREES FOR ENCLOSED SPACES,
FRONT GARDENS

EGG-SHAPED
TILIA CORDATA 'ERECTA' *(SMALL-LEAVED LIME)*
FOR FORMAL SITUATIONS WITH TREE ROWS
AND AVENUES, URBAN OPEN SPACES

FUNNEL-SHAPED
CATALPA BIGNONIOIDES (INDIAN BEAN TREE)
FOR TREE ROWS AND GRIDS

UMBRELLA-SHAPED
CATALPA BIGNONIOIDES (INDIAN BEAN TREE)
FULLY GROWN TREES FOR SHELTERED SEATING
OR SMALL AREAS REQUIRING SHADE

PINE-SHAPED
POPULUS NIGRA 'AUSTRIACA' (FORMALLY CLIPPED
AUSTRIAN BLACK POPLAR).
SILHOUETTE WITH A POWERFUL EFFECT IN OPEN
LANDSCAPES WITH HILLS AND MOUNTAINS

BOX-SHAPED
TILIA PLATYPHYLLOS (FORMALLY CLIPPED
BROAD-LEAVED LIME).
FOR FORMAL SITUATIONS, GREEN ARCHITECTURE

Different characteristics of trees

ROUND, SPHERICAL
PLATANUS ACERIFOLIA (MATURE PLANE)
FORMAL SITUATIONS WITH ROWS,
AVENUES AND GRIDS

ROUND/EGG-SHAPED
ACER PLATANOIDES 'CLEVELAND' (NORWAY MAPLE)
OPEN URBAN LOCATIONS, INCLUDING SQUARES,
STREETS AND PARK LAYOUTS

IRREGULAR, LOOSE-CROWNED
GLEDITSIA TRIACANTHOS (HONEY LOCUST)
INFORMAL SITUATIONS AS A SINGLE TREE,
IN MIXED DISPLAYS

MULTI-TRUNKED
ACER PALMATUM (JAPANESE MAPLE)
IN CONNECTION WITH BUILDINGS FOR EMPHASIS

CONE-SHAPED
CORYLUS COLURNA (TURKISH HAZEL)
GROUP PLANTINGS OR AS A FOCAL POINT
BETWEEN OTHER PLANTS

PILLAR-SHAPED
POPULUS NIGRA 'ITALICA' (BLACK (LOMBARDY) POPLAR)
OPEN LANDSCAPES, FLAT EXPANSES AND GENTLE RISES,
TO EMPHASIZE LINEAR ELEMENTS (AVENUES).
A CONTRAST TO MARKEDLY HORIZONTAL CONSTRUCTED
ELEMENTS AND ENTRANCE AREAS

OVERHANGING
BETULA PENDULA (SILVER BIRCH)
SOLITAIRE TREE WITH ARTISTIC FORM FOR SOLO
PLACEMENTS AND LOOSE GROUPS, FOR SCENIC PARK
LAYOUTS AND BUILDINGS WITH ELABORATE DIVERSE FORMS

48

GROWTH HEIGHT AND THE HORIZONTAL PLANE

The effect made by planting also differs in terms of the horizontal plane, and in fact according to the height to which their plants grow, but also by the height of the beds or their framing. An impression of openness and breadth is created by flat, low-growing designs at ground level. Calm stretches of water acting as a mirror can further enhance this effect. Up to a height of about 50 cm, plants or beds can have a structuring effect and control traffic. Raising them to about 1 m shapes the space without blocking sightlines. The vegetation shifts closer to viewers, and the tactility and fragrance of the plants makes a greater impact.

The 50 cm high plant containers on the private London sun terrace **49** AND → **p.74** structure the space and raise the vegetation to the eye level of a seated viewer. If plants form a boundary at or above eye level, the planting dominates, and makes a powerful contribution to shaping the space. A 'green wall' of this kind can seem more or less transparent, or solid, according to the density of the plant varieties and the distance between the plants. A solid quality can then seem protective if it frames a seating niche, or it can make the pathways easier to identify, thus inviting visitors to explore the garden, as in Monika Gora's 'Glass Bubble' conservatory **51** AND → **p.78**. In the Outback Hall in the Lufthansa Aviation Center, the slightly undulating beds are set like islands in an area covered with white chips, and are unframed **50**. This makes the very tall woody plants look light and emphasizes the height of the space even more, while the broad areas of chip cover make it easier for people to move around.

49 The uniform tall plant containers structure the space in an enclosed London roof garden, and users have a sense of the vegetation in terms of both tactile quality and fragrance.
50 The beds in the Outback Hall at the Lufthansa Aviation Center form reddish-brown islands in the white chips that cover the atrium floor.
51 The vegetation in the raised beds towers over visitors to the 'Glass Bubble', so that the garden has to be explored in stages.

49

50

51

Thinking in terms of the horizontal plane, it is possible to divide plants into one stratum with trees, one with bushes, one with grassy plants, and one with soil or moss, as well. The special forms of climbing plants can bring the three growth patterns together, and such plants can be used as ground cover, or can climb to the height of the tree stratum. Interior gardens are usually planned as combinations of different habits: for instance, large woody plants in the tree stratum with low grassy underplanting.

The grassy stratum and bush stratum represent the largest groups of plants suitable for interior planting. The grassy stratum includes plants up to a height of 30 cm. Many of these plants are creepers, close to the ground, and they form cushions or, in the case of many grasses, tufts. They can frame solitaire plants, act as ground cover for the substrate, create geometrical patterns in combination with different textures or other materials such as gravel or sand, or make interior landscapes look natural. The bush stratum includes bushes, shrubs, and young trees up to a height of 5 m. The soil or moss layer with mosses, lichens, and fungi is usually chosen for natural-looking planting, such as in combination with a stream.

Trees, bushes or shrubs can make a particular impact as solitaires either in their natural form, or trimmed or modified in some other way as an individual plant. They are suitable for container planting, and also for fixed beds, with or without underplanting. Tall woody plants have the advantage of leaving sightlines open and possibly letting more light through for the underplanting.

TEXTURE

The texture of plants gains in significance from close up. This includes the number and density of the leaves; as well as the shape, size, orientation, and qualities of the individual leaves, shoots and stems, including the extent to which they reflect (matte to shiny).

The selection of plant textures can relate to the texture of the building materials in order to develop certain harmonies or contrasts. A fine texture can also look very good as an abstract graphic area in architectural surroundings with little contrast, whereas a combination of exclusively large-leaved plants will tend to convey an impression of unease and excess in a space with a large variety of shapes and colours.

ATMOSPHERE

Individual aspects and combinations of the above-mentioned effects can be used to express many different qualities for the atmospheric impact of planting. These may include luxuriance, naturalness, or have a minimalist approach, exotic or homely, natural or abstract. This can be expressed by individual plant varieties, as well as by combining the vegetation with decorations or interior landscaping. It is possible to go for displays placed at individual points, subordinate placing, or displays that dominate the space, and these may change either a little or a great deal with the seasons. Harmonies or contrasts can accentuate, combine, conceal, divide, or impose a structure. Individual large trees look majestic and convey size or independence. Clearly ordered patterns suggest seriousness and decisiveness. The cool elegance of steel and glass architecture can be warmed by plants with small or particularly soft leaves and embedded more harmoniously in nature, or straight lines can be further emphasized by trimmed shrubs in angular or metal containers. Expanses of water can create a sense of breadth when used as mirrors, while reflecting light and vegetation; they make a change in the floor covering and can complement pathways. Water – as a pool, stream, well, fountain, wall of water, cascade, or fish pond – has a calming effect on most people. And the murmur of a stream or fountain can mask extraneous sounds such as traffic noise pleasantly and enhance the experience and sense of recreation offered by the planting.

52–56 Example of different textures: fine, semi-fine, semi-coarse, coarse

52

53

54

55

56

Principles of design

BY REGINE ELLEN WÖHRLE, HANS-JÖRG WÖHRLE

In order to create a good planting plan, the different appearances of plants – size, form, colour and texture – must be combined to form an inner coherence. This requires a unifying idea, a main theme. Thematic ideas form the content of the design, which is given shape by space, plants and materials. Knowledge of universally applicable principles of design, such as contrast and balance, repetition, rhythm and order, and so on, gives us the tools to make our ideas clear and recognizable, independent of images of exemplary plant combinations from numerous gardening books.

CONTRASTS

Contrast is one of the most important principles in design using plants. It is required in order to create the tension and attraction that will interest the viewer. By means of contrast, differences become much more noticeable. A contrast arises when at least two opposing effects coincide. In the atrium of the Covent Garden building → **p. 84**, for example, the dense covering with homogeneous under-planting contrasts with the form, growth and habit of the very open planting of the tall trees.

The deliberate association of plants with contrasting forms, sizes and colours is an important tool in emphasizing the impact of individual plants. Strong contrasts, such as colour contrasts, are perceived quickly, with little concentration required. Weak contrasts, for example in texture, require a longer observation time and more intense concentration on the plants. Contrasts require balance. A quiet background, such as a building's wall, or cold and neutral plant colours (green, grey), or a transition mediated by displays graduated by height and colour, will accentuate a contrasting counterpart. Small plants and plants with subdued colours should be planted in greater numbers than larger plants and those with brilliant colours. Too many strong contrasts have an exhausting effect, whereas too much similarity and a lack of clarity will appear unsatisfactory and dull. Contrasting pairs that are suitable for design using plants include:

— Habit contrasts
— Texture contrasts
— Colour contrasts
— Light–dark contrasts
— Figure–background contrasts
— Fullness and emptiness
— Light–shadow contrasts
— Negative–positive contrasts (concave/convex)
— 'Yin and yang'

Habit contrasts

Habit contrasts heighten the static and dynamic effect of plantings. By enlisting its polar opposite, the habit of a plant with its own peculiar qualities can be expressed more strongly than is possible in isolation. Contrasting pairs are perceived as such only when they are of equivalent size. Suitable habit contrasts include:

— Vertical and round, without direction
— Horizontal and loose
— Overhanging and inclining
— Loose and firm, round
— Loose and strict
— Linear and without direction, round
— Linear and flat
— Graphic and artistic

As the spherical form is directionless and has a static effect, a contrast to it can be created using flowing forms with a non-constant direction. A curved ribbon of plants, or spherical plants flanking a winding path, may fulfil this function. In large-scale interior planting planted atria, for instance this motif can crop up in the form of erratic boulders and river gravel located in winding riverbeds, as in the Alltours building → **p. 114**. Linear leaf forms (e.g. grasses or irises) create a contrast to broad, round and flat leaves (hosta, water lily). Horizontally oriented plants with horizontal branches and a broad umbrella crown (Indian bean tree, catalpa) or clipped hedges offer a recumbent contrast to curved ground forms and surfaces or vertical forms (pillar-shaped woody plants, buildings). Ground cover planting using a low herbaceous plant variety may also create a simple but effective habit contrast with vertical tree trunks. Vertical forms always appear nearer than the usually distant horizon line. For this reason, pillar forms in a landscape are striking even when seen from a distance. On curved ground, vertical forms appear fixed by comparison; balancing this using plants with a non-constant direction (e.g. inclining or overhanging plants) brings dynamism into the display. Trees with compact, continuous contours and trees with a graphic, linear effect, for instance, create a juxtaposition that is effective in design terms.

Textural contrasts

Textural contrasts lend creative force to a plant schema. This is especially clear in a planting that is quiet in terms of colour. In a layout with varying levels of green, the viewer's attention is directed to the interplay of the contrasting foliage and the way the plants are formed. White blossoms or white-edged or variegated leaves may heighten the effects of textural contrasts, as they do not detract through colourfulness.

Textural contrasts in plants may be:
— Loose and dense
— Fine and coarse
— Lustrous and matte
— Soft and firm
— Felted and smooth
— Rough and smooth
— Delicate and tough
— Transparent and leathery
— Linear and broad
— Linear and directionless

Coarse-textured plants give an impression of strength and stability, while fine-textured plants radiate peace and understatement. Seen from an equal distance, large-leaved plants appear nearer to the observer than plants of the same size with a fine texture.

Colour contrasts

Colour contrasts make displays livelier and heighten the effect of colour. The most important colour contrast effects are:
— Light–dark contrasts
— Cold–warm contrasts
— Complementary contrasts
  (opposing colours in colour wheel)
— Quality contrasts
  (colour contrast of brilliant and dull with
  texture contrast of lustrous and dull)
— Quantity contrast
  (colour surfaces of different sizes)

The strongest colour contrasts are achieved through the use of two-part and three-part harmonies, that is, using colours that are opposite to each other on the colour wheel (complementary colours). Flower colours should harmonize with each other as well as with the surrounding leaves (the base colour). Leaves vary in their spring shoots, summer and autumn colours, and also vary depending on the plant species (yellow-green, green, blue-green, red-brown).

Light–shadow contrast

The play of light and shadows on trees and the play of shadows on the ground can be very attractive. Depending on its intensity, light creates strong gradations of light and dark. Depending on the colour tones of leaves, bark and soil, and the nature of the foliage and branch/twig structure, a unique pattern of shade is created: shot-through-with-light, light, dark, heavy, sharp, soft, colourful, full of contrasts, diffuse. Beneath trees, the shadows on the ground change continually. The form of the shadow tells us the time of day. At midday, sunlight is bright and hard, and shadows are short, while in the late afternoon the light is soft and yellow, and the shadows grow increasingly long, strengthening the impression of three-dimensionality in an open space.

RHYTHM

In order to give coherence and structure to a garden, a park, or a display, it is necessary to include the same or similar plants or groups of plants repeatedly. Simple repetition alone does not create rhythm, merely a connection between certain areas of a display. Rhythm, and with it a unified overall layout, arises with regularly recurring characteristic vegetation elements; close and distant areas are linked with one another visually. In a large interior garden, atmospheric coherence can be created for the whole layout through uniting its individual areas by means of rhythmical elements of different characters. If a typical plant species is used in an open layout in large numbers, it characterizes the unmistakably, becoming a theme: this shows particularly clearly in the thematically differently designs of the atrium halls in the Lufthansa Aviation Center → **p. 98**.

THEME PLANTS

Theme plants supply a starting point for planning a display; a framework. Their arrangement holds the display together, creates visual stability, and makes the planting easier to understand. Plants are placed, grouped and repeated according to their ranking. Woody planting is most strongly defined by trees. The size of the trees should harmonize with the architecture and the available space. Small trees, large bushes and solitaire woody plants are, like trees, structuring woody plants. They serve to emphasize size relationships, connect architecture with the rest of the garden space, and create a transition to bushes.

Expanses of herbaceous plants are structured using solitaire and theme herbaceous plants. Tall species with an apposite and effective form or colour are used. Additional herbaceous plants accompany the theme herbaceous plants rhythmically in greater numbers and should therefore be more modest in appearance. Filling-type herbaceous plants are used to create surfaces or as ground cover. The transitions between the different types are fluid. One and the same plant type can occupy a different position depending on the theme of the garden. For instance, iris may be the theme plant for one theme, and the accompanying plant for another.

TIERING

One possibility when arranging herbaceous plants is a three-tiered structure of tall, medium and short species. The rhythmical repetition of herbaceous plants should not be schematic, as this will cause the display to lose interest and liveliness. The intervals between the theme plants, and the number of individual theme plants, should be varied, with the relative expanse of each of the tiers changing along its length.

The lower plants in a bed can extend farther forward or less distance backward. Intermediate or tall plants can be placed forward, move forward, or recede. An even distribution of lower plants in the forward part of the bed, medium plants in the middle, and tall plants in the rearward expanse (or, in a bed that can be viewed from all sides, in the middle) produces a dull, lifeless effect.

Another compositional possibility is a two-level construction. This involves placing taller plants individually or in small groups amid surface-covering lower varieties. Displays of woody plants and combinations of woody plants and herbaceous plants are also tiered according to an established ranking system.

REPETITION AND HEIGHTENING

The simplest form of repetition is to position identical elements at regular intervals. This creates clear continuity with a high degree of unity. For instance, trees may form a row, avenue, or tree block. The effect of these elements is strict and formal. The resulting regular arrangement can be extended as far as desired. Repetition emphasizes a selected plant and reinforces its significance. The repeated element may be the intervals between plants (e.g. a grid pattern), their colour, or their texture **44** AND → **p. 57** (ESO Hotel). The heightening of a plant theme can achieve an even more expressive overall effect by graduating flower colours, sizes and textures. This involves using different varieties of the same plant or alternations of accompanying plants. Note: the choice of species, in particular the theme herbaceous plants, should be restricted, for good design with plants involves clarity and simplicity above all.

A further form of heightening involves accentuating existing constructed or topographical features using plants. For instance, a regular tree block echoes the orthogonal form of a building, a grouping of trees emphasizes a hill, or an avenue of trees accompanies a path.

SYMMETRY AND ASYMMETRY

The reflection of an individual plant, shaped plants, or area figures on an axis creates a symmetrical effect. Trees arranged in pairs identify the boundary of a space **40** AND → **p. 33** AND → **p. 158** a change in function in the course of a path, or a construction relating to the space such as an entrance gate, a bridge or a flight of steps. A symmetrical arrangement can be repeated several times in its entirety (e.g. as an ornament). Planted parterres and sightlines in Baroque gardens are typical examples of planning using axes of symmetry. In such a layout, ornamental area figures are surrounded by formally clipped hedges, in order to reinforce the symmetrical impression. Symmetrically arranged areas can also be surrounded by formally clipped hedges, with trees and bushes growing naturally behind them.

EQUILIBRIUM

Equilibrium is a common aim of design. It describes a state of balance and harmony between different design components. We experience a balanced design as harmonious and not as stiff as a symmetrical framework. Balance and symmetry may be achieved together within a landscape, park, or garden by means of a central built element. The exact positioning of plants on each side creates symmetry, while small variations in planting create balance. The more the building obtrudes visually, the less it is necessary to resort to symmetry in the planting. One possibility is to place plants with striking forms, textures or colours at appointed intervals on either side of an axis of symmetry, while structuring the planting in between less strictly.

The creative approach

The design principles relating to space, contrast, order, rhythm, tiers, balance and repetition discussed above can be applied in different ways when looking for a specific form for concrete planning according to the scale of the planned project, either in outline or in detail.

When planting is introduced later, it is often possible to plan only the form or the individual design elements. In extreme cases, it is possible to carry out alterations to the building in relation to the interior area to be planted, and in some cases the architecture can be adapted to different requirements, for instance by enlarging window apertures to meet the plants' need for light.

When planning a new building, it is best for the architecture and the planting to be planned by the same person, or in close co-operation between architect and green planner.

FORMAL VARIETY

Two-dimensional forms (areas) such as the triangle, square, rectangle, circle or rhombus, or three-dimensional forms (solids) such as the cube, cuboid, sphere or cone, are some of the basic design elements that can form the foundation of a design. All sorts of forms and ground plans can be developed by addition, subtraction or transformation – by folding and bending, for example. Provided that the physical principles of the basic form remain recognizable, and provided that the succinct impact of a simple geometrical solid making its impact in a large space does not have something else superimposed, then the geometrical concept of the design will remain intelligible.

Examples of geometrical design concepts: the ground plan of the ESO Hotel on the Cerro Paranal in Chile **57** AND → **p. 54** is made up of lucid basic geometrical forms, with the circular form of the planted entrance hall setting a clear accent. The distinctive shape of the 'Glass Bubble' **58/59** AND → **p. 78** stands out clearly from the linear architecture of the existing building, and the ground plan for the Can-West inner courtyard **60** AND → **p. 60** integrates several circular seating niches into the curved lines of the plant beds.

Natural forms, whether they are organic or created by the environment (e.g. driftwood, polished pebbles or rocks) can also be used as a design base. Here the complicated natural structures are abstracted and

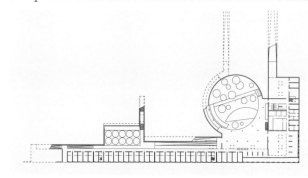

57

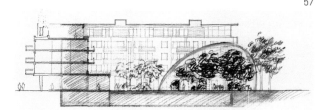

58

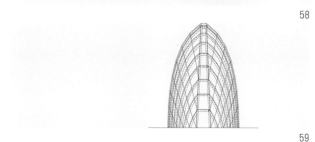

59

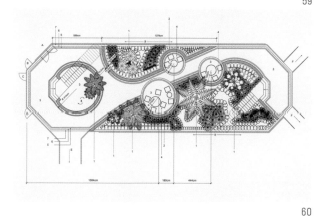

60

57 Ground plan of the ESO Hotel by Auer+Weber+Assoziierte.
58/59 Section and top view of Monika Gora's 'Glass Bubble'.
60 Ground plan of the National Post inner courtyard by Oriole Landscaping.

developed into architectural forms that can be implemented. Free-form shapes often make a dynamic and symbolic impact. The organic shapes of the plant containers in the Design Centre, for example, were designed specially for the modernization programme for the three atria. Their individual shape and finish emphasize the Design Centre's role as a showroom for product and furniture design **61/62** AND → **p. 49**.

Solids define an architectural space. Here, interaction can be created by combining a variety of different solitaire forms – such as the square plant bed under the triangular roof surfaces in the Seattle Public Library → **p. 38** – or by juxtaposing similar solids. In planting that is intended to break down the boundaries between indoor and outdoor space, fluent spatial sequences are often created between clearly outlined spaces and clearly intelligible solid bodies. In the One Kowloon building in Singapore **63**, plant containers, stone blocks, stairs and framing define different fluent spatial sequences within the clearly outlined foyer, and these continue, sometimes seamlessly, into the outdoor area.

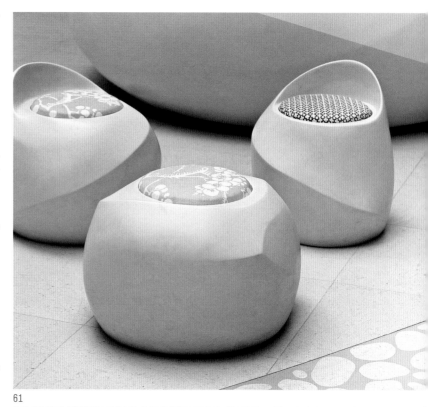

61

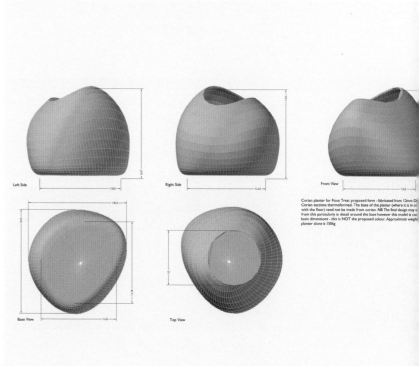

62

63

64

65

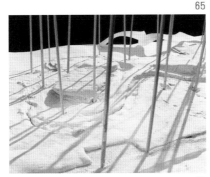

66

67

68

As for any planning task, ordering principles and rules of proportion can help when designing interiors in moving towards defining dimensions and arrangements for the different elements creating the space and the way they relate to each other. When designing the Design Centre, ideas and possible solutions were repeatedly examined using sketches, drawings and models, until the design both met the individual requirements and, as a structure, lent order to the individual elements and defined how they would relate to each other **63–65**. The landscaped terrain modelling for the planted areas in the greenhouse in the new botanical gardens in Bordeaux by Hélène Jourda and Mosbach Paysagistes was also dimensioned and arranged in a model **66**.

To maintain a sense of scale for landscape designs in particular, it is important not to plan for too many different or large plants, as the development of the vegetation could overwhelm the design in quite a short time. The model and rendering for the new National Geographic 'Explorers Hall' in Washington, D.C., by Travis Price Architects **67/68** illustrates this: all the trees are shown as fully grown and at the appropriate distance apart, even though the trees were younger and thus smaller at the time of planting.

61/62 Plant containers by Jinny Blom in the Design Centre
63–65 Jinny Blom's working models for the Design Centre.
66 Terrain modelling for the interior landscape in the model for the
        greenhouses at the botanical gardens in Bordeaux (architect:
        Françoise Hélène Jourda; planting planning: Mosbach Paysagistes).
67/68 Model and rendering for the new National Geographic
        'Explorers Hall' by Travis Price Architects.

ARCHITECTURAL AND DESIGN DEVELOPMENT

As indoor gardens need good lighting and ventilation, the commonest architectural types used are the greenhouse, a glazed extension, an atrium, a patio, or a light roof. But any other form may also be considered for use provided that it meets the requirements of the users, and that the location conditions permit the plants to flourish. The size, shape, orientation and finish for the plant containers and beds can be defined freely in the design so long as the minimum requirements for a long-term solution are met, such as for adequate root space in the planted areas.

The detailed development of the design and the choice of materials influences the spatial effect, the budget, and the lighting conditions in the interior. Beds can accommodate more plants than individual containers and offer more scope for luxuriant or landscaped designs, or those that cover a large area, and thus look more natural. Raised edging for the beds where they meet the space around them can be considered for creative reasons, but also from a practical point of view, to prevent material being discharged from the beds; or to offer seating, but without creating a risk of tripping.

69

70

71

72

69 Square stepping stones in baby's tears planted as ground cover give access to the area and also create a graphic pattern in the wide area of finely textured planting.

70 The striking shape of the bamboo beds makes an impact through the raised stone edging, which can be used as a bench, and the light-coloured stone floor. The intricate foliage of the bamboo, planted as a grove, livens up the straight lines and hardness of the architecture.

71 This large area of wall planting in the Hydrolab in Zurich looks homogeneous from a distance because of its shades of dark green.

72 Design for including the old, tall trees on the plot in the interior of a private home: Hayes House, by Travis Price Architects (completion 2011).

73/74 A glass wall in front of this narrow wall planted with a variety of textures in the Fragile fashion firm in Antwerp protects both plants and users. The glass wall finishes flush with the floor covering and is held in place by steel fastenings.

75 The translucent facades of the box-shaped greenhouses in the botanical garden in Bordeaux mean that viewers have only a hint of the vegetation inside. Wood is seldom used as a material for planted interiors, but it creates a distinctive atmosphere in this space.

73

74

75

USE REQUIREMENTS AND DESIGN

The intended use of an interior garden affects the design. At the planning stage, questions arise about who will use the building or the planted space, what they will need and what functions they would like to use in what way. In private projects, planners can usually discuss such matters thoroughly with the client and draw up a detailed list of requirements. When designing a public building, perhaps an office building with visitor traffic, or a kindergarten, the needs of various user groups (employees, public traffic) have to be analysed and evaluated precisely. Planting in a care home for the elderly, for example, or in a medical facility, should be visually attractive in a way that meets the needs of patients and staff and that makes it possible to discover and experience from various points of view. The overall effect would be essentially calming. In contrast with this, gardens for children must be designed robustly, as the users touch the plants and substrate in this case – of course, none of the plants can be poisonous – and like to walk on the beds. The design can stimulate active use by children with user-friendly elements, such as stones for seating, or by a choice of plants appropriate to a school garden; all this will make the garden part of the children's daily routine.

In a prestigious company building with visitor traffic there will be a need to promote corporate communication and client loyalty, but the needs of the employees for identification and recreation should also be taken into account.

Interior gardens can count as main use areas, traffic routes, or peripheral areas in the spatial programme, or they can serve merely decorative purposes, for example, in the case of vertical planting, the form of which is not derived directly from the spatial programme as a rule. A spatial programme distinguishes between workplaces, quiet areas, catering, and so forth, as well as areas needed for plant care, or that have to be accessible. The plants must also be appropriately spaced to take into account their future development, so that useful spaces are not compromised by the planting. Mobile plant containers or beds and expanses of water that can be temporarily closed with custom-built covers make it possible to expand the useful area for a time or to divide up the ground plan more flexibly. A flexible combination of this kind minimizes the need to seek extra event space in corporate buildings or permits flexible use, as in the case of the mobile elements in the Fusionopolis building → **p. 134**.

It goes without saying that standards and safety regulations must be met for all planning purposes.

Budget

Budget stipulations affect the use and nature of the planning measures as well as the choice of materials. Detailed discussions with the client about the planned use and possible subsequent changes of use should produce calculation variants that will enable the client to take a long-term view when making decisions. As a rule, retrofitting is expensive, and in some cases impossible. Plant beds in a private conservatory, for example, that are created during the building process and link directly with the outside soil save sealing and drainage costs and reduce the amount of ground that has to be sealed. Additional power and water supplies that are already anticipated and installed at the building planning and realization stage increase building costs but then make it possible to automate water and nutrient supplies subsequently, which can reduce long-term maintenance costs. Heating costs should not be forgotten as installation and consequential costs. The various building types can be divided into three temperature range categories in terms of heating type and the associated possibilities for use: cold or cool, temperate, and hot **76** . The variants from cold to temperate are cheaper to install and maintain, and can also play an active part in the building's energy balance as buffer zones. But use of the space is usually limited in the cold season, because the energy input as a result of the greenhouse effect must not be too high in winter so that the plants are not disturbed in their dormant winter period. Spaces used at room temperature throughout the year have to be appropriately insulated, and they increase the useful area of the building that has to be heated and climatized. Local building regulations also apply to conservatories and other glazed structures.

Here, safety regulations for overhead glazing and appropriate use of materials to meet recommended energy consumption values and so on make unavoidable minimum demands on the budget.

Interior planting makes very high demands on the quality of plants, as the planting has to look good from the outset, and function over the long term. Solitaires are usually planted as fully grown specimens, and ground cover and accompanying plants are ordered in large numbers. Ordering from specialized horticultural businesses generates costs for selection, transport, and any acclimatization that may be necessary.

Maintenance care involves regular checks on the plants as well as the running maintenance programme, and also major interventions such as cutting back or cleaning the entire green area over longer time intervals. Regular professional care should be factored into this budget, as it is the best guarantee for timely identification of and rapid response to under- or over-provision, diseases, or pest infestations.

Distinguishing between green spaces by temperature range.

Cold or cool Spaces that are without heating facilities or are thermally separated from the rest of the building, and in which temperatures have to be held at about 5 °C when there are minus readings outside, or can even sink to slightly above freezing point. Heat insulation is usually minimal, and glazing single. Building and maintenance costs are correspondingly low. But energy gains can be achieved to a limited extent by the greenhouse effect and by lower heat losses from adjacent facades and pre-warming of the air to ventilate the interior.

Temperate Higher thermal insulation in combination with a heating system and energy given off by the surrounding rooms maintains cold season temperatures of 8–15 °C. The energy saving possibilities described above are a little higher in this case.

Hot Spaces kept at room temperature for occupation all year round, in which insulation, heating and climate control keep the room temperature between 20 and 24 °C. A special case occurs when the temperature is temporarily lowered to save energy, for instance, at night (night reduction), at the weekend, or in the holidays.
Planting has to take this into account, as some of the tropical or subtropical plants suitable for spaces at room temperature will not tolerate such fluctuations, or the water supply will have to be adjusted accordingly.
In addition, consequential costs are triggered by tending in the installation period and as routine maintenance. Care in the installation period has to be more intensive during the growing phase, including adjustment of any automated watering and nutrient supply cycles.

PLANNING DEADLINES

Planting planners should be involved in the project plans from the outset, in order to match the planting's use and the possibilities it offers to the site conditions. Necessary access for lifting devices to set up large plant containers, bring in large quantities of substrate, or plant larger shrubs and trees must be provided and remain open. There should also be adequate intermediate storage space planned in the building, in case large trees can no longer be delivered in a later building phase. Rare or large imported plants must be chosen, ordered and acclimated in good time; this can take one to two years in extreme cases. Imported plants may also be subject to quarantine regulations.

The actual planting should always take place after the interior is complete, as finishing other interior work can damage plants; by breaking off parts of plants, trampling the substrate down, paint splashes on leaves, draughts, severe fluctuations in temperature, or through chemicals exuded by floor coverings, insulation foam, or adhesives.

If there are building delays, the planting date could be shifted to a different season. This can make it difficult to transport plants and will raise costs if tropical plants, for example, have to be delivered from the hothouse in air-conditioned lorries. But some plant varieties cannot simply be temporarily stored outdoors even in summer, because direct radiation can cause leaf-burn. Adequate time must be available for the planting itself, as fewer machines can be used inside, and more work by hand is needed.

Viewers perceive gardens in buildings differently from green outdoor areas. This means that each plant must be so placed and oriented according to its habit that it makes the best possible effect in the space. The planting should also be completed before the building opens for use, as planting work needs time and possibly also the use of machines for the above-mentioned reasons, and this could cause noise and dirt that users would find disruptive.

Materials
and construction

3

Material properties and material quality

Functioning indoor gardens are compositions, made up of various materials that have to be matched to each other in order to establish the character of the green space. The major materials here are the plants, but the substrate is also important, along with the interior finishing materials, materials for plant containers or planted areas, insulating materials, glazing, and lighting, all of which have to be carefully chosen.

PLANTS

Plants are living building materials. The planned design develops constantly after planting and can take on different forms in the course of time, for example a plant that usually develops quickly may grow slowly in a particular location, or vice versa. Important criteria for the correct selection and positioning of plants are fundamental knowledge about the relevant location conditions, clear ideas about the appearance of the different species, and aesthetic principles. Regular care systems also help to keep the development of the planting close to the design.

Each plant has its own characteristic appearance. At a first glance, this emerges from the structure, texture, and colour of the shoots and leaves (CHAPTER PERCEPTION, → **p. 160 ff.**). In addition, small details such as leaf vein systems, the type of bark, blossom forms, thorns or seed pods can also be itemized.

The time dynamic of plants as materials is an important aspect when designing indoor planting. Unlike other materials, vegetation develops dynamically after completion of the project, rather than being subject to an aging process. The peak development point occurs at different times after planting.

This development process is particularly clear outdoors, from the planting of young specimens through the cycle of the seasons. The development span is shorter indoors, as more mature plants are usually selected, and seasonal fluctuations are less marked, or do not occur at all. Despite all this, special criteria do still apply to the use of plants indoors.

---

1   The appearance of a plant is defined by:
— Trees and shrubs: deciduous, coniferous, fruit trees, palms
— Herbaceous plants: flowering plants, foliage plants, ferns, grasses, bulbs and tubers, aquatic plants
— Climbers and creepers
— Succulents, cacti
— Colour of the leaves, blossoms, fruit, bark
— Shape, size, structure and shininess of the leaves (including the appearance of the veins or development as thorns, blades, or bracts)
— Leaf shedding
— Blossom formation
— Fragrance
— Fruit and seed formation
— Shape and structure as well as growth of bark, stem, or trunk and roots, including aerial roots

Plant selection criteria

Indoor planting is viewed more closely and less tolerantly than outdoor planting. Planning should work towards a period of 10–20 years, so that the planting does not have be completely revised or replaced after a few years. This is why no annuals are planted as a rule, but plants that will live for the duration of the project. Some plants have to be replaced earlier for various reasons: some die, the plants have grown too big, the available light has changed etc. **2**.

Solitaires are usually introduced as fully grown plants, so that the planting looks as convincingly designed as possible from the outset. As well as this, plant communities – what fits in with what – have to be considered, as different varieties and families may need different soil types, for example.

Drift or block planting make a homogeneous, structuring impact more readily if plants of the same quality, size, habit and leaf colour are selected. If plants are to be able to play their part in creating a striking space or increasing humidity, for example, they must have an appropriate foliage volume at the time of planting. It can be impossible, or extremely expensive, to replace individual large bushes or trees in particular if special access had been kept open during the building phase for delivery and for setting up hoists. It is therefore essential to select individual plants carefully.

Rapid growth is not usually a factor for indoor planting. On the contrary, fast-growing plants are often cut back regularly in order to keep them in proportion with the interior space for a number of years. Decorative plants bred for rapid growth and by many traditional garden centres are not suitable for sophisticated indoor planting. Specialist firms can provide good quality specimens and will often prepare the plants for special sites in their new location: for example, in a shady hall.

---

2 Plant selection criteria are
— in relation to the building/climate
— site conditions such as lighting and room temperature → **p. 185 ff.**
— soil structure: substrate depth and composition, open and closed systems → **p. 188 ff.**
— in terms of design → **p. 142 ff.**
— purpose such as air freshening
— thematic requirement
— visual impression
— in terms of plant type → **p. 181**
— longevity
— ability to perform and regenerate
— plant communities
— care and maintenance levels

Plant types

Various woody plants, perennials, climbers, and creepers, as well as cacti and succulents, are suitable for indoor planting → CHAPTER 2, **p. 160 f.**

Woody plants are perennial plants with woody shoots above ground level. Tree usually have a main stem or trunk that is continuous or has few branches, and they shoot from a apical bud to form a crown. Shrubs do not have a trunk as the main axis but form a lot of shoots that branch out close to ground level or grow directly out of the soil.

A distinction is made between three different root systems: tap, fibrous or horizontal root systems. Deciduous trees and shrubs are seldom used indoors; broad-leafed evergreens, conifers, shrubs, and palms predominate. They create their effect mainly by their habit, leaf shape and colour. Some species can be grown as hedges or for topiary work. **Climbers** and **creepers** are also counted as broad-leafed plants. They cannot stand independently, and need strong tendril support such as walls, trellises or wires to grow upwards.

Herbaceous perennials often form clumps or tufts, like most **grasses,** or grow via runners. The vitality of the above-ground parts dwindles in some species, or they withdraw completely; then new buds form close to or below ground level. Many evergreen perennials with ornamental foliage from tropical or subtropical climates that flourish in shadier locations are suitable for indoor planting, as underplanting for solitaire shrubs and trees, for example. They make an impact through the colour, shape and texture of their leaves, which are often variegated or have white edges. Flowering perennials enhance an indoor setting with the colour, shape and fragrance of the blossoms they develop in good locations. Whether the impact made by perennial planting looks natural, structural or abstract depends on the nature of the planting scheme as well.

Mixed perennials, especially using plants from the same area of origin, look casual and natural. Drift or block plantings emanate a sense of calm and can provide harmonious underplanting to set off woody plants.

Ferns, which usually have feathery fronds and usually come from shady woodland locations, are well suited to many interiors. They can survive with less light, but need higher humidity levels. Large tree ferns look very impressive as solitaires, while varieties that serve as ground cover as dense underplanting or in vertical gardens convey an impression of luxuriance.

Many **aquatic plants** flourish indoors and make expanses of water look natural. They can be used as natural water filters, as in the Alterra → **p. 120** and Covent Garden → **p. 84** projects, or contribute to raising humidity by high evaporation levels or cooling by transpiration.

Succulents come from arid tropical and subtropical areas. They can accumulate and store water in various plant organs in order to survive long periods of drought. A distinction is made between leaf, stem and root succulents, according to the storage location, but all combinations are also possible. The cactus sub-family originally came from arid areas of the Americas. Succulents and cacti make for easy-care displays in locations with extreme conditions, such as spaces that are sunny but difficult to access.

Plant qualities

Only high-quality, robust, healthy and vital plants from specialist suppliers should be used, to ensure that the indoor planting looks good from the outset. Pot and container goods are grown in such a way as to produce compact, dense root balls, like baled plants as well, and this means that large plants can be replanted. Only container goods can be considered for imports from other countries or transport over long distances.

For perennial plants, the container volume is usually given in litres, to distinguish between the various ranges on offer. For woody plants, measurements are given in terms of height and width, as well as the trunk circumference for trees (measured at a height of one metre).

Other plant quality criteria are the number and height of shoots, and habit, in terms of variety and age. Solitaire trees and shrubs should have sufficient space in the nursery to develop a wide, evenly formed crown. Shrubs and tree crowns should have a regular structure with dense branches, while the foliage or needles should also be dense, and appropriately coloured for the species. Large woody plants intended to make an impact indoors as solitaires are quite often viewed, chosen and reserved up to two years before planting, in order to guarantee the best possible quality and the desired impression in design terms.

Plants that show signs of damage caused by inappropriate care or in transit, such as damage to bark, pest infestation, disease, or infestation with root weed should be rejected.

Acclimatization

Garden centres in various countries have specialized in breeding large, healthy and robust plants from subtropical or tropical climates that are suitable for indoor planting: centres in southern European countries such as Italy and Spain; in the southern U.S.A., especially Florida; in Mexico; and in Asian countries such as Thailand, Vietnam and China. Many plant varieties, if they are to be used for indoor planting in northern and central Europe or North America must first be acclimatized in special greenhouses or open-air cultures, especially in terms of the changed lighting conditions. This process can last for several months, as the plants need to adjust gradually. Some garden centres that import plants have specialized in this. Thanks to the Gulf Stream's benign effect on the climate in Great Britain, plants can often continue to be tended in the open air, in order to provide more robust specimens for interior planting.

Careful preparations have to be made for imported plants to be transported by sea in ventilated but dark containers; this often places plants under such strain that they not infrequently drop their leaves. This means that such plants have to be ordered in good time and appropriate acclimatization arrangements made, where the conditions are similar to those indoors. This makes it possible to guarantee that the vegetation will be vital and visually unblemished by the planting date, and can develop without any problems at the new location.

SUBSTRATE, THE VEGETATION SUPPORT LAYER

As the vegetation support layer, the substrate has a stabilizing function alongside that of providing nutrients, so that even large plants can be held stably in the long term. The vegetation layer is made up of mineral and humus components, and these provide a location for the plants, with pores that can carry water and air. Horticultural composts, especially for indoor planting, have to meet heavy demand, as plants with small root volumes have to flourish vigorously throughout the year and for long periods.[1] Multi-layered substrates should contain more mineral components at the lower level and more humus at the higher level.

Different substrates are also used for different plants. If beds are in contact with soil beneath them, often only the upper layer of substrate is replaced or fertilized. Sandy soil tends to be used for Mediterranean vegetation, to avoid waterlogging, while a genuine tropical garden prefers a substrate composition with a greater water retention capacity. For the use of hydroponics → **p. 192**.

1   Kerstjens, Karl-Heinz: 'Begrünungssysteme erstellen', in: *Handbuch Innenraumbegrünung,* ed. Renate Veth, Braunschweig, Thalacker Medien, 1998.

3 **The substrate should meet the following conditions in terms of soil physics and chemistry:***

— **Structural stability/sliding stability:** subsidence or root growth must not reduce the number of pores conveying air and water.

— **The porous volume,** that is, the water and air capacity, should be at 70–80 %.

— **Capillarity/water storage capacity:** enough to hold the water supplied in the root area against the force of gravity or to compensate from another source.

— **Prevention of caking or silt formation** in the soil particles by the use of organic substances that resist decomposition, and coarse-grained mineral substances.

— **Low algae growth:** a constantly moist soil surface and high proportions of decomposable organic substances can lead to the formation of unwanted algae or moss.

— **Low decomposition level:** for optimal supply to plants and for visual reasons, the substrate should extend to the edges of the beds and not shrink.

— **Trampling resistance:** the grain composition and mixture should not deteriorate in the long term as a result of being walked on.

— **The pH** should lie in the optimum range for most plants of 5 to 6.5, and be stable.

— **Hygiene and health:** the soil should be free of chemical, vegetable, or animal plant pathogens and not contain fungal spores, bacteria, pests, weed seeds, or weed rhizomes.

THERMAL INSULATION AND GLAZING

Buildings in which people spend long periods of time are subject to energy-saving regulations in European countries and many other parts of the world. Construction methods and the materials for indoor gardens in buildings must match each other in such a way that the building as a whole is energy efficient and the interior offers the best possible location conditions for the vegetation.

The heat transfer coefficient U, also known as the U-value, is a specific characteristic value for the heat transmission in different building materials. The g-value for transparent building components gives the thermal conductivity: how much short-wave solar radiation is transmitted that will contribute to raising the interior room temperature as long wave heat radiation, and also the degree of secondary inward heat dissipation as a result of long wave radiation and convection.

Glass qualities

The choice of glazing has a considerable effect on thermal insulation and transmission of both solar radiation and the light spectrum **3**. Heat protection or insulating glass offers U-values of 1.2 W/m^{2}K or lower and reduces energy loss when the outdoor temperature is lower than the indoor temperature. This saves heating energy, and the raised temperature inside the glass means less draught and condensation. Heat protection glazing is therefore essential for all spaces where people spend time at room temperature all year round.

But the low g-values of most heat protection glass also indicate a lower passive energy gain through the greenhouse effect → p. 186 in the cold season.

For example, a single pane of white glass has a g-value of 0.85. This means that 85 % of the radiated energy penetrates into the space and raises the interior temperature as long-wave thermal radiation. Unheated glass greenhouses work on this principle. The glass used in unheated glazed extensions such as conservatories or atria should have the highest possible g-values if the greenhouse effect is to be used. At the same time, adequate ventilation should be planned so the space will not overheat in summer.

Special solar protection glass delivers reduced g-values of 0.18–0.5; their colouring or coating offers protection from overheating in summer, as the energy is either reflected for the most part or absorbed by the glass and slowly returned to the outside atmosphere. This type of glass can be used for glass roofs and facades that can be shaded only with difficulty. Combinations of thermal and solar protection with low U-values around 1 W/m²K are offered by many manufacturers today.

4   Summary of various building materials and their U- and g-values (specimen information from various manufacturers):

Material	U-value (W/m²K)	g-value
Single glazing, 6 mm	5.9	0.85
Uninsulated concrete external wall, 25 cm	3.3	–
Insulating glazing, 24 mm	2.8–3.0	0.75–0.82
Thermal insulation glazing, double	1.0–1.2	0.58–0.75
Thermal insulation glazing, triple (passive building standard)	0.5–0.8	0.58–0.63
Solar control glass, double	1.1	0.42–0.50
Solar control glass, triple	0.6–0.9	0.18–0.38

But there is a third value that has to be taken into consideration for indoor gardens: the light transmission level, identified by the T-value, which relates to the visible radiation wavelength (380–780 mm). Various types of glass can block the wavelengths important to plants. Most plants use mainly radiation in the 500–600 mm range for blue and 600–700 mm for red radiation for photosynthesis; green radiation in the 500–600 mm range is less important, but is still also used in part → **p. 208 f.**

So it is important to ask manufacturers for the most detailed information available, and where possible materials should be selected during the planning phase that guarantee the best possible growing conditions for the plants. If no detailed information from manufacturers is available, readings should be taken on site before the plants are chosen.

White glass is well suited to planted spaces, as it contains little iron oxide, and is particularly transparent and clear. It is striking when looking from the side and in the case of multi-layered panes that the typical green cast is significantly reduced. Light transmission is usually 6–10 % higher than for traditional float glass, and the interior colours are conveyed accurately. This glass can be used like any other float glass.

People all over the world are working on 'intelligent' glass facades that make it possible to control light and heat penetration into a space individually, and that can also provide optical protection. So-called smart glass technology combines glass and electronics and uses liquid crystals, for example, or the electrochromic effect. Here, a coating takes on colour when an electric current is switched on, and this regulates transmission from maximum – with low solar radiation – to minimum – with high solar radiation. Smart glass technology has the advantage that glazed areas remain transparent and mechanical protection against the sun is not needed.

Self-cleaning glass is also of great interest for glass roofs. A weatherproof coating on the outer pane uses UV rays and photocatalysis to break down organic soiling by pollen or bird excrement. The dirt particles do not become firmly attached to the glass, and are washed away by precipitation that runs off the glazing.

Indoor site conditions

The indoor climate is determined by light and sunshine, air temperature, humidity, air movement, and the temperature of the enclosing surfaces, such as windows, walls, ceilings and floors. These factors must be in equilibrium if comfortable conditions are to be created for users and for the plants, where both feel at home. Even if a room is at an ideal temperature, is well ventilated, and has entirely suitable humidity levels, if it is too dark, plants will flourish only if sufficient artificial light is introduced. People, on the other hand, find major variations between air temperature and floor temperature uncomfortable, as a cold floor draws warmth from the body at that level, and both people and many plants are sensitive to draughts.

The plants live in the same space for 24 hours a day and 365 days a year. So the climate must be adjusted to suit them throughout the year, or plants must be selected that can tolerate extreme fluctuations; for example, if the heating is to be turned down in winter for long holiday periods. Among the many factors, the interplay of light and temperature or light and water supply have a particular effect on the plants. Tropical plants need an average temperature between 18 and 24 °C, and can tolerate short periods of fluctuation if the humidity is adjusted appropriately. If the temperature level falls for a sustained period, the plants suffer, the root system is damaged, and then consequently the plant tissue. But Mediterranean plants, for example, usually tolerate seasonal temperature fluctuations well. So they can be planted in rooms that are unheated or only slightly heated in the cold season, but then they need less water, and should definitely not have moist root balls → **p. 198**. If the plants, some of which are frost-hardy, are to be able to hibernate successfully, an unheated conservatory or atrium must be well ventilated in winter so that the room temperature is not raised unduly by the greenhouse effect, which would stimulate growth.

The ventilation flaps in the atriums of the Alterra laboratory and office building **5** are open almost all year round, so that the temperature inside is only a few degrees higher than the outside air.

5 The open ventilation flaps stop the temperature from rising too much in the atrium of the Alterra building. (Alterra laboratory and office building → **p. 120**)

5

GREENHOUSE EFFECT

The greenhouse effect raises the indoor temperature in relation to the outside temperature: a glazed area reflects a bit of the solar radiation that hits the building, and an even smaller proportion is absorbed. Most of the visible light and short-wave solar radiation penetrates the glazing and lights the space in the first place; there is little direct heat gain. Interior materials with storage capacity absorb the visible light and short-wave solar radiation energy and emit it again as long-wave thermal radiation. The glass is impermeable to most of this radiation, keeping it from radiating out through the panes, so the space heats up as a result of the long wave thermal radiation **6** .

The extent of energy gain through this greenhouse effect depends on the building location, its orientation, the climatic conditions, the time of day and season of the year. If too much energy is produced, the excess heat has to be removed by ventilation, or the thermal input reduced by shading.

For further information on climatization, lighting and shading SEE THE BUILDING SERVICES CHAPTER → **p. 206 ff.**

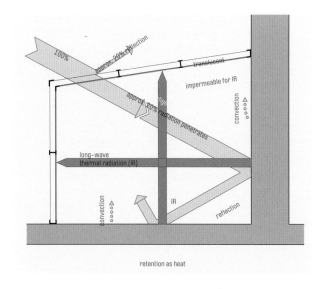

6   Schematic diagram of the greenhouse effect: the glass admits short-wave sunlight into the interior, where it is absorbed by materials capable of storing it and transformed into long-wave thermal radiation. The glass (according to its U-value) allows the thermal radiation to escape only in small quantities, so the space warms up.

LIGHTING

Adequate light is the key to having an indoor planting that works well. Lighting, whether natural or artificial, must be devised and planned correctly from the outset. The majority of planted spaces also have to accommodate people, and should therefore be comfortable for them to spend time in, while using energy efficiently. Using daylight turns out to be a crucial element here; the different needs of plants and people have to be considered in relation to quantities of light, intensity and protection from the sun.

Establishing the intensity of the interior light is complex, particularly if the building is still at the planning stage and all the data have to be calculated. But even when it is possible to use a light meter, factors influencing the amount of light that the plants can use for photosynthesis must be considered

Plants carrying out photosynthesis use a certain spectrum of sunlight, the Photosynthetically Active Reaction Area (PAR). This corresponds roughly with the wavelength visible to the human eye (38–780 nm), but is distributed differently: human sensitivity to brightness peaks in the green wavelength at approx. 555 nm, while PAR radiation has two maxima in the red and blue ranges of the spectrum. Plants use the green area of the spectrum for photosynthesis to a lesser degree, so light that seems bright to the human eye can prove inadequate for plants, according to wavelength.

Each plant needs a certain amount of light, based on intensity and the duration of the illumination. This figure is assessed all year round, and minor fluctuations are tolerated well, on the whole. If there is a temporary lack of light, the plants can use up stored energy to a greater or lesser extent to compensate for the lack of photosynthesis. But an ongoing lack of light will damage most plants. The damage includes increased susceptibility to disease, etiolation (over-rapid, rod-like growth of shoots and leaves), and shoots lightening in colour until they die. Most plants need more suitable light at higher temperatures, so lack of light has a stronger adverse effect on indoor planting at high room temperatures than when the room temperature falls at night, for instance.

Daylight intensity depends on the changing position of the sun throughout the day and year, and the extent of cloud cover and air pollution. Ideally, global radiation figures should be available from meteorological services, but if not, they should be measured on site at various times in order to acquire more reference points. It must also be taken into account that the amount of radiation reaching the outer skin of the building is reduced by various factors. These include: the type of glazing, bars in the glazed areas; the amount of dirt on the glass; shading according to the position, orientation and dimensions of the building; and the position and orientation of the planting inside it.

Reduction of radiation and variations in daylight intensity are not usually taken into consideration for daylight planning, e.g. according to DIN 5034 (daylight in interiors), but they can be very important in terms of plant choice. Some manufacturers provide PAR values as well as their products' light transmission in lux, which according to a study by the Insitut für Technik in Gartenbau und Landwirtschaft are about 10 % lower under glass than light transmission according to DIN 5034. Indoor planting planners should therefore ask for the most detailed product information possible or where necessary consider possible reductions at least as an estimated value when making calculations, so that the quantity of light is under- rather than overestimated. In the long term, plants cannot make up for a lack of light, but too much light is rarely a danger to the plants' health.

The natural light radiation level in the interior can be deliberately increased by the use of reflecting surfaces such as light-coloured floors and walls, reflective water surfaces, or other reflecting elements, as well as light-management measures → **p. 211 f.**

The market offers various programmes for calculating illumination in a simulation for the full year; these include DAYSIM (Dynamic Daylight Simulations), a program developed by the Fraunhofer Solar Research Institute and the Canadian National Research Council; or DIALUX, another lighting calculation program that can be downloaded from the internet free of charge.

In order to establish the most precise values possible with these programs the spaces with their dimensions and apertures have to be constructed similarly to AutoCAD programs, and precise information supplied about the materials.

Factors for determining interior light levels
— Building parameters: dimensions, position, orientation, apertures, shading elements in the interior such as stairs or lift-shafts
— Dimensions, position and orientation of neighbouring buildings that could shade the space to be planted
— Materials and their qualities, such as light transmission, reflection: glass, facades, floors etc.
— Reduction of light transmission by window bars, dirt, sheeting etc.
— Variations in sunlight through the position of the sun at different times of the day and year, degree of cloud, unclear air

Construction principles

The choice of building materials and the control possibilities offered by the building services both influence the climate in the glazed interior. The better the levels of energy being introduced or dissipated, ventilation, humidity, and thermal insulation are matched to each other, the pleasanter the indoor climate will be for people and plants, while optimizing energy consumption.

Detailed work on designing the space and selecting material influence both the effect it makes and the budget and the indoor lighting conditions. If the load bearing structure is kept slender, the glazed areas can be larger and more light can penetrate the interior.

The glass-grid shell of the atrium structure for the Lufthansa Aviation Center spans large areas and at the same time admits a great deal of light into the interior **7**. Thicker supports can reflect light and look more filigree if they are painted in light colours or given a mirrored surface, as in the old people's home in St. Pölten **8**.

A frame structure permits larger apertures than a post and rail structure, and this should be taken into particular consideration for small glazed extensions. Timber profiles offer advantages in relation to thermal insulation and soundproofing but can be protected against the weather only to a limited extent. Steel metal profiles are suitable for extremely stable filigree structures, but conduct heat. Then again, thermally separated profiles take up more space. In additional, the steel has to be protected against corrosion, which also occurs indoors because of the condensation moisture that accumulates on the cold profiles. Aluminium profiles are relatively slender, light, and are available in a wide variety of colours. The disadvantage here is the higher price and the poorer ecobalance.

FLOOR STRUCTURES

Plant beds can be made from a wide variety of construction materials, in gaps in a concrete floor, for example. They can be flush with the floor, or raised with borders. All materials that come into contact with substrate or plants must be free of substances that can damage plants. The target size of the planting determines the size of the beds or containers, to ensure that there will be adequate root space in the long term. Plants must be kept far enough from the facade as well, so that there is guaranteed room to reach the facade for cleaning or fire prevention purposes if the plants grow over the edge of their beds.

7

8

9

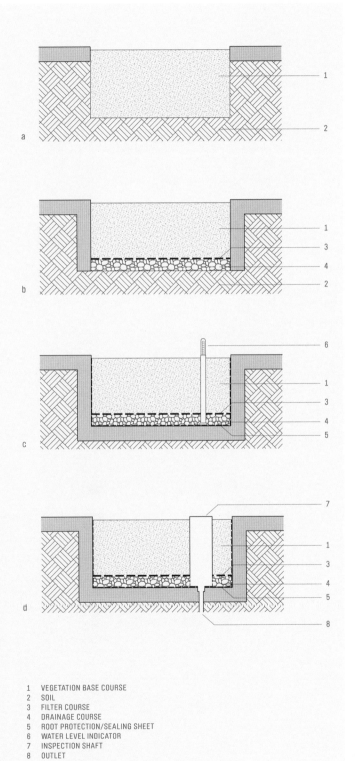

1 VEGETATION BASE COURSE
2 SOIL
3 FILTER COURSE
4 DRAINAGE COURSE
5 ROOT PROTECTION/SEALING SHEET
6 WATER LEVEL INDICATOR
7 INSPECTION SHAFT
8 OUTLET

Open and closed systems

A distinction is made between beds with direct access to the ground; open systems, in which the plants can extend their roots down to the layer of soil under the building; and closed systems **10**. Container planting is counted as a closed system, with the special advantage that containers can be placed flexibly according to size; these are not discussed in detail here (for setting up container planting and tending tub plants, see the literature information in the Appendix → **p. 222**).

Beds in direct contact with the soil usually have to be planned before the building is constructed, as the work involved in retrofitting is usually too elaborate and costly. They offer the advantage that excess water can drain out through casting flaws in the base and there is a lot of root space for the plants. Water dissipation can also be improved by drainage systems. But it is important that water-soluble components in the substrate, and the nutrients, can be flushed out, and that watering occurs at short intervals, as the plants cannot develop their root systems far below the surface to access reserves of moisture deeper in the ground.

7 The roof of the Lufthansa Aviation Center by Ingenhoven Architekten is a glass-grid shell, with a form reminiscent of a paraglider, that can span large areas with maximum transparency. It was also glazed in white glass, which lets maximum daylight through to the interior. (Project Lufthansa Aviation Center → **p. 98**)

8 The client for the old people's home in St. Pölten wanted a roof structure using concrete girders rather than a filigree metal structure; architect Georg W. Reinberg gave this a reflective surface to compensate for the lack of transparency.
(Project for the old people's care home in St. Pölten → **p. 64**)

9 In Françoise Hélène Jourda's new botanical garden in Bordeaux, the round timber columns enhance the natural atmosphere of the gently undulating indoor gardens inside the cubic greenhouses.

10 1. Bed structure in contact with soil as a gap in the flooring:
a without drainage and **b** with drainage.
2. Structure of a closed system **d** with drainage, outlet and control shaft.
3. Closed system **c** with drainage and water level indicator, typical of container planting.

10

In the conservatory in the Meletitiki private house in Greece the narrow bed was set up on an open basis. The large, 20-year-old solitaire ficus has fed and watered itself for years, as its roots go very deep, and so it is neither watered nor fertilized → **p. 34**. In the Atacama Desert in Chile, the undulating landscape in the planted rotunda of the ESO Hotel is designed in terraced form using excavated stones and earth **11**. Plant trenches were provided for large plants and all the plants set in a layer of fertilized substrate.

Beds not in direct contact with the natural soil have to be sealed so that they are watertight in relation to the building. Durable EPDM rubber sheets of the kind that have proved their worth in garden pool construction or roof planting are among the materials suitable for this. A root barrier membrane on top of the sheet secures the building against root penetration and subsequent water penetration.

Both these steps can also be managed with a combined product or, if the bed is to be set in water-impermeable concrete, there is no need for the plastic seal. If possible, materials used for indoor planting should be tested and guaranteed. In terms of guarantees, it is advisable to commission an expert to glue the sealing sheets. Beds and connecting areas should be tested for watertightness before the substrate is introduced. For safety reasons, plant beds as fixed installations should always be fitted with at least one overflow connected to the building's drainage system. This prevents water damage to the building even if the stop function on an automatic watering system fails.

Closed systems must have a multi-layered structure to ensure that the root space has an adequate oxygen supply and that the organic soil components do not rot. Water level indicators make it possible to monitor inadequate or excess watering, and control shafts deal, where needed, with the necessary draining off and replacement of all the liquid in the system.

11

12

1   AERATION/CLEAN
2   PLANTER DRAIN TYP
3   STONE COPING
4   RUBBERIZED PLAY SURFACE,
    SLOPE SUB-FLOOR TO DRAIN
5   FILTER CLOTH
6   PLANTING VOLUME
7   INSULATION FILL
8   DRAINAGE COURSE
9   PLANTER DRAIN

Soil strata

In a closed plant bed, a protective layer should first be laid over the **sealing** and **root protection** sheets. This protects the root protection sheet from damage by sharp-edged components in the drainage layer that is laid above it, and prevents chemicals from the root protection sheet, PVC softeners, for example, from leaching into the plant habitat.

The **drainage layer** absorbs and disperses excess water; the roots of the plants penetrate this layer. For this reason, mineral aggregates that are not harmful to plants should be used, such as brick chippings, lava, gravel, pumice, or expanded clay. The layer should be about 20% of the entire bed structure in thickness, and no thicker than 15 cm, as a rule. In the case of large beds, it is advisable to lay profiled channels in the drainage layer to direct the water to the outlets.

A fleece on the drainage layer prevents fine soil particles from penetrating it. Such particles would block the flow of water out of the drainage layer, making it less effective, and the roots could be damaged by an ongoing build-up of water. A wide range of geotextiles that are not harmful to plants are available, along with resistant filter fleeces, which are also used in roof planting.

The **vegetation support layer** provides the plants with nutrients, while at the same time fulfilling stabilizing functions, so that larger plants are stabilized for the long term as well. For the quality of the plant substrate → **p. 182**.

1   TREE GRATE SET IN STRUCTURAL FLOOR
2   TILE ON MORTAR BED
3   STRUCTURAL FLOOR SLAB
4   SOIL MIX
5   STRUCUTRAL FLOOR SUPPORT BRACKET AT PLANTER WALL
6   DRAINAGE MAT
7   CONTINUOUS WATERPROOF MEMBRANE ON BELOW TILE STRUCTURAL SLAB
8   EXPANDED SHALE DRAINAGE COURSE WITH CONTINUOUS FILTER CLOTH
9   CONCRETE PLANTER WALL
10 LEVEL STRUCTURAL SLAB
11 SLOPE FLOOR MIN. 1,5% TO PLANTER DRAIN
12 CONTINUOUS WATERPROOF MEMBRANE
13 PLANTER DRAIN

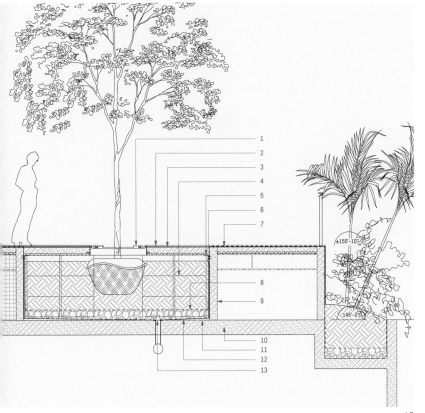

11 The extensive planted areas in the ESO Hotel entrance rotunda were arranged as a rising undulating landscape with access to the natural soil. Deeper trenches stabilize large plants and offer sufficient root space in the more nutrient-rich imported substrate → **p. 54**.
12 Different bed structures: a) with ground-level connection and control shaft, b) with outlet, without control shaft, along a run of wall. (*Devonian Gardens Project* → **p. 90**)
13 Structure of a tree pit below the flooring with a protective grid around the trunk. (*Devonian Gardens Project* → **p. 90**)

13

Hydroponics

Large and small container plantings, as well as entire flowerbeds, can also be cultivated hydroponically. Hydroponics or hydroculture means keeping ornamental plants in expanded clay containers using a soil-less process. The zone containing the water should occupy at the most 20 % of the pot height; above this is the wet zone, below it the arid zone.

Hydroponics is usually carried out at a room temperature of above 17 °C, so it is most suitable for heat-loving plants from tropical or subtropical climates that need a temperature range of 18 to 24 °C. As a rule, plants suited to cooler conditions cannot tolerate the combination of a low ambient temperature at the same time as a wet root space. All other location factors, such as light intensity or direct sunlight, affect the choice of individual plants for hydroponic culture.

The substrate is fired clay granulate, or expanded clay, which is permanently stable in structure; in other words, it does not compact. This means that the plant roots can breathe better and the plants have to be repotted less frequently. No pathogens or moulds can gain a hold in expanded clay, it is a particularly hygienic substrate, and thus suitable for people with allergies and for use on medical premises. Soil pests likewise cannot flourish in clay granulate, so the plants have fewer problems with root disease.

Hydroponic containers are available in all kinds of dimensions and finishes, and the usual planting depth is a maximum of 35 cm. Of course the containers have to be watertight and equipped with a water level indicator. All the plants in a hydroponic container have to be placed in the granulate in growing pots of the same height, so that the roots can reach the water-bearing level. For watering, the water available in the container must be filled to the maximum on the water level indicator. The plants uses the water as it needs, and the water level has to be re-filled to the maximum only when the indicator shows that the water level has been reduced to the minimum.

In a large bed containing a number of plants, the areas for the plants requiring different depths must be sealed off from each other and set up with individual water level indicators. Preparing the bed for sealing and so forth is the same as for a bed filled with soil substrate that has no access to the natural soil.

A slow-release fertilizer, or special liquid or salt fertilizers, can be used for hydroponic cultivation. Slow-release fertilizer is introduced into the water-bearing layer of the vessel roughly every three months; for large containers this can be managed very easily via the fertilizer tube. Flourishing hydroponic plants in combination with a well-ventilated mineral substrate can achieve high air filtering values and eliminate noxious substances from the indoor atmosphere, as some substances are broken down by micro-organisms in the root area.

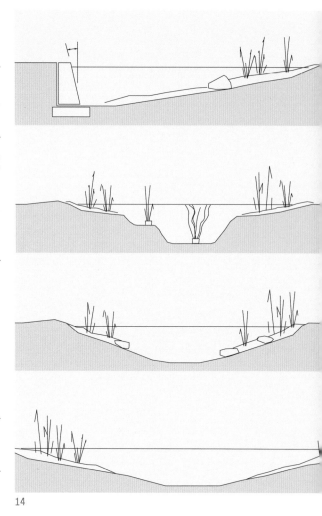

14

14 The soil retention construction method is ideal for a natural-looking water feature built into a planted area in the form of a pond.

15 Examples of different top layers for architectural pools.

16 Architectural pools can also be planted in zones of different depths. A layer of gravel on the substrate keeps it from floating off.

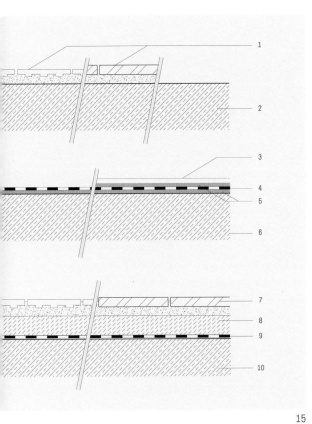

1   SURFACE/TOP COURSE NOT WATERTIGHT, E.G. TILES/NATURAL STONE ON MORTAR COURSE
2   WATERPROOF CONCRETE, PREFABRICATED POOL, IMPERMEABLE TO WATER
3   TOP COURSE, NOT WATERTIGHT (STAINLESS STEEL, SLABS LAID ON CHIPPINGS/MORTAR COURSE)
4   PLASTIC LINER
5   PROTECTIVE FLEECE
6   POOL SUPPORT STRUCTURE, NOT WATERTIGHT (E.G. MASONRY OR REINFORCED CONCRETE)
7   SURFACE NOT WATERTIGHT, E.G. SLABS/NATURAL STONE SURFACE ON MORTAR COURSE
8   LEVELING COURSE
9   PLASTIC LINER
10 POOL SUPPORT STRUCTURE, NOT WATERTIGHT (E.G. MASONRY OR REINFORCED CONCRETE)

15

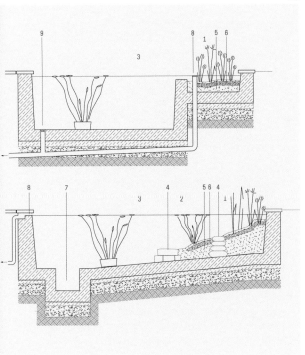

1   SHALLOW WATER ZONE
2   MEDIUM-SHALLOW ZONE
3   DEEP ZONE
4   TERRACING USING STONES/SACKS
5   GRAVEL
6   POOL SUBSTRATE
7   SUMP WHERE REQUIRED
8   OVERFLOW
9   FLOOR OUTLET

16

WATER FEATURES

It is not unusual for indoor planting to be combined with water features. Indoor water features can take the form of natural-looking ponds or cascades, or are designed as architectural pools or fountains. They can make an important contribution to humidity, increase the amount of light indoors by reflection, mask unpleasant ambient noise by the sound of the water, or fulfil a number of design functions.

When planning an indoor water feature, the load-bearing strength of the floors must be taken into account if there is no direct contact with the ground. The stability of the subsoil and, if using earth retention construction methods, the lateral boundaries must be carefully checked as well. The earth retention method involves a non-rigid structure in which the subsoil is generally sealed off with special sheeting. This approach is particularly suitable for natural-looking designs, as the water feature can be integrated into a planted bed in any desired shape **16** . Rigid or stable structures can be built in various materials, such as waterproof concrete (as in the ponds of the Alterra project **18**), reinforced concrete, masonry or natural stone. A sealing sheet must also be used in conjunction with materials that are not waterproof **16** . Small rigid pools can also take the form of metal tubs, in zinc or stainless steel, for example, provided they can be guaranteed waterproof. Rigid pools can be clad with other materials for design purposes, as was the case with copper in the 'Giardino delle Ninfee' **17** → **p. 68**. It is also possible to combine the two methods – rigid and non-rigid – by using sheeting to seal a stably framed structure against the subsoil.[1]

Indoor water features are seldom dimensioned on a large enough scale to establish biological equilibrium and guarantee the long-term quality of the water without using pond technology. A pumping plant to purify the water, including a pump sump or chamber on the bottom of the pond to pump the pond out if necessary, should therefore be planned, along with a nearby water supply. In pools without any plants, the water should be changed regularly or at least agitated, using a fountain or more elaborate water feature, for instance. In the 'Giardino delle Ninfee', the water is in constant motion, which makes the water quality better than that of standing water.

Introducing organic matter, such as falling leaves, should be avoided at all costs. Planted pools can utilize only limited quantities of organic matter, and over-fertilizing can lead to overgrowth of algae and lack of oxygen. In unplanted pools, pollution by solid matter reduces the aesthetic quality, which is particularly striking indoors. The pump filters in planted or unplanted pools have to be checked and cleaned regularly; frequent soiling leads to higher maintenance costs.

17

---

1 For further information on the construction of water features see *Constructing Landscape* by Astrid Zimmermann, Birkhäuser Verlag, Basel 2009.

17 The copper cladding on the dynamic waterfall has acquired the typical patina over time. ('Giardino delle Ninfee' Project → **p. 68**)

18 The architectural pool is made of waterproof concrete and is used above all to collect, buffer and warm the rainwater to be fed into the watering system (Alterra project → **p. 120**)

18

But very large pools can fulfil a filtering function and improve water quality even indoors. Rainwater collected outside the atriums of the Alterra laboratory and administration building **18** AND → **p. 120** is pumped into the two pools in the indoor garden; there it is buffered and warmed and ultimately used for watering. In the Covent Garden building complex → **p. 84**, several large pools planted with marsh plants act as a natural filter for treating 'grey' waste water from the building, as well as rainwater. The treated water is used for watering the roofed garden and for flushing toilets in the building.

Appropriate places for the desired plants have to be provided in planted pools. Here a distinction is made between various habitats in the marsh, shallow water (0–30 cm), medium-deep (30–50 cm), and deep water zones (deeper than 50 cm). The substrate should be low in nutrients to keep the input of organic matter as low as possible, as the plants could otherwise grow too quickly, or too much algae could thrive. A thin substrate layer of 5–10 cm is sufficient in most cases in a natural-looking pond; a gravel covering layer will prevent the substrate from floating to the surface or being eroded. In a pool that is only partially planted, the substrate layer can be restricted to the planted areas; these can even be individual plant containers. The plants can be placed in plant baskets at the appropriate depth of water. This reduces the amount of maintenance needed, as the plants can simply be taken out in their baskets if necessary, and is also a way of limiting the spread of the different species to certain areas. An indoor planted pool should be positioned so that the plants have sufficient light, but not too much direct exposure to sunlight, as this raises the water temperature. Plants with floating leaves can be used as natural sources of shade.

PLANT TECHNIQUE AND CARE

When choosing suitable plants for a particular location and the use to which the space will be put, an experienced expert should be consulted in order to extend the spectrum of design possibilities beyond the standard range and to avoid losing plants. The plants discussed below are grouped according to their origins by climate and vegetation zones. After that, various plant lists survey a selection of plants suitable for different locations.

Grouping by climate and vegetation zone

The better the location factors in the interior to be planted match the location factors at a plant's place of origin, the more the plant will flourish, that is, the more precisely the interior climate corresponds with the climate at the home location, the better the planting will flourish in the long term, as vegetation is defined by climate. But different vegetation zones have to be identified within each climate zone; these are differentiated from each other by the effects of altitude and ocean currents.

Plants in one vegetation zone have matching requirements in relation to temperature and light intensity, but they may have different needs in terms of direct exposure to the sun (sunny, semi-shaded and shaded locations) and of water and nutrient requirements. Detailed planning must take all this into account, to avoid combining sun-loving with shade-loving plants, or plants that prefer relatively barren soil to those that like high concentrations of nutrients, because this would inevitable lead to failures. Considering the vegetation zone when choosing plants is recommended, and makes harmonious and balanced design easier – and it is less likely that one plant will prove invasive in relation to the others – but it does require considerable knowledge of plants.

As a considerable simplification, the different climate zones, with their various subdivisions into humid, semi-arid and arid areas, will be divided here according to degrees of latitude into

— tropics (0–23.5°)
— sub-tropics (23.5–40°)
— temperate zone (40–60°).

More detailed classifications distinguish between four climate zones and 30 to 72 climate types, and take into consideration both the earth's radiation zones and also established and calculated values for heat and water balances.

In tropical climates the average temperature is above 18 °C throughout the year, daily temperature fluctuations are greater than annual ones, and the length of the day varies between 10.5 and 13.5 hours. In a rainforest climate (e.g. the Amazon basin, Indonesia, western central Africa) there is sufficient precipitation each month, while in the savannas (e.g. Thailand, north-eastern Australia, central Africa) the winter is a drought period. Arid regions are the tropical semi-deserts and deserts that maintain the same temperature throughout the year.

Plants in the moist and semi-arid zones are suitable for indoor use at room temperature. Rainforest plants in particular require relatively little light, as they usually grow in the shade of larger vegetation when they are young plants in their natural habitats. Typical representatives are the *Ficus* varieties; their light and moisture requirements can differ considerably from species to species. Epiphytes, hemiepiphytes, and climbers such as *Tillandsia, Anthurium* and *Philodendron,* which can emphasize verticals, are suitable for versatile designs.

In subtropical climates the temperatures are high in summer and moderately warm in winter, and nighttime and daytime temperatures differ sharply. A further subdivision is made into arid, winter-moist, summer-moist, and constantly moist subtropics. The Mediterranean vegetation zone, with its rich diversity of varieties, is a subtropical climate; summers are arid to semi-arid, and precipitation occurs mainly in the cool winter months. Mediterranean vegetation is found all round the Mediterranean Sea, but also along the coastal strip of California and Chile, on the Cape in South Africa, and in south-western and southern Australia. The dominant vegetation is sclerophyllous in the Mediterranean area, in the form of evergreen oak varieties (such as the holm oak, *Quercus ilex,* or the cork oak, *Quercus suber*) and the olive tree *(Olea europaea).* In California we find oaks and conifers, and in Australia eucalyptus varieties such as jarrah *(Eucalpytus marginata)* and marri *(Eucalyptus calophylla).*

Many Mediterranean plants are also suitable for cold and warm conservatories that may even experience slight frosts in winter and in which top summer temperatures can be very high; they are also suitable for temperate indoor planting where the temperature does not fall below 10 °C. But most Mediterranean plants miss the winter vegetation break at room temperature.

The moist subtropics are to be found mainly south of the Himalayas, in the south-eastern USA, in southern Australia, and on the North Island of New Zealand, with mixed or eucalyptus and laurel forests. Particularly decorative specimens from this vegetation zone include the tree fern, which originates mainly in Australia and New Zealand, for example *Dicksonia Antarctica,* which is suitable for relatively poorly lit interiors, provided that the humidity is high and the intensity of direct sunlight low.

The range of vegetation in the arid subtropics (e.g. Middle East, Sahara, Atacama Desert) is small. But plants from the arid areas of South Africa are well suited for easily maintained planting in extreme locations that cannot be very well climatized. It is advisable to set up a rockery in these cases, and to cover the substrate with stones containing quartz and slate, since the plants spread very slowly as ground cover.

The temperate zone shows considerable seasonal differences. The length of the day also varies considerably season to season: from 8 to 16 hours. Adequate precipitation occurs all year round; with values of around 800 mm, the temperate zone has the second-highest precipitation rate, after the tropics. Very few plants from the temperate zone are viable for long-term indoor planting.

Special planting features

Particular location conditions apply indoors, and these affect the planting techniques. In most cases, large woody specimens can be planted unanchored, as they are stabilized by the size and weight of the root ball alone, and there are no strong wind movements that could hinder the growth of the fine sucker roots. Root balls for woody plants suitable for indoor planting should be stable, with dense roots, and compact; in the case of container goods, the ball is usually flat on the bottom, which makes the plant stand particularly stably and securely.

If necessary, large woody plants can be secured by root ball anchors or other underground anchors **19a–c** , without any posts or cables above ground level to impair the aesthetic quality of the new planting. For instance, a steel mat or a metal fence panel larger than the ball can be placed at the bottom of the planting pit and the ball attached to it with straps. Here the surface of the root ball should be protected by a mat made of coconut fibre, for example. The substrate layer on the steel mat ensures adequate flexibility. It is also possible to set up underground anchoring with short wooden poles or metal anchors, but great care should be taken not to squash the root balls.

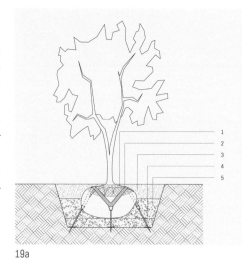

BELT SYSTEM WITH SOIL ANCH
1   ROOT BALL PROTECTION S
    (E.G. COCONUT MATTING)
2   LASHING STRAP WITH RA
3   TOPSOIL
4   SOIL ANCHOR
5   INFILL SOIL

19a

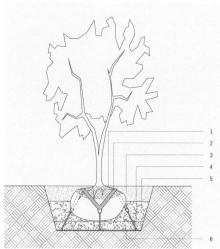

BELT SYSTEM AND STEEL MAT
1   ROOT BALL PROTECTION S
    (E.G. COCONUT MATTING)
2   LASHING STRAP WITH RA
3   TOPSOIL
4   ANCHOR
5   INFILL SOIL
6   STEEL MAT

19b

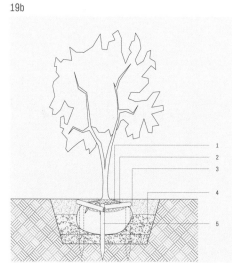

WOODEN TRIANGLE
1   ROOT BALL PROTECTION S
    (E.G. COCONUT MATTING)
2   WOODEN TRIANGLE
3   TOPSOIL
4   INFILL SOIL
5   WOODEN POST

19c

19 a–c Underground anchoring variations.
20/21 The large palms in the atriums of the Lufthansa Aviation
      Center in Frankfurt am Main had to be well protected and secured
      for planting so that they could be set up stably and in immaculate
      condition on site.

20

21

Nutrient supply

If they are to grow, plants require water, light, air and nutrients. Indoors, plants have to rely on additional nutrients in the long term, as the substrate volume is limited in closed beds and containers and the plants have to have nutrients. Consumption depends on the nature of the planting and the indoor climate, as these affect growing periods. In beds with direct connection to the natural soil, plants with deep root systems can draw nutrients from the soil strata under the building and so need correspondingly less fertilizer or possibly even none at all, as is the case for the large *Ficus benjamina* in a private house → **p. 34**.

Plants need various substances in order to grow; put simply, nitrogen (N) for leaf growth, phosphorus (P) for blossom and fruit formation, and potassium (K) for tissue stability. So these three elements are the basic ingredients of mixed fertilizer, with foliage plant fertilizer containing a particularly high proportion of nitrogen. Plants also absorb minerals and trace elements that are contained in the fertilizer or can be added appropriately: lime, which is usually dissolved in the water they are given; magnesium (MG), a component of chlorophyll; sulphur (S); iron (FE); manganese (MN); zinc (ZN); copper (CU); boron (B); and molybdenum (MO).

Soil analysis provides information about the actual pH and nutrient content. It is important to establish this in order to match fertilizer composition and dosage to the vegetation's needs. Soil analysis should be conducted at regular intervals.

Annual or semi-annual surveys provide a clear overview of the development of soil quality, and prevent under- or over-provision of certain nutrients. Professional fertilizers are not cheap, and should not be used where they are not needed, as this makes maintenance more expensive.

It is generally true that indoor gardens should be fertilized sparingly but regularly, so that the plants remain vigorous without growing too much. The pH should ideally be between 5 and 6.5. Some nutrients are not easily soluble or available for absorption at higher pH, such as the trace elements iron and manganese.

Fertilizers can be supplied in various forms. Organic fertilizers cannot be considered for indoor planting, as their components are not sufficiently broken down by micro-organisms and bacteria, and thus liquid or solid mineral fertilizers or slow-release pellet fertilizers tend to be used. When slow-release fertilizers are used, it should be noted that the moisture content of the soil and the temperature affect the release of the nutrients to a considerable extent. The coating dissolves more rapidly in constantly warm interiors than in cool conservatories: no nutrients are released at temperatures below 10 °C, and the plants do not need the minerals until after they have finished hibernating. Foliar fertilization can be administered selectively. This has the advantage that many plants absorb the nutrients very well, and the leaf surfaces are cleaned at the same time. Ion exchange fertilizers are among the other products available for hydroponic cultivation → **p. 192**. But whatever fertilizer is selected, the different manufacturers' instructions should always be followed.

The water used may contain more or less mineral substances, and also harmful substances, and so it should be analysed as well, and the nutrient supply adjusted appropriately; the composition of drinking water is also subject to local and sometimes seasonal fluctuations. Collected rainwater contains only very small quantities of minerals, while softened water or spring water can be totally unsuitable in terms of composition. Very hard water can have an adverse effect on the substrate in the long term if calcium is deposited in the soil in the form of lime, raising the pH. The solubility and availability of certain elements decreases at pH above 7, and the plants will no longer be properly nourished. If the tap water is too hard, it can be mixed with rainwater or softened water for watering the plants, but in any case the mixture should be analysed and checked. When planning the green space, the substrate can be selected and prepared in the light of the water analysis, and in the case of existing planting the risk of damage to the plants can be reduced.

Disease and pest infestations

The common combination of high indoor temperatures and low humidity offers ideal conditions for pests to appear and reproduce, while at the same time using chemical pesticides runs counter to the idea of improving the indoor atmosphere and the building's ecobalance. For this reason, the health of the vegetation should be checked regularly and at short intervals in order to be able to react at an early stage in the event of leaf damage by bacteria, fungi, or pests. Local conditions should be taken into account in every case as well, as it is possible that even temporary extreme temperature fluctuations and humidity or light intensity factors can lead to phenomena such as wilting or even the death of plants. Too-intense sunlight can cause leaf burn, and insufficient light can lead to chlorosis, etiolation or leaf loss. It often happens, particularly in buildings that are open to the public, that the substrate is 'poisoned' by having drinks poured out onto it. In the case of hydroponics, it may be possible to save the plants by completely changing the nutrient solution, or in fixed beds by washing the substrate thoroughly.

If affected parts of the plants are noticed at an early stage, it is often possible to prevent the disease spreading right through the planted area by cutting these parts back carefully or by removing the whole plant. Very few pesticides are suitable for indoor use. For this reason, beneficial organisms are often used; in other words, predators or parasites that eat or suck out the pests in their various life stages, or lay their eggs in them. Using such organisms can be more work-intensive and expensive than using chemicals. But the advantages are obvious: they have no side effects on people, animals or plants; they are odourless, do not damage the furnishings, do not lead to resistance being built up, and can even be used preventively.

VERTICAL SYSTEMS

Trimming and care

Each time the plants are checked, dead or diseased parts should be removed, for visual reasons as well, and the leaves cleaned. Dust from the air tends to accumulate on indoor plants, as there is no wind or rain to remove it. A thick layer of dust can considerably reduce a plant's photosynthesis performance, so washing the leaves is important for more than just aesthetic reasons.

Trimming and pruning of plants should be carried out only by experts, whether it is to limit size or to achieve the desired shape as the plant grows. Radical intervention of the kind possible outdoors is not usually tolerated by users indoors. For this reason, cutting back often has to be done over a timescale of a few weeks, which raises maintenance costs.

Problems arise if a container is too small. Deciding on the size of a container for planting must take into account location factors, the vegetation, and its anticipated development over a period of years, as part of the advance planning. Extensive cutting back of roots after only a few years or replacing the entire plant should be avoided at all costs.

Vertical gardens, by definition, need little or no ground space. They save space, and are therefore particularly appealing to buildings in the city core with high prices per square metre. Well-known examples of vertical gardens are the hanging gardens of Semiramis in Babylon, espalier fruit cultivation, or plants such as vines or ivy growing up the sides of buildings.

Climbing plants in beds or containers

Climbers and creepers make it possible to design space-saving gardens in a variety of ways, and epiphytes can also be used to plant and emphasize the vertical. Various types and techniques are available for climbers **22**: trellis climbers need some frame support. This includes climbers and creepers that do not form special retaining organs, but need suitable supports to wind themselves round. Twining plants also attach themselves with side shoots, spines or thorns to existing vegetation, especially woody plants. They have to be tied to smooth climbing aids such as stretched wire. Natural attachment by climbing plants should also be stabilized by tying.

Climbers that have clinging roots or suckers by which they attach themselves to a base are the only ones that can survive without climbing aids. Here it is important to establish that the base is permanently stable and that the material will not be damaged by the attachment organs, otherwise unattractive 'scars' can be left when they are cut back. The shoots should be guided in the right direction in the initial stages; later, overly luxuriant growth should be cut back to shape, so that balustrades, windows or ventilation apertures do not become overgrown.

The material and shape of the climbing frame can help vertical planting with climbers to create very different spatial effects, but the structure – more vertical or more horizontal orientation and struts – must be matched to the plants' climbing technique. This is demonstrated very clearly in the St. Pölten old people's home **23/24** AND → **p. 64**:

The rapidly growing climbing chestnut vine develops very long shoots whose weight needs a stable trellis.

Climbing aids must always be well secured and large enough to support the considerable weight of metre-long plant shoots without difficulty. The time dimension is usually very clear when planting climbers, as even larger plants achieve the full height on site only gradually. So especially at the initial stages, decorative underplanting can enhance the visual effect. But this has to be modified frequently over the years, as plants growing towards the light allow less and less light in spaces that are lit from above to penetrate below. Then only shade-loving plants can be considered as ground cover, or the underplanting has to be provided with artificial light.

GROWTH FORM		CLIMBING SUPPORT	
SELF-CLINGING PLANTS		WALLS TREES SURFACES (HORIZONTAL, AT AN ANGLE, VERTICAL)	SUCKERS / CLIMBING ROOTS / WALL
TWINERS		TRELLIS GROWING TRELLIS STEEL MESH VINE WIRES STRETCHED HORIZONTALLY AND VERTICALLY	
VINES		VINE WIRES, STRETCHED PERGOLA LOGGIA	
RAMBLERS		WALLS TREES	WALL

22

23

24

22 Growth forms of climbing plants and climbing supports.
23/24 In the St. Pölten old people's home, the climbing aid consists of wire cables stretched between stainless steel beams fixed into the beds and the upper storey. (Project for the old people's care home in St. Pölten → **p. 64**)

Wall planting systems

Patrick Blanc pioneered a new horticultural technique for vertical gardens in the 1980s in France. He invented a form of wall planting that covers the entire surface of inside and outside walls with plant growth, with no connection to the floor. His starting point was to observe plants that settle in extreme locations, such as steep cliffs, in various climates. Given the lack of nutritious soil, these plants use their base primarily as a grip, and absorb the substances necessary for their survival from precipitation and the air via their roots and leaves, so long as adequate light is guaranteed.

Many different individuals have developed this system derived from nature for wall planting that is complete in itself, in which plants grow on vertical bases and are fed by drip irrigation. They market these systems under various names, such as

— 'Fytowall'/Fytogreen (Australia),
— 'Plantwall'/Green Fortune (Denmark),
— 'Mur végétal'/Patrick Blanc (France),
  'Equilibre'/Héliotrope (France),
— 'Grüne Wand'/Indoorlandscaping (Germany),
  'BioWall'/Biotechture (UK),
— 'Living Wall'/Nedlaw (USA) among others.

The first free-standing planting systems are now available as well. They simply stand in front of a wall, or they can be set up in other places. But it is more common to plant on a supporting wall that has to meet certain requirements in terms of its load-bearing capacity. First of all, a root-proof sealing layer is attached to the wall, and this protects the base in the long term from damage caused by damp. Then a support structure is mounted on the wall. The base for the plants is attached to this, and it also contains the fittings for the hidden irrigation system. Water and power supplies must be in place for the irrigation system; many systems also need an outlet to allow any excess water to drain away.

The wall planting can be built into a niche or be surrounded by a frame. A frame conceals the substructure from the side, and also protects the substrate and prevents too-rapid evaporation.

Some systems work with standardized plant modules that can be hung easily, rapidly and precisely on the prepared wall. The modular technique permits pre-cultivation of the wall elements in a greenhouse, so that the vegetation has reached a certain density and size by the time of installation.

The qualities of the substrate soil in terms of its structural stability, rot resistance, sterility, and capacity to store and transport water are crucial for the concept of wall planting and watering, and for the long-term functioning of the system. Structurally stable inorganic substances, such as mineral wool or foamed resins, are most often used. Other wall planters work with textile substrates such as felt or geotextiles; these are fixed to the substructure, and pocket-shaped plant holes can be cut into them.

Plant walls are not in direct contact with the ground and are irrigated via drip hoses. These hoses are laid at regular intervals – between the modules, for example – and the water reaches the roots by seeping slowly down through the substrate from top to bottom. Different substrates distribute the moisture at different rates, and some carry a proportion of the irrigation water upwards, via the capillary effect. The quantity of water and duration of the irrigation process is managed automatically by a control unit. This does not necessarily have to be in the immediate vicinity of the wall, but can be set up in a different room or a cupboard. Liquid nutrients are added to the irrigation water as needed; this process can also be automated. A drip tray collects excess water at the bottom edge of the planted area. This water is either reintroduced into the water cycle or diverted directly into the building's drainage system.

A functioning wall is very easy for users to tend. It is however essential to have an acoustic and/or visual warning system in case too little or too much water is supplied, or if the power fails, as the plants have to have sufficient water and nutrients on a regular basis and the substrates have only limited reserves for storing moisture.

According to location, adequate light must be supplied or secured for the plants through artificial lighting. Careful recording of all the location factors and the choice and grouping of ideal vegetation are basis requirements for the durability and vital growth of wall planting. Decorative arrangement of the various species suitable for the location requires additional planning skills. Patterns and structures that enhance the indoor space are created according to design principles – especially relating to grouping and effects over large areas **29–31** .

Trained staff should check the vegetation at regular intervals for pests or disease, cut plants back where needed, control the nutrient supply and modify it if necessary, clean the drainage gutters, and make sure that the control system is working properly.

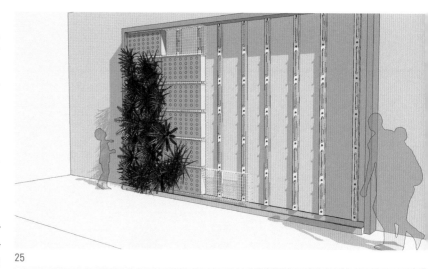

25

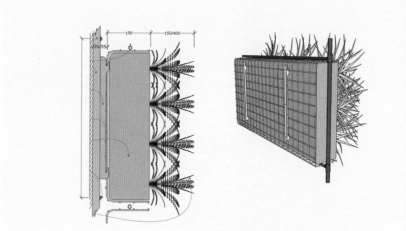

26

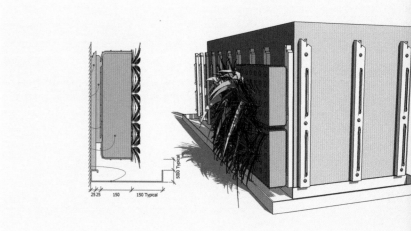

27

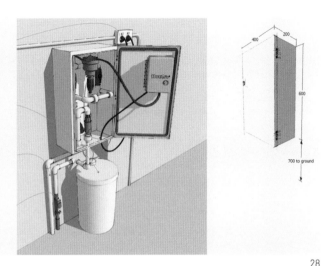

28

29

If wall planting is to last in the long term and function without too much maintenance, detailed knowledge and a wide range of experience with suitable plants is required. Much research and experimentation takes place in this field. It is certainly the most dynamic form of interior planting, and its diversity offers enormous potential in terms of use, design and structure. Some companies are now trying to persuade architects and interior designers that planting a wall represents an interesting alternative for wall cladding that is no more expensive in terms of construction costs than other high quality materials, and one that enhances the space considerably.

Other vertical planting schemes, with or without direct contact with the soil, continue to be developed and can fulfil functions relating to interior design, indoor climate, and even micro-agrarian functions. A start has been made on using mobile planted shelves as flexible room dividers or for saving space when planting food such as lettuce or tomatoes in urban areas.

25 Typical structure for the 'Fytowall' wall planting system (Australia): modules pre-planted in a greenhouse are simply placed in position on the substructure mounted on the supporting wall.

26 The 'Fytowall' consists of individual modules suspended from the prepared supporting wall on metal hooks. The drip hoses for watering are placed between the modules.

27 A drip tray at the bottom of the planted wall area captures excess irrigation water and protects the interior against damage by moisture.

28 The automatic watering control unit can be accommodated in a wall cupboard; the container under the tank is used for fertilizer supply.

29-31 For this 150 m² plant wall, BioTecture drew a pattern reminiscent of woven fabric made up of 11,000 plants from 15 different species. (Anthropologie store, London, UK)

30

31

Building services

In order to create a pleasant indoor climate in glazed interiors, the quantities of energy that are introduced or removed, ventilation, the moisture content of the air, and thermal insulation all have to be matched to each other.

HUMIDITY, EVAPORATION, AND EVAPORATIVE COOLING

The recommended indoor relative air humidity that people find pleasant is 45–65%. However, some tropical or subtropical plants require higher values of 55–85%, while desert plants are happy with just 10%.

Plants emit some of the water into the air in the form of water vapour through their leaf stomas, thus raising humidity. This evaporation process – the transition from a liquid to a gaseous state – also draws energy out of the indoor climate, effectively cooling the air. Both these effects are in proportion to the total surface area of the leaf masses. Humidity can also be increased by introducing expanses of water, or water features, and also by using water-loving plants such as ferns, sour grasses *(Cyperaceae)*, or sparrmania, as this will mean that the substrate stays wetter all the time.

If the indoor climate is too dry for the plant – this happens most often when the space is being heated – too much water evaporates and leaf tips and leafs turn brown. Blossom buds drop off and pests such as spider mites appear more frequently. In such cases, the humidity in the space must be raised, by regularly spraying the plant, for instance, or by using humidifiers or water features with fountains. But overwatering is also counter-productive, as in many climates the period when heating is needed coincides with less daylight, and the plants stop growing for a time.

CLIMATIZATION: HEATING AND VENTILATION

As well as the above-mentioned evaporative cooling, the building itself can contribute to balancing the climatization in the interior: a glazed extension acts as a buffer zone to help prevent undue heating or cooling of the facade and so that the air can be pre-heated or cooled down.

Large glazed facades, extensions, and conservatories all acquire thermal energy from direct sunlight and the greenhouse effect. But in most climates, indoor gardens that are used year-round must also be heated in the cold season. Systems such as fan convectors that circulate the air are suitable for this, as they can also be used for ventilation at the same time, by including outside air, and in summer for air conditioning.

The heating elements should be in several rows, if possible, so that they emit both radiant and convection heat, which warms the air more evenly. Both people and plants find this more pleasant. It is an advantage that room temperatures can be individually regulated by thermostats. Both plants and interior furnishings must be at least 20–50 cm away from the heater. The substrate in plant containers placed on floor heaters dries out more rapidly, so more watering is needed and there is a danger that water will condense on the cooler glazed surfaces. An energy-saving storage heater in the floor combined with a heat pump can also heat large spaces evenly, as well as saving energy.

Facade apertures make it possible to ventilate a space naturally, and this can be controlled manually or automatically. The ventilation apertures have to be sufficiently large to make it possible to exchange enough air relative to the size of the room. A standard value of 15–20 % is used for glasshouses and glazed facades. An air exchange rate of three to five times the volume of the space per hour is recommended, and a higher value for cooling can also make sense in the hot season. Fitting the apertures at different heights makes it possible to exploit thermal lift.

Natural ventilation has the advantage that it can be adapted rapidly and easily to changes in weather conditions. The positioning of the ventilation flaps can be problematic for the plants in terms of draughts, or if cold air flows in directly and in large quantities in winter. The structural conditions should also be considered when recording climate data for a space, so that such extreme values are not interpreted uncritically and so distort the overall result of a set of readings. Mechanical ventilation via extractor equipment or air-conditioning plants is also possible, but operational noise should be kept to an absolute minimum. Ventilation flaps for manual ventilation from the outside should still be available when needed.

WATERING

Whether plants flourish depends on continuous and appropriate water supplies, regardless of the predominant location factors in the space. If this cannot be assured through having responsible staff, an automatic watering system should be installed. If this is to be done, all the connections for water and power should be constructed as integral to the structure, and sealed so that they cannot be damaged by root growth over the long term. The quality of the irrigation water available should also be analysed at an early stage, so that the nature and quantity of its contents can be matched to the requirements of the plants, and the fertilizer levels adjusted where necessary.

Various watering systems are available: reservoir systems mean that water can be stored until required, and can also be automatically controlled by a float switch arrangement. It should be noted that reservoir systems are mainly used for supplying deep-rooted plants, and roots in higher layers of the substrate can be ignored.

Micro-spray systems serve to water the surface, and spray-mist devices (fog or mist systems) can also be used to create a particular visual effect in a planted area – on high poles in a bamboo grove or in a luxuriant tropical forest, for instance. These mist devices can also raise the humidity if needed without damaging the plants, as the fine water droplets disperse completely in the air.

Systems laid on or in the substrate with porous hoses or drip systems produce water a drop at a time, usually over a certain area with hose systems, but more deliberately close to each plant for drip systems. In some systems (micro-drip) the capacity can be set individually to the needs of particular plants.

Any watering system should be robust for maintenance reasons, and not easily calcify or become blocked. Readily available spares or repair parts make it easy to swap parts out quickly if it is discovered that something has been damaged by trampling in larger beds. Also, a water supply and drainage facility should be available near the beds in larger planted areas for manual watering and cleaning.

Tension sensors or electrodes

Watering systems can be controlled by moisture sensors in the substrate, so that a plant's actual needs are taken into consideration, as more moisture evaporates from the leaves in bright sunshine, for example, and more water is needed. Watering that happens only at pre-determined times can supply too much or too little water over the long term, with corresponding consequences for the vegetation.

In a tension sensor, mechanical sensors measure the soil suction power using a Plexiglas tube filled with water and a clay mass. When the substrate is dry, the clay gives off water, pressure in the Plexiglas tube is reduced, and a switch is activated by a membrane, thus opening the water supply valve when the set value is reached. The clay draws water back out of the moistened substrate, the pressure in the tube rises, and the water supply is switched off again. The moisture values to be set on the tension sensor usually lie between 50 and 70 hectopascals (hPa) for moisture-loving plants, and up to 300 hPa for plants that favour dry conditions. In each case, there must be good contact between the metering cell and the plant substrate. The distance from the next drip cell should be at most 10 cm: measuring sensors should not be constantly in the shade or in direct sunlight. The soil dries out more rapidly from the top between watering intervals; this will affect the depth at which the tension sensors are placed.

Another way of controlling watering is by measuring the electrical conductivity between two electrodes inserted into the substrate; the amount of water needed is calculated from the reading. To do this, the specific conductivity of the available water should be set, as this can affect the amount of water discharged. It is advantageous if the conductivity sensor can be stuck completely into the ground, as it will then be better protected against wilful manipulation or damage. Disadvantages are that the electrodes are complicated to handle and intolerant of fertilizer with a high salt content.

Simple, battery-powered control equipment can be used for smaller planted areas. Larger planted areas, especially when the indoor planting affects the air conditioning in the building, are best regulated by computer-controlled systems, and these usually control heating, cooling and ventilation as well. In large planted areas with several watering circuits, a central header unit with shut-off valve and pressure regulator can reduce the water pressure to about 0.5 to 1.5 bars so that smaller headers fitted with magnetic valves and filters can distribute the water into the various watering circuits. The magnetic valves are opened and closed by control equipment with moisture sensors. A watering system of this kind can also be regulated by a time switch if there are times when no watering is required: for example, in buildings that are open to the public, or when stimulating flowering plants by planned dry periods. In such cases the time-switch clock can prevent watering even when the moisture sensors indicate that it is needed. Fertilizer levels can also be automated.

Automatic watering systems should always have an alarm to indicate defects and over- or under-supply, and be equipped with an emergency overflow.

Because plants sometimes need more moisture in their growing phase, the automatic watering system settings should be checked more frequently in the early stages, and additional watering should be carried out by hand where needed.

All the connections should be covered and inaccessible to unauthorized persons, especially in publicly accessible indoor planted areas, and drip hoses should be laid a few centimetres below ground level. All the control systems and their sensors, as well as the control shafts for the outlets, should be accessible to specialist personnel at all times, so that checks can be made on whether they are functioning efficiently.

LIGHTING

For lighting an area by daylight, see the chapter on location conditions/daylight → **p. 186**. The quantity of incident daylight can be exploited better by the use of light-direction systems → **p. 211 f**.

Artificial light

Of course the full range of the illumination programme for ensuring safety and orientation, structure and atmosphere, and for lighting areas where work is being done, and so on, is fully available in an indoor planted area, provided that the minimum requirements for the particular location are met, such as insulation against penetrating damp.

It is a way of prolonging the possible use of a planted space effectively into the evening and night hours. In a glazed extension, lighting points or floodlights can be built directly into the support structures. For smaller spaces, such as private conservatories, cable systems can span the full width of the space with spotlights, hanging lamps, or floodlights fitted and adjusted along the line of the cable; wall and standard lamps can also be installed for flexible use. It is important that the intensity of light indoors and outdoors is carefully matched, to avoid reflections or the impression of black walls in the case of complexes with dark exteriors.

The plants can be presented using effect lighting, for instance, by floor-level floodlights set close to the trunk of a tree to stress its vertical quality. The entire habit of the tree is emphasized by positioning the lights a little farther from the trunk and using floodlights with broader beams, whereas spotlights pointing upwards at the lower branches of a tree make the crown seem to float.

If daylight will not be able to provide sufficient light for the plants, additional artificial lighting has to be installed 32. Most lamps can combine effect or safety lighting with increasing the overall amount of light. To do this, artificial light sources should be chosen that emit a great deal of light that plants can exploit, such as HID lamps 33 – survey of lighting technologies). Very bright lights must be mounted in such a way as to cause minimum glare.

32 Basic lighting technology values

— **Light visible to the human eye** is in the electromagnetic radiation wavelength of about 380–780 nanometres (nm). Ultraviolet and infrared radiation lie below and above this range. The wavelength determines the colour of the light.
— A **lamp** is the **light source** placed in a lantern or luminaire, e.g. a bulb in a ceiling light.
— **Luminous flux** is measured in **lumens (lm).** It indicates the radiation output of a light source in all directions in the visible field.
— **Luminous intensity** is measured in **candelas (cd)** and measures the luminous flux emitted in a particular direction. A normal household candle has a luminous intensity of 1 cd, emitting a luminous flux of about 12 lumens over the entire solid angle.
— Various **lantern forms and reflector lamps** distribute the luminous intensity in the space in different ways, e.g. concentrated at points or asymmetrically.
— **Illuminance** is the measure of luminous intensity emitted by a light source over a defined area. Here 1 lux (lx) denotes even lighting of a square metre with one lumen of luminous flux: $1\,lx = 1\,lm/m^2$.
— The **distance from the light source** affects the illuminance; illuminance is calculated in lx from the quotients of the luminous intensity of a point light source in cd and the square of the distance in m, e.g. the illuminance of a candle at a distance of 2 m is 0.25 lx.

$$1\,cd/(2\times2) = 0.25\,lm/m^2 = 0.25\,lx$$

— Illuminance is measured with a lux meter.
— Typical values are
summer day, no cloud: 100,000 lx
summer day, cloudy sky: 20,000 lx
operating theatre: 10,000 lx
room lighting: 800 lx
corridor lighting: 100 lx
street lighting: 10 lx
— The term **footcandle** is mainly used in English-speaking countries: here one unit corresponds to one lumen per square foot. One footcandle equals 10.764 lx, i.e. in practice a footcandle is converted into lux by a factor of 10.
— **Reflectivity** indicates what proportion of the luminous flux hitting a surface is reflected. The lighter the surface, the higher the reflectivity. A white wall reflects up to 85% of the luminous flux.
— Living things that practise **photosynthesis** use a certain spectrum of **solar radiation**: the photosynthetically active radiation (PAR) level. In terms of wavelength, this corresponds roughly to the wavelength of radiation visible to the human eye, but it is divided up differently: human sensitivity to light is at its highest in the green wavelength range at approx. 555 nm, while PAR radiation has two maxima, in the red and blue areas of the spectrum. Plants use the green area of the spectrum for photosynthesis to only a limited extent, so what seems like considerable brightness to the human eye could still mean inadequate provision for the plants.

33 Survey of lighting technologies suitable for indoor planting

— In principle, a **halogen lamp** works like an incandescent lamp, in which current flows through a wire and makes it glow. Halogens are added to the gas-filled glass cylinder, and these increase the amount of light emitted. A distinction is made between low-voltage and high-voltage halogen lamps. Some models are dimmable, and adding inert gases makes halogen lamps more energy efficient.

— In **fluorescent lamps** and **compact fluorescent lamps** a fluorescent substance transforms the ultra-violet radiation created by an electrical charge into visible light. An electronic ballast (EB) is needed to operate the lamp; in some versions it is actually integrated into the lamp (in a classic lamp shape). Advantages here are the light spectrum, which is appropriate for plants, the low purchase price, and the low thermal emissions; one disadvantage is its limited range: the lighting has to be quite close to the plants. LED lamps (Light Emitting Diodes) use a semiconductor material and can transform current into light directly. They are very small, so they can be integrated in a wide range of locations. The mains voltage has to be reduced by transformer; this is already built into some lamp types, so that they can be used in standard fittings in a wide variety of fixtures in the form of LED retrofit lamps, in place of conventional bulbs.

— **High intensity** or **gas discharge lamps** use various gases that create enough heat to vaporize plasma-forming substances. They need an electronic ballast and are used mainly in sealed lamps for safety reasons. High-pressure gas discharge lamps, also known as HID (high intensity discharge) lamps, have a higher flux and luminance than low-pressure lamps. HID lamps are particularly suitable for use with indoor planting and in market gardens, as they emit light that is similar to daylight with high luminous intensity but with little heat produced, and they use less energy than halogen bulbs. Their range is very wide, but they are also expensive to buy.

34 Behnisch Architekten designed a 'chandelier' made up of prismatic plates to increase and distribute the daylight in the atrium of the Genzyme Center in Cambridge, Massachusetts, which is lit exclusively from above.

34

SHADING

Shading systems are intended to prevent the building from overheating. They are more effective when fitted externally, because then the interior does not heat up at all. Even deciduous trees outside a glazed facade can provide effective protection from the sun; they are particularly worthwhile outside east- or west-facing windows. Shading devices can also help to protect privacy, which is an important consideration when planning a conservatory in a private house, for example.

The market offers a large number of different construction methods for externally mounted sunshading systems, some of which can be built into the facade: roller blinds, Venetian blinds, awnings (with their many variants, such as facade, drop-arm, and articulated-arm awnings), and shutters. Externally mounted systems are exposed to the elements and therefore have to be robust and sturdy. If the system is automatically controlled, wind speed and precipitation should be metered so that the sunshading comes into play at the right time, and the material is not damaged by moisture or gusts of wind.

Venetian blinds in aluminium, PVC or wood are robust and can usually be finely regulated, as the variable positioning of the slats admits different amounts of light into the interior and the view of the outside world is not entirely blocked, as is the case with roller blinds. Venetian blinds can be combined with light-directing systems → SEE ABOVE; for example, when the upper section can be controlled separately or the upper slats are perforated, thus admitting more light into the interior. In terms of design, they offer the advantage that the slats are supplied in a wide range of colours and surface finishes. The more solar radiation the blinds reflect, rather than absorbing it, the less the sunshading device and the surface of the glass will warm up, hence the interior stays cooler as well.

In the case of awnings of any kind, the quality of the material used for the guide rails and fabric is very important, to ensure that the sunshading continues to function without difficulty and to look good even in the case of frequent precipitation or after a winter break. Light-coloured and partially transparent fabrics admit diffuse daylight into the interior of the room, make it pleasant to spend time and work in the glare-free space without additional artificial light, and often make it possible to look out at the outside world if the slats are sufficiently transparent.

A shading system inside the building is less efficient: it will be more effective if there is ventilation between the shading and the glazed envelope. However, interior shading systems can be used at night or in winter as additional insulation for the glazed surface, so that the room temperature falls less rapidly. This effect is deployed in the atria of the Alterra lab and office building → p. 120 using the coated cotton blinds familiar from tomato growing, which boosts the energy efficiency of the building.

Sunshading systems can be combined with light-directing daylight systems. The light direction should control the available daylight as needed; it is usually directed from the level of the windows via the ceiling into the back of the space. The almost parallel direct radiation from the sun is simpler to direct than diffuse light from the sky in general. The latter is really useful only if the area is heavily built up, where situation light direction systems that absorb or reflect some of the light themselves can direct some of the light into the back of the space.

If a facade is in direct sunlight, even a very narrow strip of light-directing glass can increase the amount of light in a space considerably. Other systems use movable or stationary prism prismatic plates, Y glass, or mirror slats; these can offer the advantage of guaranteeing shading, preventing glare, while also permitting an outside view and good lighting in the space. Such systems are well suited to raising the amount of daylight available to plants, and the design scope they offer means that they can be used in different types of buildings.

AUTOMATIC CONTROL

In the Genzyme Center **34** AND → **p. 128**, static and mobile prismatic plates direct the daylight into the lower and side areas of the central atrium, thus improving the quality of the light indoors for both people and plants.

Light direction systems can provide interiors with daylight even without windows. These use an exterior light collector, a light direction medium, and an optical system to distribute the daylight. This system is still very rarely used, as in most cases it is still not financially viable, and people are not able to enjoy looking out of the window. The light available from these systems is not adequate for plants.

Manual regulation of the individual components can definitely be used to guarantee a pleasant and constant indoor climate where plants can flourish in the long term. This requires only a few monitoring instruments, such as thermometer, hygrometer and moisture sensors in the substrate. But it is essential that the instruments function perfectly, and that the appropriate adjustments to climatization, shading, watering, and so forth are carried out responsibly, in good time, and throughout the year.

To ensure efficient energy use and greater user-friendliness for the system, heating, climatization, shading and ventilation, and the supply water and nutrients for the plants can be controlled and auto-mated via the technical facilities in the building. Various metering sensors such as thermometers, pho-to-electric cells, and anemometers take into account the internal and external weather conditions and also respond to special phenomena, such as strong winds that make the use of external shading devices temporarily impossible. Switches and control panels for this regulating technology, and also those relating to the plants, should be readily accessible, as this makes monitoring and care easier. It is ideal in larg-er systems to provide a special space for the technical facilities, one that can also accommodate garden tools and supplies such as fertilizer or spare parts for the watering system.

Appendix
4

Plant lists

BOTANICAL NAME	ENGLISH NAME	PLANT FORM	GROWTH HEIGHT	FOLIAGE
ARBUTUS MENZIESII	PACIFIC MADRONE	TREE	5-20 m	YOUNG LEAVES LIGHT GREEN, ORANGE-RED IN THE 2ND YEAR
CINNAMOMUM CAMPHORA	CAMPHOR TREE, CAMPHOR LAUREL	TREE	1.5-15 m	DARK GREEN, FRAGRANT
OLEA EUROPAEA	OLIVE TREE	TREE	1.5-15 m	UPPER SIDES GREY-GREEN, UNDERSIDES SILVERY. SMALL LEAVES.
QUERCUS ILEX	HOLM OAK	TREE	5-20 m	YOUNG LEAVES SILVERY-WHITE, OLDER LEAVES DARK-GREEN
CERATONIA SILIQUA	CAROB TREE	TREE, SHRUB	1.5-15 m	PINNATE, LEATHERY, GLOSSY
CUPRESSUS SEMPERVIRENS	MEDITERRANEAN CYPRESS	CONIFER	3-15 m	DARK GREEN
CUPRESSUS ARIZONICA	ARIZONA CYPRESS	CONIFER	4-20 m	BLUE-GREY
CHAMAEROPS HUMILIS	MEDITERRANEAN FAN PALM	PALM	1-7 m	FAN-SHAPED, WITH THORNS ON THE STEM
PHOENIX CANARIENSIS	CANARY ISLAND DATE PALM	PALM	3-12 m	PINNATE, EXTENSIVE
TRACHYCARPUS FORTUNEI	CHINESE WINDMILL PALM	PALM	2-20 m	FAN-SHAPED. UP TO 90 CM LONG.
ACCA SELLOWIANA	PINEAPPLE GUAVA	LARGE SHRUB	2-8 m	DARK GREEN, MATTE
ARBUTUS ANDRACHNE	GREEK STRAWBERRY TREE	LARGE SHRUB, TREE	3-5 m	EGG-SHAPED. DARK GREEN. UNDERSIDE GREY-GREEN.
LAURUS NOBILIS	LAUREL	LARGE SHRUB	1-12 m	LEATHERY, HARD
FICUS CARICA	COMMON FIG	LARGE SHRUB, TREE	2-10 m	DECIDUOUS, LARGE-LEAVED
NERIUM OLEANDER	OLEANDER	LARGE SHRUB	1.5-6 m	SPEAR-SHAPED. UP TO 20 CM LONG.
PISTACIA LENTISCUS	MASTIC	LARGE SHRUB	1-6 m	LEATHERY, PINNATE
PITTOSPORUM TOBIRA	JAPANESE MOCK-ORANGE	LARGE SHRUB	1-5 m	DARK-GREEN, GLOSSY
FATSIA JAPONICA	JAPANESE ARALIA	LARGE SHRUB	1-5 m	PALMATE, LEATHERY
FREMONTODENDRON CALIFORNICUM	CALIFORNIA FLANNELBUSH	LARGE SHRUB	2.5-6 m	SEMI-EVERGREEN, LEATHERY, HAIRED
ERICA ARBOREA	TREE HEATH	SHRUB, TREE	1-6 m	NEEDLE-LIKE, VERY SMALL
PUNICA GRANATUM	POMEGRANATE	SHRUB, TREE	1.5-5 m	DECIDUOUS, LARGE-LEAVED
MYRTUS COMMUNIS	MYRTLE	SHRUB	1-3 m	SMALL-LEAVED, DARK-GREEN, GLOSSY
FORTUNELLA JAPONICA	ROUND KUMQUAT	SHRUB, TREE	1-4 m	SPEAR-SHAPED, THORNS
VIBURNUM TINUS	LAURUSTINUS VIBURNUM	SHRUB	1.5-3 m	DARK-GREEN, LEATHERY
YUCCA GLORIOSA	ADAM'S NEEDLE YUCCA	SHRUB	1.5-3 m	NARROW, POINTED. UP TO 60 CM LONG.
CISTUS HYBRID	ROCKROSE	SMALL SHRUB	0.5-1.5 m	SMALL, SPEAR-SHAPED
ROSMARINUS OFFICINALIS	ROSEMARY	LOW-GROWING SHRUB	0.5-1.6 m	NEEDLE-SHAPED, WHITE UNDERSIDES
LAVANDULA SPEC.	LAVENDER	LOW-GROWING SHRUB	0.3-1 m	SILVERY GREEN, NEEDLE-SHAPED
RUTA GRAVEOLENS	COMMON RUE	SMALL SHRUB	0.4-1 m	BLUE-GREEN, FINELY DIVIDED, FRAGRANT
DANAE RACEMOSA	POET'S LAUREL, ALEXANDRIAN LAUREL	SMALL SHRUB	0.4-1.2 m	EVERGREEN, ELONGATED, POINTED
CAPPARIS SPINOSA	CAPER	DWARF SHRUB	0.5 m	SMALL, ROUNDED OVAL LEAVES
ROSMARINUS OFFICINALIS 'REPENS'	VARIETY OF ROSEMARY	LOW-GROWING SHRUB	15 cm	NEEDLE-LIKE
FUCHSIA PROCUMBENS	CREEPING FUCHSIA	LOW-GROWING SHRUB, CREEPING	5 cm	SMALL, ROUNDED OVAL LEAVES
CLEMATIS ARMANDII	EVERGREEN CLEMATIS	CLIMBING PLANT	2-6 m	LEATHERY, GLOSSY. UP TO 15 CM LONG.
JASMINUM OFFICINALE	COMMON JASMINE, POET'S JASMINE	CLIMBING PLANT	2-10 m	DECIDUOUS TO SEMI-EVERGREEN
PARTHENOCISSUS TRICUSPIDATA	JAPANESE CREEPER, BOSTON IVY	CLIMBING PLANT	2-20 m	DECIDUOUS
PASSIFLORA CAERULEA	COMMON PASSION FLOWER	CLIMBING PLANT	2-8 m	SEMI-EVERGREEN
TRACHELOSPERMUM JASMINOIDES	STAR JASMINE	CLIMBING PLANT	2-6 m	DARK-GREEN, GLOSSY
HEDERA SPEC.	IVY	CLIMBING PLANT	2-20 m	TYPES WITH DIFFERENT GROWTH FORMS, SOME VARIEGATED
BIGNONIA CAPREOLATA	CROSSVINE	CLIMBING PLANT	2-10 m	EGG AND LANCE-SHAPED, DEEP GREEN
AGAPANTHUS HYBRIDS	AFRICAN LILY	PERENNIAL	80-100 cm	STRAP-SHAPED. SOME TYPES ARE DECIDUOUS.
PHORMIUM TENAX	NEW ZEALAND FLAX, HARAKEKE	PERENNIAL	1-2 m	SWORD-LIKE, STIFF, OFTEN EDGED
LIRIOPE MUSCARI	LILYTURF	PERENNIAL	20-45 cm	GRASS-LIKE, SOMETIMES STREAKED WITH YELLOW
OPHIOPOGON JAPONICUS	MONDO GRASS/FOUNTAIN GRASS	PERENNIAL	20-30 cm	GRASS-LIKE, RICH GREEN
CAMPANULA POSCHARSKYANA	SERBIAN BELLFLOWER	CUSHION PERENNIAL	5 cm	SMALL-LEAVED, A STRONG GREEN
ALOE ARBORESCENS	KRANTZ ALOE	SUCCULENT	0.5-6.0 m	GREY-GREEN, SERRATED
HYDROCHARIS MORSUS-RANAE	FROGBIT	WATER PLANT	5 cm	LIKE A WATER-LILY BUT SMALLER
TRAPA NATANS	WATER CHESTNUT	WATER PLANT	5 cm	DECIDUOUS

NON-HEATED GREENHOUSE WINTER TEMPERATURE CIRCA 0 °C, LIGHT FROST OF UP TO –5 °C

COLOUR OF FLOWERS, FRUIT	BLOSSOM/FRUIT	LOCATION	ORIGINS	OTHER
	❀/🍎✕	◐	THE WEST COAST OF NORTH AMERICA	SLOW-GROWING. BRIGHT RED-BROWN PEELING BARK
	❀/🍎	○◐	JAPAN, EAST ASIA	CAMPHOR OIL IS DERIVED FROM THE BARK AND THE WOOD
	❀/🍎✕	○◐	THE MEDITERRANEAN (MAQUIS)	SLOW-GROWING. OLD PLANTS CAN BE RELOCATED.
	❀/🍎	○◐	THE MEDITERRANEAN (MAQUIS)	TOLERATES HEAVY FROST.
	❀/🍎	○	THE EASTERN MEDITERRANEAN, THE MIDDLE EAST	CAN BE PLANTED IN OUTDOOR LOCATIONS THAT ARE AS WARM AS A ROOM, IF THERE IS SUFFICIENT LIGHT.
	❀/🍎	○	THE EASTERN MEDITERRANEAN, THE MIDDLE EAST	DIFFERENT TYPES HAVE DIFFERENT COLOURING. SOMETIMES WEAK-GROWING
	❀/🍎	○	CALIFORNIAN HARD-LEAF AREA (CHAPARRAL)	
	❀/🍎☼	○◐	THE MEDITERRANEAN	FORMS SIDE-SHOOTS, GROWING LIKE A BUSH. ROBUST.
	❀/🍎	○	THE CANARY ISLANDS	SINGLE-TRUNKED PALM WITH A FULL CROWN
	❀/🍎	○◐●	CENTRAL AND EAST CHINA	ROBUST
	❀/🍎✕	○	BRAZIL, URUGUAY	CAN BE A STANDARD TREE. CAN GROW IN ROOM-TEMPERATURE LOCATIONS. LOW-MAINTENANCE.
	❀/🍎✕	◐	THE MEDITERRANEAN	TOLERATES HEAVY FROST.
	❀/🍎☼	○◐●	THE MEDITERRANEAN	ROBUST. CAN BE FORM-CLIPPED OR A HALF-STANDARD TREE. FRAGRANT LEAVES. DROPS ITS LEAVES.
	❀/🍎✕	○◐	THE MEDITERRANEAN, THE MIDDLE EAST	TOLERATES HEAVY FROST
	❀/🍎☠	○	THE MEDITERRANEAN	MAY BE A STANDARD TREE. ALL PARTS OF THE PLANT ARE POISONOUS. ☠
	❀/🍎[1]	○◐●	THE MEDITERRANEAN	TOLERATES HEAVY FROST AND LOW AIR HUMIDITY
	❀/🍎	○◐●	CHINA, JAPAN	PERFUMED. MAY BE A HALF-STANDARD TREE. FORM-CUT.
	❀	○●	EAST ASIA	PREDECT FROM OVERHEATING
	❀/🍎	○	CALIFORNIAN HARD-LEAF AREA	HAIRS ON LEAVES CAUSE SKIN IRRITATION. THE ROOT BALL IS INTOLERANT OF DAMP AND HEAT.
	❀	○◐	THE MEDITERRANEAN (MAQUIS)	YOUNG PLANTS HAVE WHITE HAIRS ON THE TWIGS
	❀/🍎[2]	○	THE MEDITERRANEAN, THE MIDDLE EAST	TOLERATES HEAVY FROST
	❀/🍎	○◐	THE MEDITERRANEAN (MAQUIS)	CAN BE FORM-CLIPPED. THE ROOT BALL SHOULD NOT BE ALLOWED TO DRY OUT.
	❀/🍎✕	○○	SOUTH CHINA	TOLERATES HEAVY FROST. LOW LEAF LOSS.
	❀/🍎	○◐●	THE MEDITERRANEAN	PERFUME. PLENTY OF FLOWERS. SLOW-GROWING. MAY BE A HALF-STANDARD TREE. CAN BE FORM-CLIPPED.
	❀/🍎 RARE	○	THE MEDITERRANEAN (MAQUIS)	CUT BACK AFTER FLOWERING. VULNERABLE TO SOIL FUNGI.
	❀☼	○.	THE MEDITERRANEAN	EDIBLE, FRAGRANT FLOWERS. CAN BE FORM-CLIPPED.
	❀/🍎 PLAIN	○	THE MEDITERRANEAN (MAQUIS)	A POPULAR FRAGRANCE. CAN BE FORM-CLIPPED AFTER FLOWERING.
	❀☼	○	THE MEDITERRANEAN, ASIA	CAN CAUSE CONTACT ALLERGY REACTIONS. POISONOUS IN HIGH DOSES.
	❀/🍎☠	○	THE MEDITERRANEAN, ASIA	CAN CAUSE CONTACT ALLERGY REACTIONS. POISONOUS IN HIGH DOSES. ☠
	❀/🍎	○◐●	IRAN, SYRIA	ROBUST. UNREMARKABLE FLOWERS. DECORATIVE FRUITS. A GROUND-COVERING PLANT.
	❀/🍎	○	THE MEDITERRANEAN	TREAT LIKE A CACTUS. DO NOT OVERWATER. GROWS WELL IN A DRY STONE WALL.
	❀	○	SOUTH EUROPE	FRAGRANT LEAVES. LOW SHAPE.
	❀/🍎	◐●	NEW ZEALAND	CREEPS VERY LOW TO THE GROUND.
	❀/🍎	○◐	CHINA	WINDING LEAF STALKS, STRONG-GROWING
	❀/🍎☼	○◐	IRAN TO INDIA, WEST CHINA	STRONG GROWING. SHOULD BE TIED.
	❀/🍎	○◐	JAPAN, CHINA, KOREA	BEAUTIFUL AUTUMN COLOURS. STRONG-GROWING. A SELF-SUPPORTING CLIMBER (WITH SUCKERS).
	❀/🍎	○	SOUTH AMERICA	SELF-SUPPORTING CLIMBER. NEEDS TRELLIS.
	❀☼/🍎	○◐●	CHINA, JAPAN, KOREA	POISONOUS! CAN BE A GROUND COVERING PLANT. SOME TYPES ARE VARIEGATED. ☠
	❀/🍎☠[4]	◐●	CENTRAL AND SOUTH EUROPE	CLINGING PLANT OR GROUND COVER; ADULT PLANTS HAVE POISONOUS FRUITS.
	❀/🍎 RARE	○◐	CALIFORNIAN HARD-LEAF AREA	CLINGING PLANT. STABLE TRELLIS. TENDRILS HANG DOWN IN A CASCADE.
	❀/🍎	○◐	SOUTH AFRICA'S CAPE REGION	VERY LOW MAINTENANCE. A VARIETY OF FLOWER COLOURS.
	❀/🍎	○	NEW ZEALAND	INTOLERANT OF WATERLOGGING
	❀/🍎	○◐●	EAST ASIA	A GROUND-COVERING PLANT. LOW LIGHT NEED. CAN BE PLANTED IN ROOM-TEMPERATURE LOCATIONS.
	❀	○◐●	SOUTHEAST ASIA	A GROUND-COVERING PLANT. HUMIDITY: 45% MIN.
	❀	○◐	SOUTHEAST EUROPE	LOW-NUTRIENT SUBSTRATE. VERY LONG FLOWERING PERIOD
	❀	○	SOUTH AFRICA	BUSH AND SHRUB-LIKE GROWTH. THE LEAVES GROW IN ROSETTES. ATTRACTIVE, LONG-LASTING INFLORESCENCES.
	❀/🍎	○◐	EUROPE, ASIA	SPROUTS RUNNERS
	❀/🍎✕[3]	○◐	MITTEL- UND SÜDEUROPA, SÜDOSTASIEN	CENTRAL AND SOUTH EUROPE, SOUTHEAST ASIA LEAVES GROW IN ROSETTES

❀ BLOSSOM SIGNIFICANT ❀ BLOSSOM RARE/INSIGNIFICANT 🍎 FRUIT ✕ EDIBLE ☠ POISONOUS ☼ HEAVILY PERFUMED

[1] FOR PLANT GROUP [2] DECORATIVE TYPES [3] COOKED [4] ADULT PLANTS

○ SUNNY LOCATION ◐ HALF-SHADE LOCATION ● SHADE LOCATION

Plant lists (cont.)

BOTANICAL NAME	ENGLISH NAME	PLANT FORM	GROWTH HEIGHT	FOLIAGE
ALBIZIA JULIBRISSIN	PERSIAN SILK TREE	TREE, SHRUB	5–10 m	DECIDUOUS, DELICATE, DOUBLE PINNATE
BAUHINIA VARIEGATA	ORCHID TREE	TREE	3–6 m	ROUNDED, SPLIT
EUCALYPTUS FICIFOLIA	ALBANY RED FLOWERING GUM	TREE	2–7 m	DARK GREEN, LEATHERY, MATTE, SCENTED
GREVILLEA ROBUSTA	AUSTRALIAN SILVER OAK	TREE	2–20 m	SEMI-EVERGREEN, MULTIPLE PINNATE
PSIDIUM LITTORALE (SYN. CATTLEIANUM)	STRAWBERRY GUAVA	TREE	2–3 m	LEATHERY, GLOSSY
PODOCARPUS MACROPHYLLUS	KUSAMAKI, INUMAKI	CONIFER	1–3.5 m	DARK GREEN. UP TO 10 cm LONG.
CHRYSALIDOCARPUS LUTESCENS	GOLDEN CANE PALM	PALM	7–10 m	FROND-SHAPED. UP TO 2m LONG.
PHOENIX ROEBELINII	MINIATURE DATE PALM	PALM	1.5–3.5 m	PINNATE FRONDS
WASHINGTONIA ROBUSTA	MEXICAN FAN PALM, MEXICAN WASHINGTONIA	PALM	5–25 m	FAN-SHAPED, LIGHT GREEN. THORNS ON THE STEM.
CITRUS LIMON	LEMON	SHRUB	1.5–7 m	OVAL, RICH GREEN
CITRUS RETICULATA	MANDARINE, CLEMENTINE	SHRUB	3–4 m	LANCE-SHAPED, DARK GREEN
PLUMBAGO AURICULATA	BLUE PLUMBAGO, CAPE LEADWORT	SHRUB, CLIMBING PLANT	1–2 m	SEMI-EVERGREEN
SEDUM	STONECROP	PERENNIAL, LOW-GROWING SHRUB	5–50 cm	THICK-FLESHED, SUCCULENT
AGAVE SPEC.	AGAVE	PERENNIAL	20–200 cm	LANCE-SHAPED, WITH DIFFERENT BASIC TONES. ALSO VARIEGATED.
DROSERA MENZIESII	PINK RAINBOW SUNDEW	PERENNIAL	15–30 cm	TRAP LEAVES WITH MOBILE TENDRILS
HELLEBORUS CORSICUS (SYN. ARGUTIFOLIUS)	CORSICAN HELLEBORE	PERENNIAL	50–60 cm	HEAVILY SERRATED, DARK GREEN
MUSA BASJOO	JAPANESE FIBRE BANANA	PERENNIAL	3–6 m	UP TO 3 m. EVERGREEN
PUYA CHILENSIS	CHILEAN PUYA, GIANT BROMELIAD	PERENNIAL	40–150 cm	POINTED, SPIKY
SAXIFRAGA STOLONIFERA	CREEPING SAXIFRAGE	PERENNIAL	15 cm	HAIRED, ROUND OR KIDNEY-SHAPED
YUCCA ELEPHANTIPES	GIANT YUCCA	PERENNIAL	2–10 m	SWORD-SHAPED, SERRATED. UP TO 110 cm LONG.
SOLEIROLIA SOLEIROLII	BABY'S TEARS	CUSHION PERENNIAL	5 cm	SMALL-LEAVED, ROUND
CYRTOMIUM FALCATUM	JAPANESE HOLLY FERN	FERN	20–80 cm	DARK-GREEN, BROAD, LANCE-SHAPED. LIKE HOLLY.
BOUGAINVILLEA GLABRA	LESSER BOUGAINVILLEA	CLIMBING PLANT	5–8 m	SEMI-EVERGREEN, ELLIPTICAL
FICUS PUMILA	CLIMBING FIG	CLIMBING PLANTAS GROUND COVER: 10–20 cm	SMALL LEAVES, EGG OR HEART-SHAPED
JASMINUM POLYANTHUM	JASMINE	CLIMBING PLANT	2–8 m	SEMI-EVERGREEN
PASSIFLORA EDULIS	PASSION FRUIT	CLIMBING PLANT	2–8 m	LARGE, TRILOBATE
PASSIFLORA VIOLACEA	VIOLET PASSIONFLOWER	CLIMBING PLANT	2–5 m	EGG-SHAPED
APONOGETON DISTACHYOS	WATER HAWTHORN	WATER PLANT	5 cm	LINEAR OR EGG-SHAPED. FLOATING LEAVES.

BOTANICAL NAME	ENGLISH NAME	PLANT FORM	GROWTH HEIGHT	FOLIAGE
FICUS RELIGIOSA	SACRED FIG	TREE	4–25 m	BRIEFLY SHEDS LEAVES. SOFT, TAIL-SHAPED TIP.
MICROCITRUS AUSTRALIS	ROUND AUSTRALIAN LIME	TREE	2–20 m	DECIDUOUS, LEATHERY, DARK GREEN
PSIDIUM GUAJAVA	COMMON GUAVA	TREE	2–12 m	SEMI-EVERGREEN
EUGENIA UNIFLORA	SURINAM CHERRY	SHRUB, TREE	2–7 m	LEATHERY, GLOSSY, FRAGRANT
MICHELIA CHAMPACA	CHAMPAKA	SHRUB, TREE	1.5–5 m	LARGE, SLIGHTLY WAVY EDGE
SPARMANNIA AFRICANA	AFRICAN HEMP	SHRUB	2–6 m	LIGHT GREEN, HEART-SHAPED. UP TO 25 cm LONG.
MUSA X PARADISIACA	BANANA	PERENNIAL	3–8 m	OVERHANGING, VERY LARGE.
STRELITZIA NICOLAI	WILD BANANA	PERENNIAL	3–6 m	VERY LARGE, LIKE A BANANA
STRELITZIA REGINAE	BIRD OF PARADISE	PERENNIAL	1–2 m	LANCE-LIKE. LONG STEM.
ALOE SPEC.	ALOE	SUCCULENT	10–600 cm	SUCCULENT, GENERALLY TRIANGULAR, SERRATED
EUPHORBIA TIRUCALLI	PENCIL TREE, MILK BUSH	SUCCULENT, SHRUB	1–7 m	VERY SMALL, SUCCULENT BRANCHES
PELARGONIUM ODORATISSIMUM	APPLE GERANIUM	HERB, SHRUB	30 cm	BRIGHT GREEN, FRAGRANT
BLECHNUM SPEC.	HARD FERN	FERN	20–100 cm	FRONDS EDGED WITH PINNATE LEAFLETS
DICKSONIA ANTARCTICA	SOFT TREE FERN	FERN	1.5–2 m	PINNATE FRONDS
PTERIS CRETICA	CRETAN BRAKE	FERN	20 cm	LIGHT-GREEN, DARK EDGED. UP TO 30 cm LONG.
MANDEVILLA SPEC.	MANDEVILLA	CLIMBING PLANT	2–3 m	OVAL, DARK-GREEN, ELONGATED
HOYA CARNOSA	WAX PLANT	CLIMBING PLANT	0.5–2.5 m	FLESHY, GLOSSY
TETRASTIGMA VOINIERIANUM	CHESTNUT VINE	CLIMBING PLANT	2–15 m	PALMATE, LARGE
CYPERUS INVOLUCRATUS	UMBRELLA SEDGE	WATER PLANT, SWAMP PERENNIAL	1–1.5 m	A ROUND STEM WITH A STAR-SHAPED EFFLORESCENCE
NELUMBO NUCIFERA	INDIAN LOTUS	WATER PLANT	20–50 cm	LARGE, WAVY EDGE, LONG STEMS
ZANTEDESCHIA AETHIOPICA	ARUM LILY	WATER PLANT, SWAMP PERENNIAL	40–80 cm	ARROW-SHAPED LEAVES

NON-HEATED GREENHOUSE – WINTER TEMPERATURE 0-10 °C, FROST-FREE

COLOUR OF FLOWERS, FRUIT	BLOSSOM/FRUIT	LOCATION	ORIGINS	OTHER
	✿/🍎	○	ASIA	AN ATTRACTIVE SHADE PLANT.
	✿/🍎	○	INDIA, SOUTHEAST CHINA	LARGE FLOWERS. DECORATIVE LEAVES.
	✿	○	SOUTHWEST AUSTRALIA (KWONGAN)	STRIKING FIERY RED FLOWERS. STRONG-GROWING. TOLERATES CUTTING-BACK.
	✿/🍎	○◑	AUSTRALIA, NEW CALEDONIA	A LIGHT SHADE PLANT. FLOWERS ONLY AFTER SEVERAL YEARS (USUALLY CULTIVATED TYPES.)
	✿/🍎✕	○	BRAZIL	CAN GROW IN ROOM-TEMPERATURE LOCATIONS
	✾/🍎	◑●	SOUTHEAST ASIA	ROBUST. SLOW-GROWING. CAN BE FORM-CLIPPED OR A BONSAI.
	✿/🍎	○◑	SOUTH AFRICA, MADAGASCAR, REUNION	SPROUTS RUNNERS. FORMS DENSE CLUMPS. CAN GROW IN ROOM-TEMPERATURE LOCATIONS.
	✿/🍎	○◑●	SOUTHEAST ASIA	ROBUST. MOISTURE-LOVING. ONE OR SEVERAL TRUNKS.
	✾/🍎	○	ARIZONA, USA	SINGLE TRUNK. FAST-GROWING. PHOENIX CANARIENSIS HAS LOW LIGHT NEED.
	✿/🍎	○◑	SOUTHEAST ASIA	FEW THORNS, BUT RISK OF PRICKING ONESELF.
	✿/🍎✕	○◑	SOUTHEAST ASIA	ROBUST. GROWS SLOWLY. ROUND CROWN. SPIKY.
	✿/🍎 RARE	○	SOUTH AFRICA	A SPREADING CLIMBER. MUST BE TIED. CAN BE FORM-CLIPPED.
	✿/🍎	○◑	THE SUBTROPICS, TEMPERATE ZONES, WORLDWIDE	A GROUND-COVERING PLANT. ROBUST. UNDEMANDING. DIFF. TYPES HAVE A WIDE VAR. OF LEAVES AND FLOWERS.
	✾ RARE	○	MEXICO	LEAF ROSETTES. SPIKY. SOME TYPES NEED A LOT OF SPACE.
	✿	○	SOUTHWEST AUSTRALIA (KWONGAN)	THE PLANT CONTRACTS IN SUMMER.
	✿	○◑	THE MEDITERRANEAN	TOLERATES DRYNESS
	✿/🍎	○◑	JAPAN	SOLITAIRE PLANT. SPROUTS RUNNERS. NEEDS SPACE. THE FRUITS ARE NOT EDIBLE.
	✿/🍎	○	CHILE (MATORRAL)	THRIVES IN DRY CONDITIONS. HAS A SINGLE SPECTACULAR FLORESCENCE, MAX. 250CM IN HEIGHT.
	✿	○◑●	JAPAN, CHINA	A GROUND-COVERING PLANT. SPROUTS RUNNERS. THE 'TRICOLOR' TYPE CAN GROW IN ROOM-TEMP. LOCATIONS.
	✿/🍎	○◑	CENTRAL AMERICA	TRUNK THICK AT THE BASE. A GOOD SOLITAIRE.
	✾ RARE	◑	THE MEDITERRANEAN	A GROUND-COVERING PLANT. NEEDS PLENTY OF MOISTURE. ALSO ROOM-TEMPERATURE.
		◑●	EAST ASIA, SOUTH AFRICA	NEEDS A COOL LOCATION, INCLUDING IN SUMMER.
	✿ WITH BRACTS	○	BRAZIL	A SPREADING CLIMBER. MAY BE A SMALL TREE. SPIKY.
		◑●	SOUTHEAST ASIA	A GROUND COVER PLANT. VARIEGATED TYPES NEED A WARMER LOCATION.
	✿ ☼	◑	WEST CHINA	STRONG-GROWING. CREEPER
	✿/🍎	◑●	BRAZIL, SOUTH AMERICA	A SELF-SUPPORTING CLIMBER REQUIRING A TRELLIS.
	✿	○◑	BRAZIL, SOUTH AMERICA	ROBUST. STRONG-GROWING. FLOWERING.
	✿✕	○◑●	SOUTH AFRICA	FORMS TUBERS. LEAVES GROW IN ROSETTES.

MODERATELY WARM LOCATION – WINTER TEMPERATURE 10-17 °C

COLOUR OF FLOWERS, FRUIT	BLOSSOM/FRUIT	LOCATION	ORIGINS	OTHER
		○◑	INDIA, SRI LANKA	LOW LIGHT NEED. HIGH HUMIDITY NEED.
	✿/🍎✕	○	AUSTRALIA	DENSE, NARROW CROWN. YOUNG PLANTS HAVE NEEDLE-SHAPED LEAVES, OLDER PLANTS HAVE POINTED OVAL L.
	✿/🍎✕	○	SOUTH AMERICA	CAN GROW ALL YEAR ROUND IN A ROOM-TEMPERATURE LOCATION
	✿/🍎✕	○	GULF OF MEXICO, BRAZIL	CAN GROW IN A ROOM-TEMPERATURE LOCATION
	✿ ☼	○◑	INDONESIA, MALAYSIA	LOW LIGHT. NEED. SPECIAL PERFUME. LOSES LEAVES.
	✿/🍎	○◑	SOUTH AFRICA	STRONG-GROWING. MAY BE A STANDARD TREE.
	✿/🍎✕	○	ALL TROPICAL REGIONS	SPROUTS RUNNERS.
	✿	○◑	SOUTH AFRICA	LIKE BIRD OF PARADISE FLOWER BUT BIGGER. CAN ALSO GROW IN ROOM-TEMPERATURE LOCATIONS.
	✿/🍎	○◑	SOUTH AFRICA	EXOTIC ORANGE AND BLUE FLOWERS FROM LATE AUTUMN TO EARLY SPRING.
	✿/🍎 RARE	○	EAST AND SOUTH AFRICA, THE ARABIAN PENINSULA	INCL. LOW-GROWING AND TRUNKED TYPES. SHRUB-LIKE GROWTH. CAN ALSO GROW IN ROOM-TEMP. LOCATIONS.
	✿	○	EAST AND SOUTH AFRICA	SHRUB-LIKE GROWTH WITH SLENDER TWIGS LIKE PENCILS.
	✿	○	SOUTH AFRICA	CAN ALSO GROW IN ROOM-TEMPERATURE LOCATIONS.
		◑●	MEXICO	A TRUNK-LIKE RHIZOME. OFTEN TREATED AS A SHRUB.
		◑●	EAST AUSTRALIA, TASMANIA	A SOLITAIRE PLANT WITH A HAIRY STEM.
		◑●	THE MEDITERRANEAN	CAN ALSO GROW IN ROOM-TEMPERATURE LOCATIONS, WHERE IT MAY PRODUCE VARIEGATED LEAVES.
	✿ ☠	○	BOLIVIA, BRAZIL	CREEPER, ☠. LOW LIGHT NEED AND MOISTURE NEED. CAN ALSO GROW IN ROOM-TEMPERATURE LOCATIONS.
	✿	◑●	EAST ASIA, AUSTRALIA	LOW LIGHT NEED. SHOULD BE TIED. CAN ALSO GROW IN ROOM-TEMPERATURE LOCATIONS.
	✾/🍎	◑●	EAST ASIA	VERY STRONG-GROWING. A SELF-SUPPORTING CLIMBER. STABLE TRELLIS NEEDED. ROOM-TEMP. LOCATIONS.
	✿	○◑	AFRICA	LOW LIGHT NEED. FORMS CLUMPS.
	✿/🍎✕	○◑	ASIA	SPROUTS RUNNERS. CAN ALSO GROW IN ROOM-TEMPERATURE LOCATIONS.
	✿	○◑	SOUTH AFRICA	LOW LIGHT NEED. ☠

✿ BLOSSOM SIGNIFICANT   ✾ BLOSSOM RARE/INSIGNIFICANT   🍎 FRUIT   ✕ EDIBLE   ☠ POISONOUS   ☼ HEAVILY PERFUMED

1 FOR PLANT GROUP   2 DECORATIVE TYPES   3 COOKED   4 ADULT PLANTS

○ SUNNY LOCATION   ◑ HALF-SHADE LOCATION   ● SHADE LOCATION

Plant lists (cont.)

BOTANICAL NAME	ENGLISH NAME	PLANT FORM	GROWTH HEIGHT	FOLIAGE	
BUCIDA BUCERAS	BLACK OLIVE	TREE	2–20 m	SMALL-LEAVED, DARK GREEN	
FICUS CYATHISTIPULA	BRANCHED RUBBER TREE	TREE	1.5–5 m	LARGE-LEAVED, EGG-SHAPED	
FICUS ELASTICA	RUBBER TREE	TREE	1.5–40 m	LARGE-LEAVED. UPPERSIDES DARK-GREEN, UNDERSIDES LIGHT GREEN.	
FICUS LYRATA	FIDDLE-LEAF FIG	TREE	1.5–30 m	VIOLIN-SHAPED. UP TO 50 cm LONG.	
FICUS MICROCARPA (SYN. RETUSA) 'COMPACTA'	CHINESE BANYAN	TREE	1–25 m	SMALL-LEAVED, GLOSSY	
FICUS RUBIGINOSA	PORT JACKSON FIG, RUSTY FIG	TREE	2–30 m	LARGE-LEAVED, EGG-SHAPED. UNDERS. RUST-COLOURED/FELTED	
INGA EDULIS	ICE-CREAM BEAN, GUAMA	TREE	2–12 m	DARK-GREEN, PINNATE	
SCHEFFLERA ACTINOPHYLLA	UMBRELLA TREE	TREE	1.5–15 m	PALMATE, HANGING. LONG LEAF STEMS.	
SYZYGIUM JAMBOS	ROSE APPLE, MALABAR PLUM	TREE	2–8 m	NARROW, LEATHERY, GLOSSY	
COCCOLOBA UVIFERA	SEA GRAPE	TREE, SHRUB	3–6 m	LARGE LEAVED, LIGHT BLUE-GREEN	
COFFEA ARABICA	ARABICA COFFEE	TREE, SHRUB	1.5 m	ELLIPTICAL, GLOSSY	
CHAMAEDOREA ELEGANS	NEANTHE BELLA PALM	PALM	2–5 m	PINNATE	
CHAMAEDOREA SEIFRIZII	BAMBOO PALM	PALM	2–3 m	PINNATE, DARK GREEN	
HOWEIA (SYN. KENTIA) FORSTERIANA	KENTIA PALM, THATCH PALM	PALM	1.5–15 m	BROADLY PINNATE	
RHAPIS EXCELSA	BROADLEAF LADY PALM	PALM	1–1.5 m	LARGE, PINNATE	
ALLAMANDA CATHARTICA	GOLDEN TRUMPET	SHRUB, CLIMBING PLANT	0.8–2 m	POINTED, LEATHERY	
CLERODENDRUM PANICULATUM	PAGODA FLOWER	SHRUB	1.5–3 m	LARGE-LEAVED, DARK-GREEN	
DRACAENA FRAGRANS	CHINESE MONEY TREE	SHRUB	1.5–6 m	BROAD, STRIPED	
DRACAENA MARGINATA	MADAGASCAR DRAGON TREE	SHRUB	1.5–4 m	NARROW, EDGED	
MURRAYA PANICULATA	ORANGE JASMINE	SHRUB	1.5–4 m	DARK-GREEN, GLOSSY, FRAGRANT	
PLUMERIA-HYBRIDEN	FRANGIPANI	SHRUB	2–7 m	DECIDUOUS, POINTED. UP TO 50 cm LONG.	
SCHEFFLERA ARBORICOLA	DWARF UMBRELLA TREE	SHRUB	2–3 m	PALMATE, LARGE-LEAVED	
ENSETE VENTRICOSUM	ABYSSINIAN BANANA	TREELIKE PERENNIAL	2–7 m	PADDLE-SHAPED. UP TO 6 m LONG AND 1 m WIDE.	
ALPINIA ZERUMBET	SHELL GINGER	PERENNIAL	60 cm	LANCE-SHAPED. LONG STEMS.	
ANTHURIUM SCHERZERIANUM	FLAMINGO PLANT	PERENNIAL	30–50 cm	DARK GREEN. 15–30 cm LONG.	
ELETTARIA CARDAMOMUM	TRUE CARDAMOM	PERENNIAL	80–150 cm	LANCE-SHAPED. UP TO 60 cm LONG.	
GUZMANIA SPEC.	BROMELIAD	PERENNIAL, EPIPHYTE	5–50 cm	DECORATIVE, COLOURFUL BRACTS	
HELICONIA SPEC.	HELICONIA	PERENNIAL	30–50 cm	LARGE, POINTED	
SPATHIPHYLLUM SPEC.	PEACE LILY	PERENNIAL	30–60 cm	ELONGATED, POINTED	
TILLANDSIA SPEC.	AIR PLANTS	PERENNIAL, EPIPHYTE	5–80 cm	GREEN TO GREY	
ZINGIBER SPEC.	GINGER	PERENNIAL	80–200 cm	LONG, ELONGATED	
ASPLENIUM SPEC.	SPLEENWORT	FERN	80 cm	PINNATE OR FORKED	
PLATYCERIUM BIFURCATUM (SYN. ALCICORNE)	ELKHORN FERN	FERN	50–100 cm	VERY LARGE, HAIRED, ANTLER SHAPE	
CISSUS RHOMBIFOLIA	GRAPE IVY	CLIMBING PLANT	2–5 m	DIAMOND SHAPE, HEAVILY SERRATED	
CISSUS ROTUNDIFOLIA	VENEZUELAN TREEBINE	CLIMBING PLANT	1.5–3 m	ROUND, LEATHERY, DARK GREEN	
JASMINUM SAMBAC	ARABIAN JASMINE	CLIMBING PLANT	3 m	GLOSSY. UP TO 10 cm LONG.	
MONSTERA DELICIOSA	SWISS CHEESE PLANT	CLIMBING PLANT	2–8 m	VERY LARGE LEAVES. UP TO 150 cm LONG.	
PHILODENDRON SCANDENS	HEARTLEAF PHILODENDRON	CLIMBING PLANT	AS GROUND COVER: 20 cm	LEATHERY, VERY LARGE	
SCINDAPSUS PICTUS	SATIN POTHOS	CLIMBING PLANT	AS GROUND COVER: 20 cm	DARK GREEN, WITH SILVER SPECKLES AND SILVER EDGE	
CYPERUS PAPYRUS	PAPYRUS SEDGE	WATER PLANT	2.5–4 m	STEMS AND FLOWER HEAD DOMINATE	

ROOM-TEMPERATURE LOCATION – TEMPERATURE 20–24 °C ALL ROUND

COLOUR OF FLOWERS, FRUIT	BLOSSOM/FRUIT	LOCATION	ORIGINS	OTHER
	❀/🍒	○◑	CENTRAL AMERICA, THE CARIBBEAN	LOOSE-CROWNED. CAN GROW IN COOLER LOCATIONS.
	✽/🍒	◑	TROPICAL AFRICA	LOW-MAINTENANCE. DECORATIVE RED-BROWN HAIRED LEAF STALKS.
	✽/🍒	◑●	SOUTHEAST ASIA. FORMS AERIAL ROOTS.	LOW LIGHT NEED. MANY DIFFERENT SORTS.
	✽/🍒	◑●	TROPICAL AFRICA	LOW LIGHT NEED.
	✽/🍒	◑	SOUTHEAST ASIA	LOW LIGHT NEED. VERY COMPACT GROWTH. A POPULAR BONSAI PLANT.
		○◑	TROPICAL AUSTRALIA	LOW LIGHT NEED. SHRUB-LIKE GROWTH.
	❀✿/🍒✕	○◑	CENTRAL AND SOUTH AMERICA	LONG FRUIT PODS, WHICH TASTE LIKE ICE-CREAM. AN UMBRELLA-SHAPED CROWN.
	❀	◑●	NORTHEAST AUSTRALIA	☠
	❀/🍒✕	○○●	SOUTHEAST ASIA	ATTRACTIVE FLOWERS. ELEGANT LEAVES. CAN GROW IN COOL LOCATIONS.
	❀/🍒✕	○	FLORIDA, THE CARIBBEAN, CENTRAL AND S. AMERICA	LOW LIGHT NEED.
	❀✿✿/🍒	◑	TROPICAL AFRICA	SENSITIVE TO OVERHEATING. NO DIRECT SUNLIGHT.
	❀	◑●	CENTRAL AMERICA	LOW LIGHT NEED. NO DIRECT SUN. VERY ROBUST.
	✽/🍒	◑●	CENTRAL AMERICA	VERY LOW LIGHT NEED. GROWS LIKE BAMBOO.
		◑●	LORD HOWE ISLAND (AUSTRALIA)	VERY LOW LIGHT NEEDS. TOLERATES DRY AIR.
	✽/🍒	◑●	CHINA, TAIWAN	LOW LIGHT NEEDS. ROBUST. GROWS LIKE BAMBOO.
	❀	○	SOUTH AMERICA, VENEZUELA	STRONG-GROWING. BRIGHT YELLOW LEAVES. ☠
	❀	○	CHINA, BURMA, MALAYSIA	SPECTACULAR FLOWER SHAPE. CUT BACK AFTER FLOWERING.
	❀	◑●	TROPICAL AFRICA	VARIETIES HAVE DIFFERENT STRIPED LEAVES.
	✽	◑●	TROPICAL AFRICA	VERY ROBUST. VARIETIES HAVE DIFFERENT STRIPED LEAVES.
	❀✿✿/🍒	○◑	INDIA TO NORTH AUSTRALIA	MULTIPLE TRUNKS. REGULAR BRANCHES. CAN BE FORM-CLIPPED.
	❀✿/🍒	○	CENTRAL AMERICA	NEEDS LITTLE WATER. COMBINES WELL WITH SUCCULENTS AND CACTI. ATTRACTIVE FLOWERS.
		●	TAIWAN	☠
	❀/🍒	○◑	CENTRAL AFRICA	NEEDS SPACE. DOES NOT FORM CLUMPS LIKE MUSA.
	❀✿	◑●	EAST ASIA	CAN SURVIVE COLD WINTERS, WHEN IT NEEDS LITTLE MOISTURE.
	❀/🍒	◑●	CENTRAL AMERICA	DIFFERENT FLOWER COLOURS. CAN BLOOM ALL YEAR. IRRITATING TO THE SKIN. ☠
	❀/🍒 RARE	◑●	INDIA, SRI LANKA	LOW LIGHT NEED. THE FLOWERS SMELL OF CARDAMOM. ROBUST.
	❀	○◑	CENTRAL AMERICA	MAY GROW AS AN EPIPHYTE OR IN A SOIL CULTURE
	❀	○	WEST INDIES	DIFFERENT FLOWER COLOURS AND SHAPES. DECORATIVE LEAVES.
	❀/🍒☠	◑●	CENTRAL AND SOUTH AMERICA	ELEGANT FLOWER SHAPES. IRRITATING TO THE SKIN. ☠
	❀	○◑	SOUTH AND CENTRAL ASIA	DIFFERENT TYPES HAVE DIFFERENTLY COLOURED FLOWERS.
	❀/🍒	○○●	ASIA	EXOTIC FLOWER SHAPES. FORMS EDIBLE RHIZOMES.
		◑●	SOUTH ASIA	CAN TOLERATE LOWER THAN 60% HUMIDITY
		◑●	NORTHWEST AUSTRALIA	MAY GROW AS AN EPIPHYTE
	✽ RARE	◑●	WEST AUSTRALIA, CENTRAL AMERICA	FLOOR-COVERING PLANT. ALSO A HANGING PLANT.
	✽	○◑	EAST AFRICA	UNSUPPORTED CLIMBER.
	❀✿✿	○◑	INDIA, SRI LANKA	SUPPORT NEEDED. SHOULD BE TIED. THE FLOWERS PROVIDE THE AROMA OF JASMINE TEA.
	❀	◑	CENTRAL AMERICA	LOW LIGHT NEED. ☠
		◑●	MEXICO	FLOOR COVERING PLANT. TO BE TIED TO A TRELLIS. IRRITATING TO THE SKIN. ☠
		◑	MALAYSIA	GROUND-COVER PLANT. LOW LIGHT AND HUMIDITY NEED. IRRITATING TO THE SKIN. ☠
	❀	○◑	TROPICAL AFRICA, THE MIDDLE EAST	NEED FOR LIGHT INCREASES WITH TEMPERATURE. IN LOW LIGHT, THE STEMS BEND.

❀ BLOSSOM SIGNIFICANT   ✽ BLOSSOM RARE/INSIGNIFICANT   🍒 FRUIT   ✕ EDIBLE   ☠ POISONOUS   ✿ HEAVILY PERFUMED

1 FOR PLANT GROUP   2 DECORATIVE TYPES   3 COOKED   4 ADULT PLANTS

○ SUNNY LOCATION   ◑ HALF-SHADE LOCATION   ● SHADE LOCATION

Picture Credits

TYPOLOGY OF INDOOR GARDENS

A PLANTED WALL IN THE INNER COURTYARD OF THE MORRIS
HOUSE IN RICHMOND, AUSTRALIA
fig. 1: © Shania Shegedyn
figs. 2, 3: © Morris Partnership Architecture and Planning
Pty Ltd
figs. 4a, 4b: © Fytogreen
PLANTED LIFT SHAFT AND CANTEEN FOR THE HEADQUARTERS OF
THE TRYG INSURANCE COMPANY, DENMARK
figs. 1–3, 5, 6: © Kim Fridbjorg and Masoud Alavi
(Built Identity)
figs. 4, 7–11: © Built Identity
VERTICAL GARDEN AT LAW FIRM MANNHEIMER SWARTLING,
STOCKHOLM, SWEDEN
figs. 1, 3, 5: © Green Fortune
fig. 4: © Åke E:son Lindman
fig. 2: Strategisk Arkitektur
ROOFED PATIO WITH GARDEN TERRACE IN THE FOOTHILLS FAMILY
HOME IN POKENO, NEW ZEALAND
figs. 1, 4, 5: © Emily Andrews
figs. 2, 3: © Strachan Group Architects
LOFT APARTMENT WITH INDOOR GARDEN, DÜSSELDORF, GERMANY
figs. 2, 6: © planungsgruppe agsn
figs. 1, 3, 4, 6–8: © Graf Luckner/Picture Press
A TREE IN AN ATHENS APARTMENT, GREECE
figs. 2, 6: © Meletitiki – Alexandros N. Tombazis and
Associates Architects
figs. 1, 2, 4, 5, 7: © Alexandros N. Tombazis, Nikos Daniilidis
PLANTING CONCEPT FOR THE SEATTLE PUBLIC LIBRARY, USA
figs. 1, 3, 4, 6:© Inside Outside
fig. 5: © Iwan Baan
PLANTING CONCEPT FOR THE OFFICE SPACE AT THE COMBINED
TRADERS COMPANY IN HAARLEM, THE NETHERLANDS
figs. 3, 5, 6, 9, 11: © Marc Koehler Architects
figs. 1, 2, 4, 7, 8, 10: © primabeeld photography
TREE INSTALLATION IN THE CHELSEA HARBOUR DESIGN CENTRE,
LONDON, UK
figs. 2, 7–13, 16: © Jinny Blom Ltd
fig. 4: © Jaap Oaake
figs. 1, 3, 5, 6, 14, 15: © Richard Lewisohn
INDOOR GARDENS IN THE ESO HOTEL IN THE ATACAMA DESERT, CHILE
figs. 2, 3, 4, 5, 6: © Auer+Weber+Assoziierte
fig. 7: © ESO/Heyer
fig. 8: © ESO
figs. 1, 9, 11: © Roland Halbe
TROPICAL GARDEN IN THE ROOFED PATIO OF THE POSTMEDIA
BUILDING IN TORONTO, CANADA
figs. 1–8: © Oriole Landscaping
PLANTED ATRIUM IN THE ST. PÖLTEN RETIREMENT AND CARE
HOME, AUSTRIA
figs. 4–6: © Georg W. Reinberg
fig. 7: © Anna Detzlhofer
fig. 8: © Pez Hejduk
figs. 1–3: © Eva Pudill

PLANTED PATIO, GIARDINO DELLE NINFEE, BOLOGNA, ITALY
figs. 2–5, 9: © Tamassociati + Agrisophia Progetti
figs. 1, 11: © Matteo Monti
fig. 9: © Gian Augusto Mattioli
figs. 6, 8, 10, 12: © Simona Ventura
LOFT APARTMENT WITH GARDEN COURTYARD IN LONDON, UK
figs. 1–7: © Olivebay
GLASS BUBBLE GREENHOUSE IN MALMÖ, SWEDEN
figs. 2–6: © Gora art&landscape
fig. 1: © Åke E:son Lindman
figs. 7, 8, 10–13: © Werner Nystrand
fig. 9: © Monika Gora
PLANTED ATRIUM IN THE COVENT GARDEN BUILDING COMPLEX
IN BRUSSELS, BELGIUM
figs. 1–9: © Art&Build
DEVONIAN GARDENS INDOOR GARDENS IN CALGARY, CANADA
figs. 1–11: © Janet Rosenberg + Associates
THEMED GARDENS IN THE ATRIUMS OF THE LUFTHANSA
AVIATION CENTER AT FRANKFURT AIRPORT, GERMANY
figs. 2, 4–6, 8–18: © WKM Landschaftsarchitekten
figs. 1, 3, 7, 19, 21, 22: © H. G. Esch, Hennef
ATRIUM HALL IN THE ALLTOURS HEADQUARTERS, DUISBURG,
GERMANY
fig. 2: © WKM Landschaftsarchitekten
figs. 1, 3–7: © thomasmayerarchive.de
TWO PLANTED ATRIUMS FOR THE ALTERRA LABORATORY AND
ADMINISTRATION BUILDINGS, WAGENINGEN, THE NETHERLANDS
figs. 5, 7: © Behnisch Architekten
figs. 1, 2, 4, 6, 11, 12: © Frank Ockert
figs. 10, 13: © Stefan Behnisch
fig. 3: © Christian Kandzia
fig. 8: © Martin Schodder
figs. 9, 14: © Copijn Garden- and Landscape Architects
INDOOR PLANTING FOR THE GENZYME CENTER OFFICE BUILDING,
CAMBRIDGE, USA
figs. 2–7: © Behnisch Architekten
figs. 1, 8–10: © Anton Grassl
'GARDENS IN THE SKY' IN THE FUSIONOPOLIS COMPLEX,
SINGAPORE
figs. 2, 4, 7, 9, 10, 14: © Symbios Design – Oculus/Terragram
figs. 1, 5, 6, 8, 11–13, 15–17: © Minitheatre Productions
fig. 3: © Kisho Kurokawa Architect & Associates

GENERAL BASIC PLANNING

fig. 1   Tryg Insurance, © Built Identity
fig. 2   Tryg Insurance, © Green Fortune
figs. 3–5   William Beaumont Hospital by Grissim, Metz,
Andriese Associates, © Justin Maconochie Photography
fig. 7   ANDREA air filter, © Véronique Huyghes
fig. 8   ANDREA air filter, © Studio Mathieu Lehanneur
fig. 9   Combined Traders company, © primabeeld
photography
fig. 10   Combined Traders company, © Marc Koehler Architects

fig. 11 Tryg Insurence, © Kim Fridbjorg and Masoud Alavi (Built
Identity)

fig. 12 DWS Investment GmbH by Breimann & Bruun Landschaftsarchitekten, © Tim Corvin Kraus, www.tckraus.de

fig. 13 ING Direct Bank by Green over Grey/www.greenovergrey.
com, © Green over Grey

fig. 14 Seattle Public Library, © Nico Tillie

fig. 15 One Kowloon by Shunmyo Masuno + Japan Landscape
Consultants, © Shunmyo Masuno + Japan Landscape
Consultants

fig. 16 Alterra, © Christian Kandzia

fig. 17–18 Lufthansa Aviation Center, © WKM Landschaftsarchitekten

fig. 19 Alltours, © WKM Landschaftsarchitekten

fig. 20 Design Centre Chelsea Harbour, © Jinny Blom

fig. 21 Design Centre Chelsea Harbour, © Richard Lewisohn

figs. 22, 23 St. Pölten retirement and care home, © Eva Pudill

figs. 24, 25 Alltours, © WKM Landschaftsarchitekten

fig. 26 Garden courtyard in London, © Olivebay

fig. 27 Foothills House, © Strachan Group Architects Ltd.

fig. 28 Can West building, © Oriole Landscaping

fig. 29 Covent Garden, © Art&Build

fig. 30 DWS Investment GmbH by Breimann & Bruun Landschaftsarchitekten, © Tim Corvin Kraus, www.tckraus.de

fig. 31 Glass Bubble, © Werner Nystrand

fig. 32 Law firm Mannheimer Swartling, © Åke E:son Lindman

fig. 33 Tryg Insurence, © Green Fortune

fig. 34 Terraform 'Hanging Garden' von Robert Cannon,
© Robert Cannon

fig. 35 Terraform 'Ursuline Garden, 2' by Robert Cannon,
© Robert Cannon

fig. 36 Giardino delle Ninfee, © Matteo Monti

fig. 37 Alltours, © WKM Landschaftsarchitekten

fig. 38 Fusionopolis, © Minitheatre Productions

fig. 39 A tree in an Athens apartment, © Nikos Daniilidis

fig. 40 Loft apartment with indoor garden, © Graf Luckner/Picture
Press

fig. 41 Lufthansa Aviation Center, © H. G. Esch, Hennef

fig. 42 Covent Garden, © Art&Build

fig. 43 Lufthansa Aviation Center, © WKM Landschaftsarchitekten

fig. 44 Investment GmbH by Breimann & Bruun Landschaftsarchitekten, © Tim Corvin Kraus, www.tckraus.de

fig. 45 Morris House, © Fytogreen

fig. 46 Anthropology shop in London, green wall by Biotecture,
© Biotecture

fig. 47 Covent Garden, © Art&Build

fig. 48 in reference to: R. E. Wöhrle, H.-P. Wöhrle: Basics Designing
with Plants, Birkhäuser Verlag, Basel 2008

fig. 49 Loft apartment with indoor garden, © Olivebay

fig. 50 Lufthansa Aviation Center, © WKM Landschaftsarchitekten

fig. 51 Glass Bubble, © Werner Nystrand

figs. 52–56 © Haike Falkenberg

fig. 57 ESO Hotel, © Auer+Weber+Assoziierte

figs. 58, 59 Glass Bubble, © GORA art&landscape

figs. 60–65 Design Centre Chelsea Harbour, © Jinny Blom

fig. 66 Botanical Garden Bordeaux by JOURDA Architectes Paris
in collaboration with Mosbach Paysagistes, © Mosbach
Paysagistes

figs. 67, 68 Explorers Hall for National Geographic by Travis Price
Architects, © Travis Price Architects

fig. 69 Carré Mainzer Landstraße by Breimann & Bruun Landschaftsarchitekten, © Tim Corvin Kraus, www.tckraus.de

fig. 70 AKN Hilversum by West 8, © West 8

fig. 71 Hydrolab by Copijn Garden- and Landscape Architects,
© Copijn Garden- and Landscape Architects

fig. 72 Hayes house by Travis Price Architects, © Travis Price
Architects

figs. 73, 74 Fragile by Copijn Garden- and Landscape Architects,
© Copijn Garden- and Landscape Architects

fig. 75 Botanical Garden Bordeaux by JOURDA Architectes Paris in
collaboration with Mosbach Paysagistes, © JOURDA
Architectes Paris

MATERIALS AND CONSTRUCTION

fig. 5 Alterra, © Stefan Behnisch

fig. 7 Lufthansa Aviation Center, © WKM Landschaftsarchitekten

fig. 8 St. Pölten retirement and care home, © Eva Pudill

fig. 9 Botanical Garden Bordeaux by JOURDA Architectes Paris
in collaboration with Mosbach Paysagistes,
© JOURDA Architectes Paris

fig. 11 ESO Hotel, © Gesswein Landschaftsarchitekten

figs. 12, 13 Devonian Gardens, © Janet Rosenberg + Associates

figs. 14–16 from: Astrid Zimmermann: Constructing Landscape,
Birkhäuser Verlag, Basel 2009

fig. 17 Giardino delle Ninfee, © Matteo Monti

fig. 18 Alterra, © Frank Ockert

fig. 19 Astrid Zimmermann

figs. 20, 21 Lufthansa Aviation Center, © WKM Landschaftsarchitekten

fig. 22 from: R. E. Wöhrle, H.-P. Wöhrle: Basics Designing with
Plants, Birkhäuser Verlag, Basel 2008

figs. 23, 24 St. Pölten retirement and care home, © Eva Pudill

figs. 25–28 © Fytogreen

figs. 29–31 Anthropology shop in London, green wall by
Biotecture, © Biotechture

fig. 34 Genzyme Center, © Stefan Behnisch

We have taken great care to identify all rights owners.
In the unlikely event that someone has been overlooked, we
would kindly ask that person to contact the publisher.

Literature

PATRICK BLANC: *The Vertical Garden: From Nature to the City,* W. W. Norton & Company, New York 2008

ANN BONAR: *The Complete Guide to Conservatory Plants,* The Overlook Press, Woodstock 1996

G. S. BRAGER, R. DE DEAR: *Developing an Adaptive Model of Thermal Comfort and Preference,* Final Report, ASHRAE RP-884, Berkeley 1997

ETHNE CLARKE: *Gardening with Foliage, Form and Texture,* David & Charles PLC, Devon 2004

BARBARA L. COLLINS: *Professional Interior Plantscaping,* Stipes Publishing, Champaign 2002

PAUL COOPER: *Interiorscapes: Gardens Within Buildings,* Mitchell Beazley, London 2006

HENRY J. COWAN: *Encyclopedia of Building Technology,* Prentice Hall, Englewood Cliffs 1988

NIGEL DUNNETT: *Planting Green Roofs and Living Walls,* reviewed and updated edition, Timber Press, Portland 2008

BRIAN HACKETT: *Planting Design,* McGraw-Hill, New York 1979

JOHN L. HAVLIN: *Soil Fertility and Fertilizers: An Introduction to Nutrient Management,* 7TH edition, Prentice Hall, Englewood Cliffs 2004

MICHAEL A. HUMPHREYS: 'Quantifying Occupant Comfort: are Combined Indices of the Indoor Environment Practicable?', *Building Research & Information 33(4),* pp. 317–325, 2005

CHARLES KIBERT: *Sustainable Construcion: Green Building Design and Delivery,* 2ND edition, Wiley, Hoboken 2007

NOËL KINGSBURY: *Gardens by Design,* Timber Press, Portland, OR 2005

HELMUT KÖSTER: *Dynamic Daylight Architecture: Basics, Systems, Projects,* Birkhäuser Verlag, Basel 2000

ANNA LAMBERTINI: *Vertical Gardens,* Verba Volant, Florence, London 2007

VIRGINIA LOHR: *Indoor Plants Increase Worker Productivity,* Washington State University, www.wsu.edu/~lohr/

VIRGINIA LOHR, C. H. PEARSON-MIMS: 'Physical Discomfort May Be Reduced in the Presence of Interior Plants'. *Hort Technology 10(1),* pp. 53–58, 2000

VIRGINIA LOHR, C. H. PEARSON-MIMS, G. K. GOODWIN: 'Interior Plants May Improve Worker Productivity and Reduce Stress in a Windowless Environment'. *Journal of Environmental Horticulture 14(2),* pp. 97–100, 1996

AXEL LOHRER: *Basics Designing with Water,* Birkhäuser Verlag, Basel 2008

HANS LOIDL, STEFAN BERNARD: *Opening Spaces,* Birkhäuser Verlag, Basel 2003

GEORGE H. MANAKER: *Interior Plantscapes: Installation, Maintenance and Management,* 3RD edition, Prentice Hall, Englewood Cliffs 1997

LIAT MARGOLIS, ALEXANDER ROBINSON: *Living Systems, Innovative Materials and Technologies for Landscape Architecture,* Birkhäuser Verlag, Basel 2007

PIET OUDOLF, NOËL KINGSBURY: *Designing with Plants,* Conran Octopus, London 1999

FRED D. RAUCH: *Plants for Tropical Landscapes: A Gardener's Guide,* University of Hawaii Press, 2000

MARK S. REA: *The IESNA Lighting Handbook: Reference & Application,* 9TH edition, Illuminating Engeneering Society, New York 2000

JANE TARRAN, TORPY FRASER, MARGARET BURCHETT: 'Use of Living Pot-Plants to Cleanse Indoor Air, Research Review', *Proceedings of Sixth International Conference on Indoor Air Quality, Ventilation & Energy Conservation in Buildings – Sustainable Built Environment,* Sendai, Japan, Vol. III, pp. 249–256, 2007

THE ROYAL HORTICULTURAL SOCIETY, CHRISTOPHER BRICKELL, TREVOR COLE, H. MARC CATHEY: *Encyclopedia of Plants and Flowers,* Dorling Kindersley, New York 2006

ROGER S. ULRICH: *Health Benefits of Gardens in Hospitals, Center for Health Systems and Design,* Colleges of Architecture and Medicine, Texas A & M University, College State, USA, Paper for conference, Plants for People, International Exhibition Floriade, The Netherlands, 2002

MANFRED WEIDNER, JAIME A. TEIXEIRA DA SILVA: *Potential and Limitations of Ornamental Plants for Indoor-air Purification,* Floriculture, Ornamental and Plant Biotechnology, Vol. IV, Global Science Books, UK 2006

SUSAN WEILER: GREEN ROOF SYSTEMS: *A Guide to the Planning, Design and Construction of Landscapes over Structures,* Wiley, Hoboken 2009

DANIEL E. WILLIAMS: *Sustainable Design: Ecology, Architecture, and Planning,* Wiley, Hoboken 2007

REGINE ELLEN WÖHRLE, HANS-JÖRG WÖHRLE: *Basics Designing with Plants,* Birkhäuser Verlag, Basel 2008

B. C. WOLVERTON: *How to Grow Fresh Air: 50 House Plants that Purify Your Home or Office,* Penguin, London 1997

B. C. WOLVERTON, A. JOHNSON, K. BOUNDS: *Interior Landscape Plants for Indoor Air Pollution Abatement,* Final Report, NASA, USA, 1989

ASTRID ZIMMERMANN: *Constructing Landscape,* Birkhäuser Verlag, Basel 2009

ACKNOWLEDGEMENTS

The author wishes to thank everyone who helped to make this book possible. Particular thanks go to essay authors Peter Guinane (CEO Oriole Landscaping Ltd.) and Hans-Jörg Wöhrle (W+P Landschaften, Wöhrle + Partner) for granting permission to reproduce the text "Principles of Design" (p. 165), Astrid Zimmermann (Dipl. Ing., landscape architect) for reworking the drawings, Jan-Hendrik Elter (Dipl. Ing. (FH) landscape architecture) for the detailed information on the subject of light planning and light intensity calculation, Heike Lechenmayr (Dipl. Ing. landscape planning and gardening) for the information on plant selection and to all the planning firms and their employees, whose support and provision of text and images helped to make the information in this book comprehensive. The project was ably supported by Norbert and Erika Falkenberg and Christophe Ceard.

Many thanks!

IMPRINT

CONCEPT AND EDITORIAL LEADERSHIP: Annette Gref, Birkhäuser Verlag
PROJECT COORDINATION AND EDITORIAL SUPERVISION: Odine Oßwald, Birkhäuser Verlag
TRANSLATION FROM GERMAN INTO ENGLISH: Michael Robinson
COPY EDITING: Susan James
GRAPHIC DESIGN AND TYPESETTING: Andreas Hidber, Basel
TYPESETTING: Amelie Solbrig, Maria Ackermann, Birkhäuser Verlag
TYPEFACES: Tiempos Text and Brauer Neue
PAPER: Plano Plus
PRINTING AND BINDING: Kösel, Altusried-Krugzell

A CIP catalogue record for this book is available from the Library of Congress, Washington D.C., USA.

Bibliographic information published by the German National Library.

The German National Library lists this publication in the Deutsche Nationalbibliografie; detailed bibliographic data are available on the Internet at http://dnb.d-nb.de.

This book is also available in a German language edition (ISBN 978-3-0346-0623-3).

© 2011 Birkhäuser GmbH, Basel
P.O. Box, CH-4002 Basel, Switzerland

Printed on acid-free paper produced from chlorine-free pulp. TCF ∞

Printed in Germany

ISBN 978-3-0346-0620-2

9 8 7 6 5 4 3 2 1   www.birkhauser.com

hydroplant^G
Grün belebt.

1

2

Nature is good for you.

Plants have a special effect on people. Their exuberant green colour has a positive effect on the spirit and well-being. There is a simple reason for this: biotechnical greening indoors not only provides a bit of refreshing nature to be seen and touched, but also perceptibly improves the indoor climate.

With the comprehensive services offered by Hydroplant, plants flourish more than ever. The service ranges from expert advice and thorough planning, through individual solution packages to plant rental to create attractive conditions, including the organisation of relocation or transport. Both for companies and for architects, office planners and interior designers looking for the correct solution for a client. Always backed up by many years of know-how in hydroponics and planting.

Vertical greening provides plant solutions of a particular type: rank planting, with mobile or fixed green walls or hanging gardens, called Verticalis. They act as natural design objects that are also outstandingly suitable as room dividers. The same applies to Prima-Klima® 'air-conditioning' plants. For functional room greening, Cyperus Papyrus, a plant known from ancient Egypt as the papyrus plant, serves as an example of both – vertical greening and an 'air-conditioning' plant – and makes a great contribution to the improvement of indoor air, provides higher relative humidity and actively livens up the whole area. Put simply, plants can be more than just plants.

1 Lively room and spirit: Example of indoor greening in the healthcare company Roche in Basel.
2 Hydroponics for high demands: Each Verticalis installation is a living work of art.

Hydroplant AG
«Creative work, display»
Neunbrunnenstr. 50
CH-8052 Zürich
T +41 (0)44 942 93 93
F +41 (0)44 942 93 94
www.hydroplant.ch